Testing the Spirits

TESTING THE SPIRITS

How Theology Informs the
Study of Congregations

Edited by

Patrick Keifert

WILLIAM B. EERDMANS PUBLISHING COMPANY
GRAND RAPIDS, MICHIGAN / CAMBRIDGE, U.K.

Published 2009 by
Wm. B. Eerdmans Publishing Co.
2140 Oak Industrial Drive N.E., Grand Rapids, Michigan 49505 /
P.O. Box 163, Cambridge CB3 9PU U.K.

Printed in the United States of America

15 14 13 12 11 10 09   7 6 5 4 3 2 1

Library of Congress Cataloging-in-Publication Data

Testing the spirits : how theology informs the study of congregations /
    edited by Patrick Keifert.
        p.   cm.
    Includes bibliographical references.
    ISBN 978-0-8028-0740-3 (pbk. : alk. paper)
    1. Religious gatherings — Christianity. 2. Discernment (Christian theology)
    3. Theology, Practical.   I. Keifert, Patrick R., 1950-
    BV700.T47   2009
    250 — dc22

                                                            2008042834

www.eerdmans.com

Contents

Foreword

Many significant shifts are taking place today at the intersection of theological education and congregations. This important book of essays provides a helpful map for charting a number of these shifts, and it offers readers keen insights into how to navigate their complexities.

One of the most important of these shifts is what Patrick Keifert refers to as "the return of the congregation to theological education." This return extends way beyond the recently developed disciplines of congregational studies and organizational effectiveness studies. Increasingly, congregations are being considered the direct subject matter that theology must engage. This invites us to a fresh imagination about the life and ministry of particular congregations, and this volume introduces some very helpful contributions regarding what this fresh imagination looks like. It does so by drawing deeply from biblical and theological sources, and through bringing theology into conversation with extensive field research. Using this combined approach, the contributing authors demonstrate the critical importance of taking the everyday life of congregations seriously as theological subject matter.

Another important shift concerns the role of the Bible in the life of congregations as they engage in moral deliberation and attempt to make decisions. This book insightfully engages the deep hermeneutical issues this shift raises, and it creatively explores the implications it has for theological education. Having worked within specific congregations for a period of years, the authors report on the extensive process they have enlisted for helping congregational leaders and members work though complex moral problems and the inherent conflicts embedded in those problems. They pay particular attention to how a regular engagement with the biblical narratives provides a framework and foundation for people with diverse views to find creative resolutions to deep differences in moral deliberation.

A third shift concerns the role of congregations living in their particular contexts as they seek to bear witness to the work of God, both in their midst and in their relationships with their larger communities. Some of these contributors present a biblical and theological framework for rethinking the public character of all congregations. They propose the metaphor of congregations as "public moral companions" as a way to rethink and reframe the life of congregations regarding what is often referred to as "civil society." The field studies that other contributors report on help to flesh out in concrete terms what this companionship begins to look like.

There are numerous audiences who will find this book instructive and illuminating, including theological educators, theological students, pastors, and denominational officials and staff. They will find in these pages substantive biblical and theological perspectives that help frame specific approaches to moral deliberation and decision-making within congregations, and through congregations for the sake of the world.

CRAIG VAN GELDER
Professor of Congregational
Mission, Luther Seminary

Contributing Authors

Ronald W. Duty holds a Ph.D. from the University of Minnesota and is an ordained minister in the Evangelical Lutheran Church in America and presently serves as the assistant director of the Department for Studies in the ELCA's Division for Church in Society.

Pat Taylor Ellison holds a Ph.D. from the University of Minnesota and is presently serving as the managing director of research for Church Innovations Institute, in addition to being an affiliated faculty member at Luther Seminary.

David Fredrickson holds a Ph.D. from Yale University and is presently serving as professor of New Testament at Luther Seminary. He is an ordained minister in the Evangelical Lutheran Church in America.

Donald Juel held a Ph.D. from Yale University and was teaching at Princeton Theological Seminary as the Richard J. Dearborn Professor of New Testament Theology at the time of his death in 2003.

Patrick Keifert holds a Ph.D. from the University of Chicago and is presently serving as professor of systematic theology at Luther Seminary. He is an ordained minister in the Evangelical Lutheran Church of America.

Lois Malcolm holds a Ph.D. from the University of Chicago and is presently serving as professor of systematic theology at Luther Seminary.

Gary Simpson holds a Th.D. from Christ Seminary-Seminex and is presently serving as professor of systematic theology at Luther Seminary. He is an ordained minister in the Evangelical Lutheran Church in America.

Framing the Agenda for Testing the Spirits

Patrick Keifert

A huge challenge faces those seeking to study congregations. Only a few re-sources are available that adequately incorporate a theological approach to this important task. In recent years numerous literatures have emerged that are intentionally more theological in focus: they include the reassess-ment of theological education, the reframing of practical theology, and the introduction of approaches for theological reflection. However, none of these deals explicitly with congregations as its primary subject matter, with emphasis on the importance of a theological perspective.

This book seeks to address this gap by bringing the everyday reali-ties of congregational life into conversation with theology. In taking this approach, the contributors to this book hope to engage at least four dif-ferent audiences with this important conversation. The first audience is theological students as they begin to prepare for ministry in serving con-gregations: our desire is to assist them in thinking about the dynamics of congregational life as they engage their studies. The second audience is the teachers of these students: we desire to help them make theological education come alive by considering more directly the realities of con-gregations. The third audience is local pastors who seek to become theo-logically informed regarding how to best serve their congregations. The contributors hope to help them learn from experiences of other congre-gations through the approach that we take in this book. And finally, we seek to address judicatory officials as our fourth audience, those who desire to become better stewards of their roles in providing leadership for congregations and their pastors.

Our Assumptions

We believe that the study of the congregation belongs as a central ingredient in contemporary theological education.[1] As this central ingredient, it belongs in biblical, historical, and constructive study as much as it does in so-called practical theology. In fact, placing the study of the congregation solely within the so-called practical disciplines continues a failed educational policy that divides theory and practice, and that tends to reduce practical theology to a series of skilled disciplines dependent on other fields for their critical reflection. This failed policy also makes it difficult for students to attend to the critical significance of the more classical disciplines in day-to-day ministry.

Over against this temptation to reduce congregational study to practical theology, the congregation has begun to come into its own within certain circles of the academy. It has drawn the interest of sociologists of religion, historians of American religion, and some theologians. However, this centrality has not, until quite recently, drawn much attention from missiologists, who tend to focus on larger organizational structures and theological considerations. Nor has it drawn much attention from those historians who are more interested in other places and times than in American history, and it has not captured the imagination of many biblical scholars.

Our Team

This volume introduces some of these neglected segments of theological education to the conversation with congregations. The contributors en-

---

1. "Congregation" in this book refers to "local religious assemblies in general." See R. Stephen Warner, "The Place of the Congregation in the Contemporary American Religious Configuration," in James P. Wind and James W. Lewis, eds., *American Congregations,* vol. 2: *New Perspectives in the Study of Congregations* (Chicago: University of Chicago Press, 1994), 54. This is not to deny that the term "congregation" can equally apply to diverse sociological realities within Roman Catholicism, for example, such as offices within the Vatican or communities of religious orders.

gage in the study of a number of specific congregations concerning the themes of moral discourse and action, of conflict and change within congregations, and of congregational efforts to respond to their immediate environment. The theological educators contributing to this volume represent different social locations for their teaching. Some teach in the congregation they serve and in other congregations within their region; others teach from a more entrepreneurial setting, that is, as consultants who enter only at the invitation of congregations and judicatories who pay for their services; others are judicatory officials and staff themselves, including an Episcopal bishop; some others teach out of denominational national offices; and still others teach in theological schools.

These teachers represent a number of denominations, though most are Lutheran. Almost all of them presently have terminal academic degrees in the various disciplines represented within the faculties of most schools of theology, in the areas of history, sociology, Bible, education, ethics, political science, and theology. These theological educators became a working team as they met face to face on regular occasions over a three-year period. We first sought to clarify our own identity and purpose by joining our own academic work to the existing field of congregational studies and the role of the congregation in the changing religious and social environment of mainline denominations (United Church of Christ, Presbyterian, Episcopalian, Roman Catholic, and Lutheran). Out of this general reading of congregational studies and reflection on the contribution our own academic work might create, we wrote a mission statement. At each subsequent meeting we reviewed this mission statement, revised it, and evaluated our progress in achieving it.

At each of our meetings we integrated three ongoing tasks. First, we updated one another on our own academic work that was related to the shared accomplishment of the mission statement. Usually this meant a discussion of a paper, some of which are in this volume. Second, we discussed and evaluated the major project of the research staff: a study of how congregations engage in talking, deciding, and acting on difficult topics, especially moral issues confronting them and their communities. Third, we invited noted scholars in the related fields to join us in reflecting on their work.

Our Mission

We named ourselves the Congregational Studies Research Team (CSRT) of the Church Innovations Institute.[2] Our mission statement reveals our growing consensus about who we are and what we seek to accomplish.

Congregational Studies Team Mission Statement

We are a theological learning organization in direct partnership with congregations, church leaders, and teachers. In concert with the Spirit of God, this partnership seeks to build up and empower congregations for mission by engaging with them in a process of conversation and action involving spiritual discernment and theological reflection about the necessary behaviors, skills, beliefs, and knowledge base for faithfully and effectively bringing people to a public identity in Christ.

We came to use a number of characteristics as we tried to identify and understand our shared work as a team. These include the following dimensions:

Learning Organization

We understand ourselves to be a theological learning community in the way that Peter Senge defines a learning organization.[3]

---

2. Church Innovations Institute describes its mission this way: "Church Innovations is a nonprofit organization devoted to renewing the church's focus on God's mission in the world. Rooted in the gospel of Jesus Christ and wholly committed to following God's leading for every congregation, we provide research and consulting tools, products and processes that increase your church's capacities to experience God's renewal and transformation." *About Church Innovations,* available at http://www.churchinnovations.org/06_about/about.html (accessed June 15, 2006).

3. Learning organizations are "organizations where people continually expand their capacity to create the results they truly desire, where new and expansive patterns of thinking are nurtured, where collective aspiration is set free, and where people are continually learning how to learn together." Peter M. Senge, *The Fifth Discipline: The Art and Practice of the Learning Organization* (New York: Doubleday/Currency, 1990), 3.

Theological

In being theological, our team took seriously our common conviction that God is the primary subject of teaching theology. We shared a perception with those scholars of contemporary theological education who have noted how a-theological much theological education has become. We as teachers sought to reflect on God in relationship to our own academic discipline and the congregation.

In Direct Partnership with Congregations

We sought to partner directly with particular congregations, which was not difficult since all of the theological educators of our team were active members of Christian congregations. Some were pastors of congregations, others were lay leaders in congregations, and others regularly functioned as teachers within congregations on behalf of judicatory or national denominational structures. Through the research model developed by the research staff of Church Innovations, we had ready access to thick descriptions of the lives of a number of congregations that had agreed to be partners in research. Members of these congregations have been taught a theological model of congregational research.

Church Leaders and Teachers

As theological educators, we were primarily interested in church leadership. Specifically, we were interested in lay leadership within congregations and how professional or paid staff leadership within the same congregations enhanced lay leadership. Secondarily, our interests were in judicatory and national leaders who support leadership development in congregations. This latter group also included leaders of schools of theology responsible for training professional and paid church leaders.

In Concert with the Spirit of God

As the CSRT pursued the relationship between our personal academic disciplines and our vocations as theological educators, we found that categories of spiritual discernment of truth joined these disparate activities. Even the most *scientific* moments of our work as historians, social scientists, philosophers, curriculum developers, exegetes, and interpreters fell within the general activity of spiritual discernment of truth within the presence of the Spirit of God.

To Build Up and Empower Congregations for Mission

This group shared the general perception that North American congregations can no longer remain passive to their immediate environment by expecting people to actively seek them out. The present circumstance demands much more active recruitment of and engagement with that environment not only for institutional survival but also for faithful achievement of Christian mission.

The group further believed that many, if not most, congregations within the church bodies represented in the group are quite passive. They tend to focus heavily on the maintenance model of Christian community, which is unresponsive to the new mission situation in the United States. We researchers and teachers further believed that the primary energy for renewing this mission dimension in congregations must come from within the congregations themselves. This group sought to empower and equip congregations by enhancing already existing capabilities rather than intervening with a new program or quick-fix techniques for evangelism or social justice. Quite to the contrary, the group assumed that strengthening the culture of the congregation and the ability of its leadership to identify the core values of that culture with respect to the needs of the immediate environment was, in the long term, a more effective way to create a climate for the renewal of the congregation's mission.

Engaging with Congregations in a Process of Conversation and Action Involving Spiritual Discernment and Theological Reflection

From the beginning, these teachers and researchers wanted to be fully engaged with congregations so that people in those congregations would become the chief actors in the research project. In addition, this engagement would be conversation and action, with all the attendant tension between talking and acting. Furthermore, the process of conversation and action would grow out of and be subject to spiritual discernment and theological reflection. The terms "spiritual discernment" and "theological reflection" were initially little more than a desire to reintegrate the more affective moments of faithful reflection with the more abstract and rational moments.

Part of the research was to uncover and renew the group's own sense of relating these two moments of theological research. This model of research joined applied ethnography with a process of spiritual and theological discernment by using a thick, participant-interpreter description approach — with members of the congregation being the primary researchers. These researchers gathered stories from their fellow members regarding times of conflict, discernment, and action regarding tough issues. The issues were moral and political both inside and outside the congregation.

We also invited the members and participant-interpreters to discern the manner in which the Spirit of God was active in their congregations' talking, deciding, and acting. We explored the diverse senses of divine agency within the membership and their own understanding of God's agency in their lives, indeed, even in the process of research.

Reflecting on such theological questions also opened the congregations to conversation that helped them discern the important differences between a Christian understanding and a more secular understanding of the same political and moral issues. In very important ways, Christian identity became less a list of peculiar Christian conclusions and more a peculiar manner of talking, deciding, and acting. This insight grew out of and was abetted by the primary biblical studies of the process of research.

Necessary Knowledge Base, Skills, Attitudes and Beliefs, and Behaviors

The team of scholars sought to examine the character of leadership, which we understood as both a personal and interpersonal phenomenon. To examine this character we believed it necessary to understand the behaviors, skills, beliefs, and knowledge base that were most often evident in the congregations we studied. The following are questions we most wanted answered by the leaders from whom we learned, leaders who included small-group leaders, pastors, and other paid staff — people we called "trustees of the vision" — and leaders of large-group discussion:

- What behaviors were typical of these leaders?
- What minimum knowledge base was necessary to use Scripture in a conversation regarding disputed moral issues?
- What beliefs informed the congregations who effectively conversed, decided, and acted together?
- What skills characterized those congregations who did this work?

For Faithfully and Effectively Bringing People to a Public Identity in Christ

The goal of this work is bringing people to a public identity in Christ. Our team's assumption was that one cannot live an effective and faithful Christian life without a public dimension. Indeed, congregations are public meeting places and are excellent schools of public life. Against the forces that would relegate religion and faith to a private sphere, this team of scholars believes that congregations must bring people to a public identity in Christ as an essential part of making disciples. Our purposes for research within the broad field of congregational studies were:

1. to increase the capacity of congregations to be renewed as unique communities of faith in service to their community and the world;
2. to join social-scientific discourse with theological discourse in service of congregational renewal;
3. to create a team of scholars and theological educators drawn from several intellectual disciplines in service to congregational renewal;
4. to facilitate the voice of congregations as communities of faith within a disciplined process of applied ethnography and theological reflection;
5. to discover the attitudes and beliefs, skills, minimum knowledge base and behavior of effective congregational leaders in moral conversation and action;
6. to develop leaders within congregations with attitudes and beliefs, minimum knowledge base, and behavior for listening, talking, deciding, and acting as Christian community.

Our Materials and Processes

In keeping with these purposes of our research, we chose to develop materials and processes that immediately respond to developing leaders within congregations. We developed a *toolbox* that was designed to enhance the existing attitudes, beliefs, minimum knowledge base, and behavior of congregations as they attend, assert, decide, and act as Christian communities. We developed the toolbox on the basis of our research in congregations that were able effectively to engage in conversation and action on tough moral issues. The toolbox includes an interactive video workshop that teaches a congregation how to identify and develop listening leaders. Then it provides resources for teaching those listening leaders how to use a process of applied ethnography to gain a clearer sense of the culture within which they will develop a process for talking, deciding, and acting about these issues.

We also developed the toolbox on the basis of our research in Scripture, tradition, and historical and social-scientific theories of society and culture, particularly community moral development and communication practices. We developed this research primarily from the reading and study of the members of our Congregational Studies Research Team, in addition to the invited scholars who participated in one or more of our meetings. This research and the experience of these congregations allowed us to test the toolbox in a number of congregations, including those involved in the original study.

This book reflects our initial reflections and tentative conclusions that are based on this research process. It also engages in a self-reflective critique of the process of research and uses the model of conversation, deciding, and acting that is in the toolbox. In our conversations as a research team, we drew on the work of James and Evelyn Whitehead[4] and Thomas Groome.[5] The research team began with the fruitful prejudice that a method of theology articulated by Bernard Lonergan would be an excel-

---

4. James D. and Evelyn Eaton Whitehead, *Method in Ministry: Theological Reflection and Christian Ministry* (New York: Seabury, 1980); see also their *Community of Faith: Models and Strategies for Developing Christian Communities* (New York: Seabury, 1982).

5. Thomas H. Groome, *Christian Religious Education: Sharing Our Story and Vision* (San Francisco: Harper & Row, 1980); see also his *Sharing Faith: A Comprehensive Approach to Religious Education and Pastoral Ministry: The Way of Shared Praxis* (New York: Harper-Collins, 1991).

lent beginning point for enhancing local theology in congregations.[6] Lonergan's theological methodology is the basis for the Whiteheads' work, with some modifications.

Our Writing

Each of the contributing authors developed his or her essay in conversation with the CSRT as a whole. We should note that, while we drew from Lonergan's work, each of us had some reservations about his methodology in theology. Most of us accept the suspicions of the critical theory of the Frankfurt school, especially that of Jürgen Habermas, which informs the work of Thomas Groome.[7] As a result, we felt that Lonergan relied too heavily on a Cartesian approach.

Rather than this Cartesian private journey of the soul, we have eschewed an overarching theoretical framework. In contrast, our work reflects more the descriptive phenomenological approach of Paul Ricoeur, his hermeneutical philosophy, and the more general hermeneutics of rhetoric.[8] For us, theological reflection involves more a communal conversation and action that *tests the spirits* rather than a progress of private insight resulting from a previously agreed upon objective method of research.

These intellectual commitments led the CSRT to imagine a future of theological education in this postmodern era in which a new age of mission in American culture requires significant engagement with local communities of faith. We hope these essays serve to engage students, teachers, pastors, and denominational officials in imagining their own ways of responding to these new cultural opportunities for doing theology.

6. Bernard J. F. Lonergan, S.J., *Method in Theology* (New York: Herder and Herder, 1972).

7. Groome, *Sharing Faith,* 102; Groome, *Christian Religious Education,* 170.

8. Paul Ricoeur, *Figuring the Sacred: Religion, Narrative, and Imagination,* ed. Mark I. Wallace (Minneapolis: Fortress, 1995); see also Ricoeur, *From Text to Action: Essays in Hermeneutics, II,* trans. Kathleen Blamey and John B. Thompson (Evanston, IL: Northwestern University Press, 1991); and "Philosophical Hermeneutics and Theological Hermeneutics," *Studies in Religion/Sciences Religieuses* 5, no. 1 (1975/6): 14-33.

PART I

DEVELOPING A THEOLOGICAL
APPROACH FOR STUDYING
CONGREGATIONS

The chapters in this section provide readers with an understanding of the necessity of taking congregations seriously in theological education. They also provide critical biblical and theological perspectives for thinking about congregations; further, they approach the everyday lives of congregations as being substantive and vital for understanding the presence and work of God in the world. The approach taken argues that it is critical to see God through the Spirit as the acting subject at work in the lived lives of congregations. It is crucial for God's people to develop the capacity for engaging in discerning the presence and the work of the Spirit in their midst.

In the first essay, Patrick Keifert makes the pivotal argument that there has been a return of the subject of congregations to the disciplines associated with theological study. On the one hand, this return marks a significant turning point, both for congregations and for theological education, in that it opens up new lines of inquiry. On the other hand, this return is not a restoration of a former time. It is a return that is fully informed by the significant social, cultural, and theological developments that have taken place over the past several centuries. This first chapter provides helpful clues for understanding how to read congregations and their contexts from a theological perspective in light of this recent return.

In the second chapter, Keifert takes up the issue of how the *Bible* is related to and interacts with this return of the study of congregations to theological education. He notes the numerous problematic ways that the Bible has been used in the past, as well as the absence of the Bible in the life of much congregational moral deliberation and decision-making. His constructive proposal toward a new movement of what he calls a "rhetorical rationality" offers a creative way to break through the problems of the past as well as the inertia of the present regarding the place of the Bible in moral deliberation and decision-making. He goes on to illustrate how taking this approach can lead to the reshaping of theological institutions and the reinventing of the teaching of theology, especially noting the resulting new interface between the church and the world.

In the third chapter, David Fredrickson creatively and imaginatively opens up the life and ministry of the congregation at Philippi in the New Testament. He carefully exegetes the letter to the Philippians and demonstrates how we need to understand that God's action in the world is taking place in significant ways in and through congregations. Further, Fredrickson demonstrates both the public and political character of this activity of God in relationship to the gospel. All of this he grounds in the work of God through Christ, which was both public and political, and which was for the sake of the world. The freedom for life that Christ extended to us through his actions now becomes the freedom for life we offer to others.

In the chapter that concludes this first section, Gary Simpson builds on Fredrickson's biblical argument by offering a theological argument from the early creeds and from Luther's writings about how congregations are to live in the world as public moral companions. He develops the concept of civil society as the arena in which this companionship takes place, and he uses Luther's conception of vocation as also applying to congregations. Congregations have a vocation of being called and sent into the world to live and work as public moral companions to the structures and organizations that make up civil society.

The Return of the Congregation to Theological Conversation

Patrick Keifert

Congregations have returned to the consciousness of students of theology. They have drawn the attention of sociologists of religion because they are the dominant social form of religion in the United States.[1] Congregations have also drawn the attention of some historians of religion, especially historians of Christianity.[2] And they have even drawn the attention of some historians of early Christianity; as a result of that attention and focus, some New Testament scholars have also become involved in studying congregations.[3]

This return of congregations to a conscious theological conversation is related to other developments taking place in theological education. In fact, four related returns are presently taking place in the contemporary study of theology: (1) practical reason; (2) interpretation and the imagination; (3) a rhetorical approach; and (4) a sense of mission. All of these deeply inform the return of congregations to the attention of theologians. My purpose in this essay is to reflect on these four related returns by engaging them in detail, and to discuss the nature of moral reflection and

---

1. Nancy T. Ammerman and Arthur E. Farnsley, *Congregation and Community* (New Brunswick, NJ: Rutgers University Press, 1997); Nancy T. Ammerman et al., eds., *Studying Congregations: A New Handbook* (Nashville: Abingdon, 1998).

2. Diana Butler Bass, *The Practicing Congregation: Imagining a New Old Church* (Herndon, VA: Alban Institute, 2004); Mark A. Noll, *A History of Christianity in the United States and Canada* (Grand Rapids: Eerdmans, 1992).

3. See, e.g., works by Peter Stuhlmacher.

decision-making in congregations. However, before exploring these various returns, let us further reflect on the nature of returning.

The Return of Martin Guerre

There is returning, and then there is returning. When I go on a trip, I return home different from when I left. The intervening time makes a difference on what the person who returns is like. Normally, the longer I am away, the more change I undergo, so that when I return from a fairly long trip, I am quite a different person. It also makes a difference in the home to which I return, for things continued to change there while I was away, and those changes also affect who I am upon my return.

The nature of the place to which one travels also makes a difference in shaping the person that returns. If I travel to a place that is, on the whole, quite like my everyday experience, I probably return quite similar to what I was like before I left. But if I travel to a place quite different from my everyday experience, I probably return quite different from who I was before I left. And if I experience a traumatic event while away, my returning self may be even more different. Traumatic events tend to profoundly change people, and more trauma usually brings greater change. Sometimes such traumatic events even include war.

War is what Martin Guerre returns from in the movie *The Return of Martin Guerre*.[4] When he returns to his home, a small sixteenth-century French village, the village has changed; but Martin has changed even more. In fact, he may not even be the Martin who left at all. The Martin who left may be dead, and this man who has returned has possibly stolen his identity. Some villagers doubt his identity, but most are unable for various reasons to question it. At first his wife also doubts his identity, but as time passes she begins to treat him as her husband.

In the American version of the movie, set in the years following the Civil War, the returning soldier clearly is not the one who left.[5] But the one who returns is very familiar with the other's story since they shared a

---

4. *The Return of Martin Guerre* [*Le Retour de Martin Guerre*], motion picture, dir. Daniel Vigne (Paris: Compagnie Commerciale Français Cinématographie, 1982); cf. Natalie Zemon Davis, *The Return of Martin Guerre* (reprint; Cambridge, MA: Harvard University Press, 1984).

5. *Sommersby,* motion picture, dir. Jon Amiel (Burbank, CA: Alcor Films, 1993).

cell in a prisoner of war camp, and their loneliness allowed them ample time to learn each other's story. The one who does return wishes to better himself, not only financially but also morally, and he pursues this course of action with diligence. Following his return, he proves to be a better husband than the former husband and a better citizen than the former citizen. He finally endears himself to the entire community — just about the time that the former Martin's past deeds catch up with him. In the end, the one who returns prefers to maintain his new identity for the sake of his children and community rather than avoid conviction for a capital offense. His return, while in many ways not a return, profoundly changes him, his wife and family, and the entire community for whom he ends up giving his life.

The return of the congregation to the conversation among those who are pursuing a theological understanding of congregations also includes, as I have noted above, the return to this discussion of practical reason, interpretation and imagination, the rhetorical, and a sense of mission. It is like the return of Martin Guerre: it is a return, and yet not a return. The congregation has never been gone, of course; indeed, without the congregation, the study of theology would seem to be purely academic. In many important ways the theologian has always imagined the congregation, especially over the past three hundred years, as the place where theology hits the road. The congregation is the location where theology is practiced.

According to this modern view, theology that is done in academia has its final application in the congregation. In recent decades, as theological education has increasingly become influenced by a system of star faculty in various theological schools, the study of theology has taken on a certain capitalist framework. The star theologian invents new theological ideas, wholesales them to her or his students, and the students retail them in the congregation. This view sees the laity primarily as consumers of these retailed theological inventions.

Of course, the schools of theology understand that living pieties have implied theologies. Students are taught, often through a key faculty star, to engage in the school's theological critique of these living pieties and to discover their implied theologies. In all of this learning the congregation is, of course, already there. However, in the following chapters of this book, the return of the congregation is not primarily about congregations being consumers of a commodity called "theology." Quite to the contrary, the congregation itself becomes a primary location that helps *generate* theology. Such theology is the result of people reflecting on the lived practices of how congregations understand the Christian thing.[6] The congregation, which lives as a community of face-to-face encounters with the God who raised Israel's Jesus from the dead, becomes in this process the primal location within which humans gain indirect knowledge of God.

Students of theology, including professional theologians, engage in theological reflection about congregations in a number of ways. Depending on the issue being considered, we find them reflecting *in, with, for,* and even *against* the lived practices of congregations. This return of the congregation is a return after a very long absence from this role. At the bare minimum, it is a return after an absence of over three hundred years, for in that time (1650-1950) students of theology sought to follow the philosophical longings and desires of the Western European Enlightenment. By such philosophical longings and desires, I mean the emotions that drive the primary themes of modern philosophy: finding certainty and security from what appeared to be intellectual and moral chaos.

This search for security and certainty sought an Archimedean point that could avoid the ugly violence of the Thirty Years War. The combatants in that war reflected the claims and counterclaims of religious groups, both Protestants and Catholics, who were seeking to provide such certainty and security. Western European philosophers — and with them most American philosophers — desired the same certainty and security that these religious communities offered, but without what the philosophers considered to be the hopelessly particular, relativistic, and irrational foundations of religion. These philosophers believed that foundations of a secure public life must be secular, universal, and rational. For the good of a secure public life, one's religion, values, particularity, and feelings needed to be kept private, and they needed to remain private even though they might be profound; but these aspects of religion were not likely to go away. The firm belief of the founding generation of the United States of America is a poignant example of this desire and longing for securing the public life in the foundation of reason, since they believed that the people are to be governed by law based in reason rather than religion.

6. David H. Kelsey, *To Understand God Truly: What's Theological About a Theological School* (Louisville: Westminster John Knox Press, 1992), 110ff.

The return of the congregation to the center of the study of theology, after such a three-hundred-year leave of absence, is a return that is more than just a return after a war. It is a return after banishment and exile. In fact, the return of the congregation is a return after being banned and exiled from theological education for 1600 years! While that seems like a long time, it indicates that part of the contemporary return of the congregation reflects changes in the relationship between the church and culture, changes so great that they equal in many respects the change initiated in A.D. 313 by the adoption of Christianity as one of the legal religions of the Roman Empire. Previous to this establishment, students of theology were more likely to have been trained by bishops in the congregational setting rather than in separate schools. I will provide more on this return in a later discussion of the return of a sense of mission.

The Return of the Congregation

For now, it is enough to say that the return of the congregation to the study of theology, as it is represented in this book, is and is not the return of the congregation to a premodern or even pre-Constantinian period of Christianity. The *not* of the metaphor is clear: the postmodern or late-modern character of the essays in this book do not pretend that a return to the past is possible. Instead, the return of the congregation will find congregations profoundly shaped by the hallmarks of modernity. Whatever way forward we may choose, we will go as students of theology profoundly shaped by modernity. Similarly, the return of the congregation from pre-Constantinian Christianity will be the return of the congregation profoundly shaped by Christendom.

Theologically, the return of the congregation is funded by the promise of God to be present through a self-giving and self-sacrificing love available through Word and Sacrament within the face-to-face gathered Christian community. Philosophically, it is funded by the return of practical reasoning, interpretation and imagination, and the rhetorical with respect to philosophical reflection. Historically, it is funded in North America by the transformation of Christendom, along with the denominational structures that depended on it, through a renewed understanding of mission.

The Return of Practical Reason

What do we mean when we refer to the return of practical reason? What other kind of reason is there? Impractical? Of course, we reason practically all the time. In this sense, practical reason was never someplace else, and thus does not need to return. However, in the events following the Protestant and subsequent Catholic Reformations, the various European parties sought to ground the life of the state, with its power of sanctioned violence, in something other than religious sources. These sources were precisely the sources under question and were even viewed by many influential interpreters as the source of illegitimate and capricious violence.

The preferred alternative was to find a kind of reason that was pure of religious foundations, a kind of reason that could function as an objective source for public life. Many candidates for pure reason were offered, most of them drawn from analogies of the natural sciences and the pure language of mathematics, especially geometry. Such pure reason and language was theoretical, above the day-to-day and practical matters. Good theory was capable of explaining diverse experiences and consistently predicting the future.

People, of course, must live out their lives making very incomplete and practical decisions. With respect to these decisions, existing theories could never quite match the complexity of particular situations, or predict reality with much consistency. According to this new theoretical awareness, people needed to learn how to apply theory. It was accepted that such application would be inexact for the time being, but as scientific research progressed, the theories would become more effectively explanatory and predictive. As a result, a great divide was created between theory and practice. For students of theology, this meant a major divide between courses in theory and courses in practical ministry.

In recent decades we have seen the return of some of the premodern frameworks with very new roles, one of which is the role of practical reason. It is now being reclaimed as an intellectual discipline, a type of wisdom that mediates between theory and practice. A number of the chapters in this book are exercises in practical reason and are understood as being part of the ongoing and self-critical tradition of Christian wisdom. In a similar manner, most of these chapters reflect a reinterpretation of the Enlightenment as a positive and direct result of the Reformation experience and reflection rather than being a failed reaction to the Reformation. This shift is important in perspective.

The authors of the following chapters, though dependent on diverse intellectual sources, also generally believe that the practices of practical reason embodied in the Reformation continue to remain useful for our late-modern or postmodern circumstances. Thus, they do not understand the Reformation as an attempt to provide alternative foundations for human culture and endeavor; instead, they see it as an exercise in prophetic critique by means of Christian wisdom and practical reason.

Practical reason is as intellectually rigorous as any claims made by pure reason or theoretical reflection. It does not replace theoretical reflection or practice; rather, it mediates among several things, including practice and action, the experience of action, and theoretical reflection and critique of practice and action in the everyday world. Practical reasoning, while it is a kind of wisdom, involves an identifiable knowledge base, skills, attitudes and beliefs, and behaviors.[7] Because these are identifiable, practical reasoning can be taught; however, it cannot be taught outside of concrete circumstances.

Because we hold that the congregation is the primary location of the Christian thing by which we engage in indirect reflection on the presence and agency of God, the congregation needs to be the primary location for learning practical reasoning as a practice of Christian wisdom. A major part of the return of the congregation to the study of theology, then, makes the primary purpose of theological education the teaching of this reasoning. This means that the return of practical reason is a mediation between theory and practice, and that can help end the false dichotomy between theory and practice. Indeed, no relatively adequate course in the study of theology can either limit itself to practice and action, or to theory, and/or to the application of theory. All relatively adequate courses in the study of theology need to engage in practical reasoning as Christian wisdom.

This approach to Christian wisdom and spiritual discernment also characterized the shared practices of the group of scholars who have contributed to this book. We deliberately conducted our research within a conscious effort to dwell within the Word of God. Our Christian practice of spiritual discernment began by dwelling on biblical texts that we under-

---

7. Aristotle, *Nicomachean Ethics,* bk. 1, ch. 13; cf. Thomas H. Groome, *Sharing Faith: A Comprehensive Approach to Religious and Pastoral Ministry* (New York: HarperCollins, 1991), 42-49; cf. Bernard J. F. Lonergan, *Method in Theology* (New York: Herder and Herder, 1972), 19.

stood historically and critically — but also theologically.[8] To say that we understood them theologically is to say that we practiced the Christian wisdom of attending to the biblical texts, and we expected and hoped to experience God speaking to us. We understood that no particular technique could guarantee that, nor did we need to exclude appropriate suspicions of our listening. Among those appropriate suspicions was attending to our social location and how it both hides and reveals how God might be speaking to us in, with, and under the biblical texts.

The authors' inherited traditions of Christian wisdom taught us that the speaking of God is not restricted to a small group of biblical experts. We also recognized the value of the powerful gifts of biblical scholars who have dedicated their lives to the study of the ancient world and to the rhetorical shapes and situations of the biblical texts. We found those historical and interpretive gifts to be crucial for contemporary Christian practical reasoning and imagination.

The Return of Interpretation and Imagination

The practice of Christian practical reasoning implies the return of interpreting and shaping this interpretation by a Christian imagination. The imagination is a faculty characteristic of all human beings. It is our ability to connect specific events and situations to abstract ideas through images. As a result, we do not live purely on the basis of the immediate and disconnected experiences of our senses, but rather our experiences are always given to us within a connected framework of images.

These images are more than just a reproduction of our senses; they reflect previous experience and the lived practices, including the speech, of the community within which we live. These lived practices, especially language, are also productive of our experiences. Though no one in our group argued that we were hopelessly caught in our particular lived practices and languages, neither did we believe that there was some kind of method or reasoning that was exempt from such particularities of the imagination. However, we believed that we were capable of distancing ourselves from our own imaginations through engagement with other imaginations dif-

---

8. See the appendix to this volume, Donald Juel's short essay "The Use of the Scriptures in Congregational Research," to better understand our approach.

ferent from our own. As theologians, of course, we believed that behind each different imagination was the irreducibly Other, that is, God. So the encounter with other imaginations, and the lived practices and speech that mutually shaped those imaginations, presented an opportunity to search for truth and shared meaning among human beings — and with God through other human beings. The encounter with the Other in the other made our work a public activity, though recognizing it was bound to the particularity of social location.

Our social location is irreducibly a Christian one, and thus it is formed within a Christian imagination. As Christians we live within and from the Word of God in our lived face-to-face communities of faith — that is, in congregations. Therefore, the congregation is inextricably part of our Christian reflection and study of theology.

This is not to say that our Christian imagination is only located in the public settings of the congregation or the larger church. On the contrary, the very public character of the Christian imagination drives us into conversation and practice in the world as the location of our vocation, which helps us live into the mission of God for the sake of the world. For the group of scholars represented in this volume, Christian imagination was neither private, though it had profound personal dimensions, nor sectarian, though it did not presume to construct the only public space within which true and meaningful practice and speech takes place. Therefore, we held that the primal location for the pursuit of truth and meaning for us was the congregation, and that the congregation is both *for* the world and *over against* the world. The Christian imagination always involves the encounter with God in Word and Sacrament; but it also includes a playful act of interpretation of culture and society and the experience of the faithful, both personal and communal.

We created a heuristic model for work within congregations and amongst ourselves. This heuristic model calls for the practical skills of attending, asserting, deciding, and acting on the basis of a process of spiritual discernment. This act of spiritual discernment grows out of attending to three sources for spiritually relevant knowledge for spiritual discernment: (a) tradition, especially Scripture, (b) culture and society, and (c) the experience of the faithful, both personal and communal. In each of these moments, the basic questions remain the same: "What is God up to here?" and "What is the Word of God for us in this place and time?"

Such a process involves a willingness to play back and forth among these sources for spiritually relevant knowledge. We took such play as both unavoidable and capable of discipline through a deliberate practice of interpreting, the discipline of connecting and disconnecting Scripture and its interpretation through time with culture and society and the experience of the faithful in a manner that is faithful to the promises of God. Reflection on this discipline of playful connection and disconnection is hermeneutics, the process of interpretation. The practice of such a faithful and playful connecting and disconnecting is Christian spiritual discernment. While involving deep personal moments, this discernment is always turned out to the Other in the other, and thus it is irreducibly public and also irreducibly rhetorical.

The Return of Rhetoric

I admit that even the use of "rhetorical" might be a rhetorical error. In fact, the contemporary use of the word *rhetoric* is usually accompanied by a word like "mere" to form expressions such as "mere rhetoric." The intended meaning here is that something expressed is either not true or is of little substance, and it is designed instead to change emotions, cloud reason, and manipulate the will. In that sense, "rhetoric" is what you do when you are not interested in pursuing the truth but when you desire to control your audience. Similarly, the contemporary sense of a "rhetorical question" is a question that presumes agreement on a major but unspoken premise. Rhetorical questions presume a lot about the audience, but "rhetoric" remains the right word precisely because it jars the sensibility and disconcerts our expectations, and that underscores how the kind of return we are speaking of is a return after a traumatic experience and a significant time away.

During the past three hundred years, moderns developed a profound distrust of rhetoric as an intellectual part of philosophy because of their desire and need for certainty and universal agreement based on objective facts. Ancient and medieval rhetoric, indeed even Reformation rhetoric, emphasized the concrete and the particular. The need was to engage in practical reasoning, persuasion, entertainment, or even an appeal to emotions, affections, and passions for the sake of a civil life. Rather than pursuing indubitably distinct ideas and logical syllogisms that were either clearly right or wrong, rhetoric suggested that most public deliberation depended on practical syllogisms that could never ultimately ground themselves in clear and distinct ideas or logic. But the character of public deliberation is that it depends on matters that are *more or less* evident rather than being clear and distinct. It depends on gathering, forming, and finally persuading one another toward a shared decision in the midst of uncertainty, and it pays profound attention to the dynamic of public discourse, especially audience.

Perhaps the only thing left of the ancient meaning of rhetoric, in our popular sense of the term, is the concern for the audience, which the following chapters view as an important concept of rhetoric. However, the return of rhetoric is not simply about audience; rather, it is about structuring the pursuit of truth and the ordering of public discourse within the interplay of three characters: the character of the speaker *(ethos)*, the character of the speech *(logos)*, and the character of the audience *(pathos)*. Varieties of rhetorical theory may emphasize one of these over the others; but, in order to be rhetorical, it must attend to all three.

The return of the rhetorical to the study of theology makes the congregation a central location and subject matter. It is in the congregation that the greatest diversity, particularity, and most common form of Christian public deliberation, persuasion, and delight take place. More often than not, the public character of the Christian is formed within the congregation, both personally and communally. Likewise, congregations enjoy access to the vast majority of diverse audiences — politically, socially, economically, and culturally. They — in concert with other social institutions, such as the households of the congregations — carry out most of the work of making disciples.

The Return of a Sense of Mission

The making of disciples introduces the fourth return within the return of the congregation to the study of theology: a sense of mission. As American culture becomes increasingly secularized, the return of a sense of mission is vital. This sense of mission needs to be one that belongs primarily to the local community rather than functioning as a surrogate of other institutional expressions of the church, such as national and judicatory bodies. This sense is vital to the congregation, and it is also vital to students of theology and to theological education.

During those centuries and in those lands where Christianity was identified either with the state or by the popular culture as the religion of choice, congregations could assume tremendous social forces supporting membership. With the rise of the secular state, those social forces began to wane. In fact, one could be considered a fine citizen — perhaps even a more trustworthy citizen — if one had no particular religious commitments. Even if religion, in general, was taken as a virtue, it was extremely important that it was a private virtue.

In a Christendom setting, the congregation functions primarily as a parish, the spiritual firehouse for a designated political and geographic area. In such settings, parishes, like firehouses, can expect goodwill from the people living in the parish. Who could complain about the existence of a spiritual firehouse since someday you might have a spiritual fire? Parishes can expect people to pay taxes for them and raise their children with a tacit, if not explicit, support of the spiritual firehouse's existence. Needless to say, like an actual firehouse, the parish as a spiritual firehouse cannot expect everyone in the parish to show up every week to celebrate its existence. More important, the congregation as parish understands its mission as maintaining and improving the status quo. The task of making disciples is no longer central since the concept of parish presumes that everyone in the parish already is a disciple.

In the congregation as parish model, the congregation can to some degree assume that the primary resources and activities for forming disciples, persons with a public identity in Christ, are present in the immediate environment of the congregation. Parents and extended families and schools and civic organizations will teach the basics of Christian identity, and the congregation is responsible to confirm these disciples in the congregation, after which the majority of them return to life as usual.

In this post-Christendom time, those congregations that are flourishing have been able to recognize this deadly formula and have sought out an alternative understanding. In most cases they have learned that they must create community and connect it to the central spiritual energies of the congregation. Rather than presume community, they actively do community development by attending to their own character *(ethos)* in relationship to the gospel *(logos)* and the audiences they seek to serve in mission *(pathos)*. They understand themselves as public communities of faith, which is in marked contrast to many congregations — especially in mainline, now old-line denominations — that continue to function as parishes.

As American culture becomes increasingly secular in its public life, the role of the congregation as parish becomes increasingly private and passive with respect to public life. Of course, those who remain interested in matters of politics and social justice may express their personal convictions and act on them out of their own conscience in a free society. But notice that public life is reduced to politics and advocacy over certain justice issues in the political sphere. The congregation is not even thought of as a public meeting house, a public space for moral deliberation and action; it is not thought of as a place where persons are fulfilled and shaped as disciples with a public identity in Christ.

The Congregation as Moral Deliberator and Actor

With the pressures of the culture pushing religion into the private sphere, Christian witness needs to draw on its public imagination without neglecting the personal dimensions of the Christian thing. Congregations are already public meetings: public worship, with its liturgy, is their most characteristic identifier. When young people participate in congregations, they experience an intergenerational public community. Congregations remain the most likely place for those marginalized in other public institutions to learn the basic skills for civic life. Likewise, congregations remain the most common place for those persons to be given the opportunity to develop leadership skills.

Latently, if not explicitly, congregations are clearly faith-based communities of moral deliberation and action. Therefore, the study of theology predicated on the return of the congregation must take as a primary activity the increasing of the capacities of congregations to engage in moral deliberation and action, making it an essential characteristic of the public life of the congregation. Such a study of theology preferably begins with the local community and engages in spiritual discernment *in, with, for,* and *against* the congregation. Such spiritual discernment needs to build community, and then it needs to connect that community to the central spiritual energies of the congregation.

In the work that we have pursued, we believed that training listening leaders to use an applied ethnographic approach was an excellent way to enter into a partnership with congregations. People who already had good listening skills were taught the basic model of applied ethnography.[9] They developed eight open-ended questions that elicited stories from members of their congregations and communities. By interviewing active and inactive members of the community, these listening leaders were creating community; in addition, they were gaining a sense of the character of their congregation *(ethos)* and audience *(pathos)* and how they related to their understanding of the Christian gospel *(logos)*. Through these conversations they began to understand their congregation as a set of moral practices, both good and bad.

The remainder of the process involved the reading of these interviews (all of which were treated confidentially) by scholars of various disciplines who were seeking to understand congregations. In addition to understanding congregations, each of these scholars was also a student of theology who was seeking to understand God truly. Thus, in seeking to understand God in the reading of these stories, they wrote a report and recommendations back to the listening leaders. And with the listening leaders and those others who held positions of public responsibility in the congregation, they introduced a process of moral deliberation and action. This process made explicit the latent discernment of God and enhanced the capacity of the congregation to gain a more public and critical theology and a practice of the Christian life. Thus is the congregation returning not only as a *consumer* of theology but also as a *producer* of it. The congregation returns as a school of theology and as a primary location for the making of disciples — and apostles, those who make disciples.

Similar to Martin Guerre, who returned from a long and traumatic absence, the congregation that is returning to theological education is, and is not, the congregation of premodern and pre-Constantinian times. These congregations will, and will not, want such a prominent place in the study of theology. The other centers of the study of theology will tend to continue thinking of congregations as either consumers of their theological products or objects of their theological critique. However, many congregations have already returned, and, like Martin Guerre, they are seeking to be better members of the household and citizens of the community than they were before.

---

9. See Pat Taylor Ellison, "Text-Dwelling, Deep Listening, and Faith-Based Conversation in Congregations" (in this volume), for a detailed description of this applied ethnographic approach.

The Bible and Theological Education:
A Report and Reflections on a Journey

Patrick Keifert

For over twenty years, my good friend and colleague Donald H. Juel and I reflected together on the place of the Bible in modern theological education. In this chapter I will sketch out why we set out on this journey and what we experienced while taking it. I also offer some brief reflections about why these travels are so necessary, not only to the life of the church, but also to the flourishing of ministry within our postmodern world. This chapter provides a backdrop for understanding the work of the Congregation Studies Research Team (CSRT) and the role of the Bible in faith-based moral conversation in congregations. We share our journey to support students of congregations, along with congregational leaders, to better understand how to use the Bible for engaging in public moral discernment.

Though we found many ways to describe what we were trying to learn, two questions serve to capture the intent of our inquiry: "When we say that the Bible is true, what do we mean? And what methods of interpretation appreciate its truthfulness?" We came to this question as we explored two places where the Bible is commonly thought to be central, indeed crucial, to theological discourse: the academy, especially theological institutions and departments of religion, and the Christian congregation.

As we searched for answers, we began to reflect on how various centers of learning within the academy understood the Bible as true, and what methods of interpretation they used to appreciate its truthfulness. We were curious about how particular methods of interpretation and application were justified within the academy, but we also wanted to know how these methods are actually used in practical situations by those who espouse them. As time passed, it became quite apparent that there was a significant amount of conflict among scholars and disciplines on these questions. And one result was our increased interest in how our colleagues in the academy actually persuaded each other to change their minds about these questions.

The Problematic: Why Is the Bible So Often Absent in Public Conversations in Church and World?

In our journey we focused on how people used the Bible to carry on moral conversations in their congregations; in particular, we looked at how scholars, teachers, and congregational leaders used the Bible to convince diverse audiences of a moral or interpretive position. In a few instances, the congregational practices we found were quite encouraging; but more often than not, we saw the opposite.

The realities of the practices common in both the academy and church caused us to reexamine the use of the Bible in theological educa-tion. The first thing we learned was that our own previous academic train-ing was, at least in part, disturbingly inadequate in preparing us to pursue these questions of truth. We also found that many of these individuals within the academy used practices of critique and persuasion that were equally inadequate. Our academic training had caused us to wonder about the relationship between traditional claims that the Bible is true and the methods we used and taught for interpreting the Bible.

For us, as with other modern students of the Bible, history was the primary "mode of intelligibility," a methodology that was key for under-standing the truth claims of the Bible.[1] However, we came to join many students of the Bible who had found that such a method has led to an un-happy and dysfunctional divide between what we, following Martin Buss, have called "critical description and capricious faith."[2] This represents the

---

1. "History as a mode of intelligibility" came into my vocabulary in a class by that title taught by Charles Wegener at the University of Chicago. See his *Liberal Education and the Modern University* (Chicago: University of Chicago Press, 1978), and *The Discipline of Taste and Feeling* (Chicago: University of Chicago Press, 1992).

2. Martin J. Buss, ed., *Encounter with the Text: Form and History in the Hebrew Bible* (Philadelphia: Fortress, 1979), 5. Describing quite different phenomena, twentieth-century

divide between either an empirical-rationalist engagement with the text as a historical document or a nonrational commitment to the Bible as the Word of God. We found the complete separation between these two approaches to the role of the Bible — critical description and capricious faith — to be present in the thought and practice of the academy as well as the congregation. Indeed, the divide was especially noticeable in the conversations and decisions of Christian congregations on morally controversial issues.

Our research on congregations in deep conflict over morally disputed topics such as sexuality, war, and worship uncovered ironic and disturbing patterns in the ways the Bible was used. The higher the anxiety on a moral issue in a congregation, the lower the likelihood that leaders would turn to the Bible in hope of even aiding, much less transforming, the conversation.[3] The pattern of avoiding discussion of the Bible altogether under those circumstances was as typical of congregational leaders who made very strong claims for the authority and truthfulness of the Bible as it was for those who made much more modest claims. In short, whatever theory of the Bible as authority for truth these leaders and their congregations embraced, a clear correlation existed between heightened anxiety and the practice of avoiding the Bible. To make matters worse, as the anxiety increased, leaders expressed fear that the Bible would contribute to, if not cause, dysfunctional conflict in their congregations.

In these crises of congregational conflict, we identified two dominant congregational habits in the use of the Bible: (a) using the Bible as a series of "Bible bullets," or (b) using the Bible to pour pious syrup on the conversation. In a majority of cases in which the Bible was used to settle morally disputed topics, parties tended to perceive the Bible as a source of ammunition to fire at the opposition. This approach was usually part of an ongoing war whose purpose was to obliterate the adverse position from the community. Not surprisingly, instead of informing or persuading any conversation partners to change their minds — or even to come to a peaceful agreement to disagree in love — such use of the Bible invariably ended the conversation. This occurred whether the text was used by "con-

---

literature on parents, Stacy Schiff notes a pattern of either "scientific or sermonic" discourse with little in between. *The New York Times Books Review* (Apr. 27, 2003), 9.

3. I describe these findings at greater length in Keifert, "The Bible, Congregational Leaders, and Moral Conversation," *Word & World* 13, no. 4 (1993): 392-97.

servatives" or "liberals." After all, bullets are intended to end a conversation with an opponent, not to foster it.

Others, especially those who hated conflict or viewed it as un-Christian, responded to increasing anxiety in the congregational system by avoiding a sustained engagement with the Bible. Instead, they often pronounced broad judgments in seeking to resolve the conflict: "The Bible's message is love, and so we should do the loving thing," or similar language, showed up often in these moments of high anxiety. Pouring such pious syrup on the conversation smothered the life out of it, ironically demanding that those in conflict simply stop the conversation. The result, though perhaps less invasively violent, was nonetheless as deadly to honest moral conversation as the Bible-bullet approach (see chap. 7 below).

When we researchers shared these observations with theological leaders, especially those with degrees from established schools of theology, we found that few were surprised by our findings. In fact, they were surprised we found them remarkable at all![4] When we probed for the reason that congregations avoided the Bible in these conflicts, congregational leaders, especially those with M.Div. degrees, admitted that they withdrew from engaging the Bible in morally disputed topics precisely because they found the use of the Bible dysfunctional to genuine conversation. Furthermore, even when they led Bible studies during times of congregational conflict, they tended to keep to a purely descriptive and factual engagement with the text. Therefore, they found that the process of making a move from the Bible to judgments on the questions at hand was threatening to their very role as leaders.[5]

To be sure, a small number of congregational leaders took these opportunities to engage the biblical text to move toward strong advocacy of their own moral positions. However, we found that the benefits of this engaged advocacy were minimal. The advocacy of the leaders tended to mobilize those in agreement with them, but it seldom expanded the numbers of those who shared the leaders' position or deepened the congregation's engagement with the issue. We concluded that, unless we were prepared to accept this sort of thinly instrumental notion of the role of the congrega-

4. Patricia Taylor Ellison, "Pioneer, Prophet, Servant-Leader: Metaphors for Leading Public Moral Conversation in Congregations" (PhD diss., University of Minnesota, 1995).

5. Ronald W. Duty, Patricia Taylor Ellison, and Patrick R. Keifert, *Growing Healthier Congregations: How to Talk Together When Nobody Is Listening* (St. Paul: Church Innovations Institute, 1997).

tion and its conversations in public life, we needed to discover another set of practices for the use of the Bible in theological conversation.[6]

Conversely, and perhaps more interestingly, we identified numerous congregational leaders who admitted that their own study of the Bible remained focused on the search for the original meaning of the Bible within its own context; but they hardly ever used it in practical reflection on contemporary morally disputed topics.[7] In fact, many congregational leaders believed that their theological education had only succeeded in helping them see the vast cultural and historical distance between the Bible and the present culture. However, the practical outcome of this lesson in distancing was that such leaders avoided normative discourse within their congregations at all costs.[8] Their education had helped them see what the Bible was *not* good for, but it had not helped them see what it *was* good for. Attaining a theological education had not helped them find a way of using the Bible even in disputes in their own congregations, among people who presumably shared many of the same commitments, much less in the larger and more morally diverse society.

This behavior, which we observed among research subjects, follows a pattern we have seen in most of our students over the past twenty years.[9] When we asked our students to write about the truth of the Bible and methods of interpretation, they spent most of their time arguing for a rejection of either a *literalist* or *fundamentalist* position. However, they were neither genuinely able to articulate a positive argument for the truth of the Bible and the appropriate methods of interpretation, nor were they able to describe how the Bible might help us see what we should do in contemporary life. Although these seminarians varied in age, ethnicity, gender, polit-

6. A denominational churchwide-sponsored consultation of over twenty organizations with processes and products designed to help congregations attend to morally disputed topics showed a "Bible-bullets" type pattern. All but one was designed around the advocacy format. See Keifert, "The Bible, Congregational Leaders, and Moral Conversation."

7. Of course, this pattern among pastors educated in the last decades simply follows the wisdom of the leadership of the biblical studies guild. Cf. Krister Stendahl, *Meanings: The Bible as Document and as Guide* (Philadelphia: Fortress, 1984).

8. Paul Ricoeur, "Philosophy and Religious Language," *Journal of Religion* 54 (1975): 75.

9. Donald Juel and I taught a course entitled "Truth and Meaning: Uses of the Bible" for fourteen years at Luther Seminary, and both of us continued teaching the course — even after he had moved to Princeton Seminary. I was later joined by two colleagues at Luther, Sarah Henrich and James Boyce, and we studied Galatians rather than Mark.

ical stance, and biblical literacy over this time period, we observed very little variation in this strange silence about the role of the Bible in our common life in the church.[10]

Toward a New Moment:
Rhetorical Rationality Encounters the Bible

We reflected at length on the set of problems associated with the use of the Bible in our own scholarship and teaching, as well as on the practices of congregational leaders. Finding strong consonance between the disturbing patterns we were witnessing and the analysis of other scholars who have called for a postmodern retrieval of the ancient rhetorical tradition to help shape secular public discourse, we engaged the work of three scholars from the University of Chicago — Wayne C. Booth, Stephen Toulmin, and Paul Ricoeur — to explore what they might be able to teach the church about its own conversations. Even though they represent three different strains of Western philosophy, these scholars concur in rather significant ways with the analysis of this problematic on the use of the Bible and on the promise of the rhetorical approach in responding to it. Our engagement with these thinkers has deepened our analysis and funded our growing sense that a rhetorical approach to theological education in general, and especially for using the Bible in that setting, holds some hope for the church.

Booth's early book *The Modern Dogma and the Rhetoric of Assent* clarified our initial diagnosis of the situation best. This volume, which contains the published lectures he delivered to undergraduates at the University of Notre Dame in the spring of 1970, reflects the realities of that turbulent time in American society. As academic dean at the time at the University of Chicago, Booth had been granted leave by student protesters, who had earlier placed him under house arrest in the university's administration building, to travel to Notre Dame and deliver the lectures.

Nevertheless, Booth's revealing lectures about the collapse of public

---

10. Interestingly enough, in my experience with them, second-career lawyers proved the exception to this general rule. My hypothesis is that they have received training and practice in one of the few intellectual disciplines where rhetorical rationality has survived the Enlightenment.

discourse on the college campuses placed less fault with the students and more on the failure of his colleagues in the elite circles of the academy. In Booth's view, these colleagues had failed to engage in sustained reflection with one another on the questions of the day, but had uncritically accepted a set of deep assumptions about the relationship of truth-seeking and the good of the community in public conversation. He called this dysfunctional set of assumptions the "modern dogma."[11] These assumptions revealed a deep divide in modernity built around the fact/value split. Booth's analysis exactly fit the pattern we found in the use of the Bible within the academy and the church, that is, the pattern of a vast gulf between the activities of *critical description* and *capricious faith.*

In response to the fact/value split, Booth called for a rhetoric of assent as his own effort to retrieve a premodern practice of rhetoric. A rhetoric of assent is intended to move the essence of critical intellectual inquiry beyond the practices of systematic doubt established by Descartes and Hume. Taking aim directly at the thought of one of the reigning philosophers of the twentieth century, Bertrand Russell, Booth demonstrates how Russell's adoption of the rhetoric of systematic doubt, along with the other contours of the modern dogma, led him to incoherence, immorality, and failed leadership as a public intellectual.[12]

Stephen Toulmin, a student of Ludwig Wittgenstein, had already developed his own itinerary for what he terms "rhetorical rationality."[13] Toulmin had explored modern human understanding and discovered some of the same patterns at which Booth had taken aim. However, Toulmin deepened Booth's analysis and response to the modern condition by exploring, in ever wider circles, the historical and cultural developments that brought about the modern dogma and effective ways of arguing or engaging in discourse that made possible sustained public understanding and truth-seeking.[14] His exploration of the use of the practical syllogism[15] and

11. Booth, *The Modern Dogma and the Rhetoric of Assent* (Notre Dame, IN: University of Notre Dame Press, 1974), 22.

12. Booth, *The Modern Dogma,* 46-47.

13. Toulmin, *Return to Reason* (Cambridge, MA: Harvard University Press, 2001), 12; see also Toulmin, *Cosmopolis: The Hidden Agenda of Modernity* (Boston: Free Press, 1990).

14. Stephen Toulmin, Richard Rieke, and Allan Janik, *An Introduction to Reasoning,* 2nd ed. (New York: Prentice Hall, 1997).

15. Toulmin, *The Uses of Argument* (Cambridge, UK: Cambridge University Press, 1958).

the ancient tradition of casuistry[16] has profoundly influenced our exploration of the place of the Bible in both the academy and the church.

Most important, Paul Ricoeur's phenomenology of the will, which he used within the framework of a rhetorical rationality, has shaped our understanding of the actual interpretation of the Bible in both the academy and the church.[17] It helped to support our sustained work toward innovating new theories of interpretation and truth. Ricoeur's dedication to engaging the greatest *aporia* of modernity and, at the same time, investigating common practices of biblical interpretation has made such innovation possible. It is an investigation that he has undertaken with great patience, subtlety, and complexity.

Donald Juel's own work on the Gospel of Mark became a shared task in our invention of new theories of interpretation and the truth of the Bible. Beginning with his dissertation, *Messiah and Temple,* he sought to move beyond the impulse of the historical-critical method to dissect the text in order to seek its truth.[18] Initially, Juel sought to understand the whole of Mark using the then-adventurous work of redaction criticism, especially the work of Willi Marxsen.[19] At the same time, he wanted to engage the historical work of his teacher, Nils Dahl, on the crucifixion.[20] In terms of our joint work, he often said that he sought to understand the book of Mark as a whole without losing its historical referentiality.[21]

---

16. Albert R. Jonsen and Stephen Toulmin, *The Abuse of Casuistry: A History of Moral Reasoning* (Berkeley: University of California Press, 1988).

17. Ricoeur and Toulmin offered a seminar in which each took his own tradition of thought (Continental and Anglo-American, respectively) and reflected on the same topics, e.g., practice and action.

18. Donald H. Juel, *Messiah and Temple: The Trial of Jesus in the Gospel of Mark,* SBLDS 31 (Missoula, MT: Scholars Press, 1977).

19. Willi Marxsen, *Mark the Evangelist: Studies on the Redaction History of the Gospel According to Mark,* trans. Donald H. Juel, James Boyce, William Poehlmann, and Roy A. Harrisville (Nashville: Abingdon, 1969).

20. Nils Alstrup Dahl, *Crucified Messiah, and Other Essays,* ed. Donald H. Juel (Minneapolis: Augsburg, 1974).

21. My own dissertation had argued that a relatively adequate theory of interpretation understood the text as a whole without losing a full range of referentiality. Of course, part of this full range included historical references. Keifert, "Meaning and Reference: The Interpretation of Verisimilitude in the Gospel According to Mark" (PhD diss., The University of Chicago, 1982).

In seeking to keep together our engagement with both the Bible as a whole and its referentiality, we sought to move beyond the fact/value split, especially beyond the modern habit of reducing truth to historical fact, a move that relegates theological meaning and significance to the category of a capricious enterprise.[22] Ricoeur's careful phenomenology of time and narrative furthered this enterprise.[23] His many-faceted descriptive phenomenology made visible the interaction of emplotment, narrative, and diverse forms of temporality that uncovered the rhetorical character of historical consciousness. The split between fact and value, once considered by modern scholars an infinite divide, becomes in his analysis a multifaceted set of relationships, rendering that split obsolete — indeed, silly. In place of reductive schemes of referentiality, we began to see multiple referentiality and polyvalence as the most intellectually persuasive and morally adequate approach to the interpretation of the Bible in the academy and the church as a whole. The use of a rhetorical rationality helped us move, in Richard Bernstein's terms, "beyond objectivism and relativism," and established a rich intellectual and teaching agenda.[24]

Reshaping Theological Institutions and Reinventing Teaching Practices

The capacity of seminaries to innovate in using rhetorical rationality with the Bible in public discourse must be shaped by developing practices that use the Bible in classes that focus on other subject matters besides the Bible itself. We believed that the paradigm for the use of the Bible in classes could be changed by two major shifts in the way we approach the Bible. First, we need to provide students and faculty with practice using the Bible to provide rhetorical warrants and backing for one's position, instead of just serving as a practical syllogism. Second, we need to reshape our prac-

22. One cannot use the phrase "meaning and significance" regarding this time period without recognizing that this desire was directed at the work of Eric Donald Hirsch, Jr., *Validity in Interpretation* (New Haven: Yale University Press, 1967), and *The Aims of Interpretation* (Chicago: University of Chicago Press, 1976).

23. Paul Ricoeur, *Time and Narrative*, 3 vols. (Chicago: University of Chicago Press, 1984, 1985, 1988).

24. Richard Bernstein, *Beyond Objectivism and Relativism: Science, Hermeneutics and Praxis* (Philadelphia: University of Pennsylvania Press, 1983).

tice of inquiry to consider God as first and always an agent, not simply a subject matter, in the educational process.[25]

This twofold shift led us toward teaching interdisciplinary courses that focused on different subject matters while we always attended to using the Bible in the work of the class. However, we wanted to explore this intellectual and teaching agenda in the real world of theological education as a whole, so we wrote a proposal to Craig Dykstra at the Lilly Endowment that led to a grant for Luther Seminary.[26] Along with our colleague in the field of practical theology, Roland Martinson, we functioned as the research and development team for the creation of a curriculum that took quite seriously this double-premised rhetorical approach to the engagement with the Bible in theological education.

First, the rhetorical approach became a critical ingredient in the interpretation of texts in the entire curriculum. We moved beyond merely studying the Bible rhetorically throughout the curriculum to also using this approach in studying other classic texts of the Lutheran tradition, the ecumenical creeds, sixteenth-century confessional documents, and other text-based parts of the curriculum. Similarly, classes based on continued living practices of the church, such as worship, integrated a rhetorical approach and were themselves integrated into the traditional text study courses.[27]

Second, we and our colleagues at Luther Seminary structured a new division of the curriculum on the rhetorical-rationality approach, which was entitled "Interpreting and Confessing." Each student of any degree plan must take required courses that teach rhetorical rationality in each year that the student is resident.[28] These courses focus on the

---

25. Eberhard Jüngel, *God as the Mystery of the World: On the Foundation of the Theology of the Crucified One in the Dispute Between Theism and Atheism* (Grand Rapids: Eerdmans, 1983); David Kelsey, *To Understand God Truly: What's Theological About a Theological School* (Louisville: Westminster, 1992), and *Between Athens and Berlin: The Theological Education Debate* (Grand Rapids: Eerdmans, 1993).

26. Our debt to Craig Dykstra, James Wind, and the Lilly Endowment goes well beyond the endowment's financial support; it includes their genuine interest, engagement, critique, and trust in our enterprise.

27. Patrick R. Keifert, *Welcoming the Stranger: A Public Theology of Worship and Evangelism* (Minneapolis: Fortress, 1992).

28. Such courses include: "Reading the Audiences" (a first-year required course in the practices of understanding the immediate environment of a congregation, its demographics, psychographics, cultures, and social systems); "Worship"; "Exercises in Biblical Theol-

mediating human faculties of practical reasoning *(phronesis)* and creative, productive activity *(poesis)* gathered together as Christian wisdom and witness.

Third, the rhetorical approach required situational reflection as a central learning activity in the new curriculum. We took certain courses and times in the student's journey as critical moments for helping students move beyond the modern dogma to practicing leadership out of Christian wisdom and witness. This move to situational reflection pressed a more integrated connection between personal student formation and formation as public leader. It also called for a move from the modernist construction of text and context, of theory and applied theory — and thus of the dominant models of contextual education — to a more situationalist understanding of learning.

Fourth, the rhetorical approach continues to serve as guiding principle in our practices for creating, introducing, and critiquing the courses that Luther Seminary offers. This has resulted in two additional overhauls in the curriculum during the past decade.

When Donald Juel moved to Princeton, our project and our conversation partners broadened and diversified. With the generous assistance of the Lilly Endowment, we were able to involve a number of colleagues from other schools of theology in conversation and critique of our rhetorical approach, which over the last decade has involved scholars, administrators, and teachers from all the disciplines within contemporary schools of theology. This conversation, continuing under the name "The Bible and Theological Education," has been furthered by the conversations of a steering committee and three project teams.[29] The team whose initial study volume was completed first explored the nature of the study

---

ogy" (a senior course using case studies from the students' internship in congregations during the previous year, which is a requirement in Lutheran seminary education). In addition, there was a series of electives generated by teams of faculty drawn from diverse disciplines around shared neuralgic themes, e.g., "God, Evil, and Suffering," taught by a systematics professor and an Old Testament scholar; "Creation and Environment," taught by a biblical scholar and an ethicist specializing in agronomy and sustainable agriculture; "Law and Justice," taught by a biblical scholar and a professor of law; "Paul, Power, and Polis," taught by a New Testament scholar and a systematics professor; and "Truth and Meaning: Uses of the Biblical Narrative," which focused on either Mark or Galatians, taught by a New Testament scholar and a systematics professor.

29. In addition to Donald Juel and me, David L. Bartlett, Beverly Roberts Gaventa, Richard B. Hays, Stephen J. Kraftchick, Dennis T. Olson, and Alan Padgett.

of theology within the rubric of rhetorical rationality.[30] This work uncovered the profoundly important role of rhetorical rationality in the preparation and practices of Christian leaders during the first four centuries of the church.[31] These researchers have concluded that, unless we view their work with an understanding of rhetorical practice, our understanding of their vision and practices will be greatly flattened and diminished. Using a rhetorical approach, this team also examined how moral questions have been examined throughout the history of the church. Among other things, we have learned how profound the differences are in how we now understand the basic teachings of the Trinity when we begin with a rhetorical approach.[32]

A second working group in this conversation has focused on the use of the rhetorical approach within the classroom.[33] Interdisciplinary teams of faculty members have attempted to rethink their classes using a rhetorical imagination: they have considered how rhetorical rationality might affect the structure of the curriculum as a whole, as well as the character of the classroom itself. To do so, they outlined how they might use learning activities appropriate to teach these necessary capacities of Christian leadership. Much of the working group's time has been spent reviewing these proposed courses created by the teams from the various schools of theology.[34]

---

30. In addition to Donald Juel and me, A. K. M. Adam, Wesley Avram, James Boyce, Donald Compiers, David W. Cunningham, Susan K. Heydahl, Frederick W. Norris, Richard R. Osmer, Janet Wearthers, and Stephen H. Webb.

31. Frederick Norris, "Nazianzus," in *To Teach, To Delight, and To Move: Theological Education in a Post-Christian World,* ed. David Cunningham and Patrick R. Keifert (Eugene, OR: Cascade Books, 2004); see also Frederick Norris, Lionel Wickham, and Frederick Williams, *Faith Gives Fullness to Reasoning: The Five Theological Orations of Gregory Nazianzen.* Vigiliae Christianae, Supplement 13 (Leiden: E. J. Brill, 1991).

32. Norris, "Nazianzus."

33. A. K. M. Adams, James Boyce, Ellen T. Charry, Sarah Henrich, Stephen J. Kraftchick, Dennis T. Olson, Marianne Meye Thompson, John Thompson, and Miroslav Volf.

34. Perkins School of Theology, Azusa Pacific University, Candler School of Theology, Duke Divinity, Yale Divinity, Princeton Theological Seminary, Fuller Seminary, St. Paul Seminary at the University of St. Thomas, the Lutheran Schools of Theology in Chicago, Philadelphia, and Gettysburg, and Luther Seminary.

Rhetoric and the Bible: For or Against Truth?

Within the conversation that we have sustained about the Bible and theological education, we have encountered both surface concerns and deeper questions about the limits of rhetorical rationality and the potential flaws in a rhetorical approach to theological education. The third team in the Bible and Theological Education project, long anticipated but only recently formed in this decade-long project, is composed of philosophers, theologians, and Bible scholars who want to respond to both ancient and modern suspicion that rhetoric is too often used as a way to avoid or confuse questions of truth.[35]

In public life, the word "rhetoric" is often used with some suspicion that the audience is being manipulated rather than convinced. This use of the term suggests that rhetoric refers to the means of communication, the outward form rather than the inner substance of a message. Or again, we commonly refer to "rhetorical questions" as those to which the answer is already assumed and thus need no discussion. Though this is not what *we* mean by rhetoric, this common usage of the word "rhetorical" captures something of the core of rhetorical rationality, namely, that rhetoric actually pays attention to the audience and what it assumes to be true in the world in which the audience lives.

Aristotle notes that all speeches reveal three characters: the character of the speaker *(ethos),* the character of the speech *(logos),* and the character of the audience *(pathos).*[36] Therefore, rhetorical rationality understands that all discourse takes place within a particular setting, is aimed at a particular audience, and is delivered by particular speakers who use assumed warrants and backing for their claims within a moral field.[37] It is about character; in

35. In addition to Donald Juel and me, David L. Bartlett, Ellen T. Charry, Stephen T. Davis, Dennis T. Olson, Alan Padgett, Marianne Meye Thompson, Mark Wallace, and Nicholas Wolterstorff.

36. Aristotle, *The Rhetoric,* 2:1.

37. Stephen Toulmin's layout of an argument in *The Uses of Argument* consists of six elements. The first element is the *claim:* the claim of the argument is the conclusion that someone is trying to justify in the argument. The second element is the *grounds:* the grounds of an argument are the facts on which the argument is based. The third element is the *warrant:* the warrant of the argument assesses whether or not the claim is legitimate based on the grounds. The fourth element is the *backing:* the backing of the argument gives additional support for a warrant by answering different questions. The modal *qualifier* is the fifth element of the argument: it indicates the strength of the leap from the data to the warrant. The

fact, we might say that it is from this moral embeddedness of all discourse in implicit values or human interests of particular times and places[38] that much of the intellectual project of modernity has sought to escape.[39]

Modernity has been skeptical of the rhetorical project, pointing to the history of human violence and oppression as its fruits. As an alternative, the chief goal of modernity was to imagine a kind of pure reason and pure language (e.g., mathematics) based on objective facts that would be so indisputable that we could avoid violent conflict in the modern world. Of course, we need to acknowledge that rhetoric was also suspect in the ancient world, and its ancient opponents, including Plato, attacked rhetoric as a rejection of the search for truth in favor of the morally suspect act of persuasion. Especially in its Latin forms, the rhetorical tradition, which attended extensively to style and aimed at the passions, seemed to confirm the suspicions of its opponents.[40]

With these issues well in mind, the Truth and the Bible team went to work.[41] The team deliberately put philosophers, theologians, and biblical scholars together with the purpose of exploring the question of truth from the point of view of these philosophical questions. This team formation was done to serve our goal of deepening the study and use of the Bible in the classroom and in local congregations.

Our study team gathered philosophers from across the spectrum of theories of truth. Some philosophers proposed that we should update the traditional correspondence theory of truth, which is the one assumed in most common conversation.[42] Others wanted to revise and apply a coherence model of truth; still others followed Ricoeur's work in conversation

---

final element of the argument is the *rebuttal:* this occurs when the leap from grounds to claim does not appear to be legitimate.

38. Jürgen Habermas, *Knowledge and Human Interests,* trans. Jeremy J. Shapiro (Boston: Beacon Press, 1971).

39. Toulmin, *Return to Reason,* 67-82.

40. Jonsen and Toulmin, *Abuse of Casuistry,* 75-88. For a description of a rhetorical approach to theology that takes seriously the Latin tradition, see Donald Compiers, *What Is Rhetorical Theology? Textual Practice and Public Discourse* (Harrisburg, PA: Trinity Press International, 1999).

41. In addition to Donald Juel and me, Alan Padgett, Marianne Meye Thompson, Stephen Davis, Nicholas Wolterstorff, Mark Wallace, David Bartlett, Ellen Charry, and Michael Welker.

42. William P. Alston, *A Realist Conception of Truth* (Ithaca, NY: Cornell University Press, 1996).

with an Anglo-American linguistic turn.[43] Finally, some members of the group proposed further development of the American pragmatist theory of truth as a vehicle for the church to consider the use of the Bible in education and moral conversation.[44]

Despite their diverse perspectives on what constitutes the most adequate theories of truth, all members of this team have participated in the study of the Bible and reflected on their proposals in light of their actual reading of the Bible. Philosophers and theologians have sought to interpret the Bible, both in the presence of and in partnership with biblical scholars, all toward serving its use in the classroom and in congregations.

Michael Welker, a systematician from Heidelberg University, best identified one of the most deeply held convictions of this study team when he pressed for the continued vocation of the church as a truth-seeking community.[45] As he articulated it, for the church to forsake this vocation would be for the church to forsake a core characteristic of its identity and to threaten its own missional character.[46]

What Is at Stake: The Church and the World

On the surface, most Christians would not question that the church has a vocation as a truth-seeking community. The church seeks truth, of course, especially in light of Jesus being "the way, and the truth, and the life" (John 14:6). However, these same Christians continue to imagine the search for truth within the troubling conditions of modernity, which profoundly threaten the life of the church and the civil community.

They are not alone. Despite the cul-de-sac created by the modern dogma that Booth and others have made visible, many public intellectuals are calling for a return to the modern project. Nowhere is this reactionary proposal more fierce — and more significant — than in the conversation

43. Mark Wallace and I.

44. Perhaps the most clear source of this approach is the work of the Chicago Pragmatists, especially John Dewey, and the Aristotlean Pragmatists, Richard McKeon and Wayne C. Booth.

45. Alan G. Padgett and Patrick R. Keifert, eds., *But Is It All True? The Bible and the Question of Truth* (Grand Rapids: Eerdmans, 2006), 1-15 (Introduction).

46. Darrell Guder, ed., *Missional Church: A Vision for the Sending of the Church in North America* (Grand Rapids: Eerdmans, 1998).

resulting from the contemporary ideological conflicts throughout the world, which for some scholars falls under the rubric "the clash of civilizations."[47] Faced with a resurgence of increasingly vocal religious communities throughout the world, including groups within Judaism, Islam, and Christianity, these reactionary modernists are proposing the same solutions that have proven only half successful. Specifically, they propose that public communities should cordon off values, especially religious values, into the private space and re-create (or preserve) a value-free public space. Here, they declare, moral and practical decisions are made based only on *objective facts.*

An inherent consequence — indeed, a hoped-for consequence — of these proposals of reaction would be that religious and moral communities would lose their place in the shaping of civil moral life. Religions would be required to forsake making truth claims, at least in public, thus avoiding irrational and unnecessary conflict, and would be required to confine their activities to their own private spaces. Some of the most subtle interpreters of modernity have been lulled into the belief that public civilization must necessarily be limited to matters of economic and political life. They assert that religion functions only in nurturing a safe and private home where people can occasionally escape the travails of the public world. These interpreters fail to see the dangers to civil life if their view should become dominant and faith communities would cease to be public meeting places that serve as bridges between the private and public dimensions of our lives.[48]

One example of this kind of reactionary proposal is Jonathan Rauch's recent *Atlantic Monthly* piece. Rauch delights in a particular form of secular tolerance he calls "apatheism," which is based on his own experience that "it has been years since I really cared one way or another" about religion. He suggests that apatheism, a disinclination to care all that much

47. By using this phrase, I am not endorsing the view of Samuel P. Huntington in *The Clash of Civilizations and the Remaking of World Order* (New York: Simon & Schuster, 1996). Still, major questions of the kind raised by Bernard Lewis in *What Went Wrong? Western Impact and Middle Eastern Response* (New York: Oxford University Press, 2002), seem vital to me.

48. Our debt to Martin E. Marty in this enterprise is clearest in these "Marty monikers" for the public church. See esp. his "Public and Private: Congregation as Meeting Place" in James Lewis and James Wind, eds., *American Congregations,* vol. 2 (Chicago: University of Chicago Press, 1994), 133-68.

about one's own religion, and an even stronger disinclination to care about that of other people, "is worth getting excited about." He praises his Christian and Jewish friends who "organize their lives around an intense and personal relationship with God, but who betray no sign of caring that I am an unrepentantly atheistic Jewish homosexual. They are exponents of the second part of apatheism, the part that doesn't mind what *other* people think about God."

Rauch cites with enthusiasm the philosopher Richard Rorty, whose opinion was that "a world of pragmatic atheists would be a better, happier world than our present one." However, he prefers apatheism to pragmatic atheism, clearly believing that both are "preferable to fanatical religiosity (al Qaeda) and tyrannical secularism (China)."[49]

But history has shown that a retreat by people of faith from making public truth claims does not empty the public square of values; rather, it fills the public square with the very fundamentalists that modernists like Rauch fear most. If the persons of faith who seek truth forsake the faith-based public practice of making truth claims, only those who disdain the careful search for truth and instead offer only capricious faith will enter the public space. In such a system, tolerance will become repressive rather than engendering of civil discourse. More ironically, a public space emptied of persons of faith searching for truth is the best place for fanaticism to flourish. Perhaps no better contemporary example comes to mind than the truncated public conversation coming from both secular and religious intellectual communities in responding to Sayyid Qutb, al Qaeda's philosopher.

Qutb, a martyr under the Nasser regime in Egypt, gathered an audience of young men who, like himself, had been raised in traditional Muslim communities and educated in European and American colleges and universities. These were not the poor or ill-educated of the Muslim world; on the contrary, they were representatives of a growing upper-middle-class Islamic culture. Yet this audience was profoundly disturbed by what they observed in contemporary Western culture. They perceived the same dysfunctional divide between fact and values, and between spirit and body, that make up the "modern dogma." Some, like Qutb, returned to their religious tradition, especially the Koran, to analyze modern Christendom. They also gathered an audience. Paul Berman suggests that Qutb's most influential works, extended commentaries on the Koran, have not at-

---

49. Jonathan Rauch, "Let It Be," *Atlantic Monthly* 291, no. 4 (2003): 34.

tracted the attention of American public intellectuals that they merit. According to Berman, Qutb's analysis is soulful and heartfelt: it is a theological analysis, but in its cultural emphases it reflects the style of twentieth-century philosophy.

Qutb's analysis asks some genuinely perplexing question about (a) the division between mind and body in Western thought; (b) the difficulties in striking a balance between sensual experience and spiritual elevation; (c) the impersonality of modern power and technological innovation; and (d) social injustice. Although Qutb has plainly followed some main trends of twentieth-century Western social criticism and philosophy, he has poured his ideas through a filter of Koranic commentary. This filter gives his commentary a grainy new texture, authentically Muslim, which allows him to make a series of points that no Western thinker is likely to propose.

Berman sees the persuasive power of such commentaries and notes how Qutb makes truth claims on the basis of the Koran, truth claims that clearly convince intelligent and technologically sophisticated Muslims about the life-and-death character of his interpretation. He underscores the power of rendering public such truth claims about a religious text, the Koran. This is the case not only for contemporary Muslim world citizens but also for the contemporary secular and religious American public intellectual who would be a world citizen.

He also notes how dangerous and ill-advised it would be to have Western politicians meddling in a discussion of these sacred matters. Indeed, to have our politicians take up this response would obviate the hard-won successes of uncoupling religious practice from state sanctions. It would also limit the diversity of secular and religious responses to such challenges to Western democratic society and culture. Instead, Berman asks: "Who will speak of the sacred and the secular, of the physical world and the spiritual world? Who will defend liberal ideas against the enemies of liberal ideas?" He answers: "Philosophers and religious leaders will have to do this on their own. Are they doing so? Armies are in motion, but are the philosophers and religious leaders, the liberal thinkers, likewise in motion?"[50] Berman sees that when religious leaders and philosophers take up the *apatheism* proposed by Jonathan Rauch, we leave the civil space to the Sayyid Qutbs.

50. Paul Berman, "The Philosopher of Islamic Terror," *The New York Times Magazine*, Mar. 23, 2003, 29.

Congregational Moral Conversation and Truth-Seeking

Varied publics to which Christians need to make the truth claims are definitely within civil space. For example, if we are to learn something useful from the challenge of Sayyid Qutb, we need to make those claims through extended and thoughtful commentary on the Bible in conversation with Islam and the Koran. At a bare minimum, we need to forsake the modernist habit of interpreting the Bible only for the faithful or reducing our notion of the *public* interpretation of the Bible to historical studies. Instead, we need to imagine commentaries on the Bible, or parts of the Bible, that are aimed to teach, delight, even persuade diverse audiences. Such regular commentary on the Bible regarding contemporary subjects and issues would better serve the civic space, especially if they are expressed by those who are highly competent in the subject under discussion and thoughtfully aware of a critical understanding of the Bible.

This approach is not likely if we take seriously Rauch's observations that "even regular churchgoers can, and often do, rank quite high on the apatheism scale." He refers to these happy Christian communities as the "softer denominations" who are "packed with apatheists." Although he does not want to identify them, I would suspect those he praises are the same mainline denominations that are in decline. In this regard he notes: "There are a lot of reasons to attend religious services: to connect with a culture or a community, to socialize, to expose children to religions, to find the warming comfort of familiar ritual." Notice that his reasons for attending religious services fall far short of seeking truth and justice, beauty and peace.

In Rauch's mind, as in those of many thinkers hankering for a return to modernism, the only alternative to these apatheist denominations is fundamentalism. In Rauch's understanding, religion is "the most divisive and volatile of social forces. To be in the grip of religious zeal is the natural state of human beings, or at least of a great many human beings; that is how much of the species seems to be wired."[51] This is a decidedly reductionist view — yet quite common.

In response to these reactive turns, Donald Juel and I, with our colleagues on the Congregational Study Research Team, tried to imagine and work out a practice for a very different Christian community.[52] Our goal

---

51. Rauch, "Let It Be," 34.
52. Members of Church Innovations Institute Congregational Studies Research Team

was to develop one that could thrive between the extremes of apatheism and religious zeal, a community that could become capable of considered, intense, conflicted truth-seeking within itself and in conversation with its neighbors. Such a community must move beyond either a propositional or a narrative approach to the Bible and into a rhetorical practice of truth-seeking.

Although the narrative approach profoundly influences our reflection on the Bible in theological education, its focus solely on one genre of the Bible and its inattentiveness to the questions of *ethos, logos,* and *pathos* in diverse publics make it relatively inadequate when compared to the rhetorical approach.[53] The finest practitioners of the narrative approach often end up moving beyond simply telling the Christian story to engaging in all the classical rhetorical inventions we call for in our proposal.

In diverse face-to-face communities, from the academy to the local congregation, from Alaska to Texas to South Africa, we have sought to regularly practice the rhetorical approach and to take seriously how human beings seem to function. It is difficult work to form a civil space where moral and religious wisdom can find a place. Drawing on critical social theory, our colleague Gary Simpson calls these congregations "prophetic public companions."[54]

We are grateful that such communities do exist, even as congregations. They approach the Bible more as beggars than soldiers in search of ammunition. They risk the pain of disagreement, even conflict, rather than smothering conversation in pious syrup. They desire to seek truth with others and witness to the truth they find rather than simply repeating the Christian story to themselves while waiting for others to be attracted to it. Their continued work of seeking the truth in an increasingly diverse and

---

were: Ann Hill Duin, Ronald W. Duty, Patricia Taylor Ellison, David Fredrickson, Nancy Hess, Donald Juel, Cynthia Ann Jurisson, Patrick Keifert, Craig J. Lewis, Mark MacDonald, Anne Marie Neuchterlein, Jose David Rodriguez, Gary Simpson, David Stark, and Arlynne Turnquist. In addition, the following were guests of the team: Mary Ann Zimmer, C. Kirk Hadaway, Lois Y. Barrett, Anita L. Bradshaw, Jonathan Case, Nathan Frambach, Scott Frederickson, Gail Riina, and Michael Welker.

53. Cf. Mark Wallace, *The Second Naiveté: Barth, Ricoeur, and the New Yale Theology* (Macon, GA: Mercer University Press, 1995), for an insightful discussion of these issues.

54. Gary Simpson, *Critical Social Theory: Prophetic Reason, Civil Society, and Christian Imagination* (Minneapolis: Fortress, 2002), 125-45; see also his essay "God, Civil Society, and Congregations as Public Moral Companions" in this volume.

dangerous world is on the cutting edge of contemporary theological education. Their practices of using the Bible are opening new opportunities for theological education. They are the primal location of such education, and our schools of theology would do well to learn from them.

Congregations, Democracy, and the Action of God in Philippians 1–2

David Fredrickson

For the apostle Paul, speaking about congregations meant speaking about God. Paul regarded the churches he had established as places where God acts for the salvation of the world. He makes crucial distinctions between God's action and the life of each community; but we miss his point if we do not see that God's sphere of action overlaps the face-to-face interactions within the gathered community of those who confess Jesus as Lord. Furthermore, if we ignore this overlap, we lose the deep connection in the Epistles between the congregation's life and God's mission in the world. To explain Pauline communities simply in sociological or anthropological terms would be to ignore Paul's repeated claim to his audiences that what is happening among them is that God is acting, and that this divine work in the congregation is the way God moves into the world for its salvation.

In this essay I attempt to describe the way in which, according to Paul, Christ and God act in local congregations. I have selected Philippians 1–2 as a resource that is rich for answering this question. I will argue that, for Paul, divine action and the interaction between members of the church at Philippi was political in nature. I will present evidence from ancient political theory to show that Paul borrows the *action* words in this portion of Philippians from the tradition of democracy in ancient Greece. Paul's description of Christ's relationship to God, of Christ's redemptive work, of the mutual relationships of community members, and ultimately of God's own relationship to the world relies heavily on key ideas associated with democracy. I wish to show that Paul's theology and ecclesiology are interrelated through the theory of democratic political relations to such an extent that we can come to see him for what he was: a pioneer in the movement to understand the triune identity of God through God's action in the congregation.

The Congregation and Political Participation

We begin our investigation with a close inspection of Philippians 1:27. Paul encourages the community of believers in Philippi to "engage politically in a manner worthy of the gospel of Christ." Unfortunately, modern translations of this imperative as "behave yourselves" or "conduct yourselves" do not permit readers to understand that Paul is in fact constructing his audience as political actors.[1] Accurately reflecting the communicative aspects of the verb, the King James translation is better: "Only let your conversation be as it becometh the gospel of Christ."

The Greek verb at issue here is *politeuesthai,* and it has the sense of "engage through speech in the formation of the city's policies, plans, and objectives." The background for this term is the practice of democracy, and particularly the characterization of citizen action within the Assembly *(ekklēsia),* the deliberating and legislative body of ancient democracies.[2] The term carries the notion of an initiation of policy in matters of the city's welfare. The

---

1. Aside from some Cynics (Pseudo-Heraclitus *Epistle* 5, and Pseudo-Diogenes *Epistle* 1) and Clement of Alexandria (*Stromateis* 4.21.130.5), this term refers to the linguistic interaction between people in political contexts rather than conformity of individuals to ethical ideals. See esp. Xenophon *Hellenica* 2.4.22, 43. For the sense of the term in democratic Athens, see N. Loraux, "Reflections of the Greek City on Unity and Division," in A. Molho, K. Raaflaub, and J. Emlen, eds., *City States in Classical Antiquity and Medieval Italy* (Ann Arbor: University of Michigan Press, 1991), 35. For later developments, see E. Gruen, "The Polis in the Hellenistic World," in R. Rosen and J. Farrell, eds., *Nomodeiktes: Greek Studies in Honor of Martin Ostwald* (Ann Arbor: University of Michigan Press, 1993), 339-54.

2. Wayne Meeks appropriately draws attention to the boldness of early Christians naming themselves "assembly" in light of this term's association with democracy. See his *The First Urban Christians: The Social World of the Apostle Paul* (New Haven: Yale University Press, 1983), 108. He does not, however, develop this insight into a principle of Paul's ecclesiology. B. Bowe (*A Church in Crisis: Ecclesiology and Paraenesis in Clement of Rome,* Harvard Dissertations in Religion 23 [Minneapolis: Fortress, 1988], 86-87) has recognized the political dimension of ecclesiology in 1 Clement; however, she makes no reference to Paul in this regard.

sense of initiation and even innovation is underscored by the fact that by the fourth century B.C.E. the term was defined in opposition to the *idiotes,* a citizen present at the Assembly who participated by voting only, not by speeches and other forms of influence.[3] Thus, in using this term that is heavily laden with public and participatory meaning, Paul orients his audience toward a political self-understanding. What goes on in the community of those belonging to Christ is to be understood analogously to the popular assemblies of democratic governments. Paul is exhorting his readers to engage actively in the affairs of their own assembly, the local church.

The question of whether individuals should engage in political activity was a hotly contested topic in the philosophical schools. Since all participants in this great debate agreed that politics inevitably involved dangers and hardships, the question in dispute was whether a life devoted to the affairs of the city was worth the trouble.[4] That the wise man does not — and should not — engage in politics was a frequently expressed sentiment. This idea is found in the Platonists, Pythagoreans, Stoics, Cynics, Epicureans, and other schools.[5]

But other philosophers declared the opposite view.[6] Arguments for participation sought to motivate the elite who otherwise were tempted to retire from political life.[7] For Plato, only the best people should rule (just think of being ruled by the worst!). For Aristotle, political participation places the individual in the position to arrive at the goal of human life. The Stoics claimed that each individual is part of a greater whole, and that it is

3. See J. Ober, *Mass and Elite in Democratic Athens: Rhetoric, Ideology, and the Power of the People* (Princeton, NJ: Princeton University Press, 1989), 106-09; M. Hansen, "The Political Powers of the People's Court in Fourth-Century Athens," in O. Murray and S. Price, eds., *The Greek City: From Homer to Alexander* (Oxford: Clarendon, 1990), 231. For Roman times, see Polybius *Histories* 23.12.9; Dio Chrysostom *Discourse* 13.17; Plutarch *Comparison of Demosthenes and Cicero* 3.1, and *Old Men in Public Affairs* 796c-f.

4. Dio Chrysostom *Discourse* 34.32-33; *Stoicorum Veterum Fragmenta* 3.172.18–19, 3.173.19–22, 3.174.26–29; see also Philo *On Dreams* 1.221–25; Ober, *Mass and Elite,* 11.

5. For the theme of withdrawal from participation, see G. J. D. Aalders, *Political Thought in Hellenistic Times* (Amsterdam: A. M. Hakkert, 1975), 48; see also Diogenes Laertius *Lives of Eminent Philosophers* 2.89, 6.29, 9.3, 10.10, 10.119; Epictetus *Discourse* 1.23.1; Plutarch *The Education of Children* 12f; *On Tranquility of Mind* 465c; *Reply to Colotes* 1125c. See also Marcus Aurelius *Meditations* 4.24; Seneca *On Tranquility* 13.1; and *On Anger* 3.6.3.

6. Diogenes Laertius *Lives of Eminent Philosophers* 6.11.

7. Retirement from political engagement has a complex intellectual and social history. See L. B. Connor, *The Quiet Athenian* (Oxford: Clarendon, 1986), 175-98.

the duty of humans to play their assigned parts, including marriage, begetting, and political leadership.[8]

The widespread debate among the philosophers concerning the wise man's participation in politics is only a partial backdrop for Philippians 1:27. But it is valuable because it helps us liberate the translation of *politeuesthai* from the modern preoccupation with the moral formation of the solitary self. Yet we should observe further that the force of Paul's exhortation has to do with the *manner* of political engagement rather that its motivation. The adverbial phrase "worthily of the gospel of Christ" seeks to define the kind of political action the community is to adopt, and it corresponds to other ancient writers' discrimination among various forms of political activity.[9] A common pattern arose among theorists in which the term *politeuesthai* was modified by an adverbial phrase,[10] and was associated with one of the following three forms of action: art,[11] force,[12] or persuasion.[13] Given the widespread theoretical reflection on the nature of political engagement in Paul's intellectual environment, it is likely that he directs his hearers to evaluate the nature of their communal interaction from a particular perspective. As we will see, this Pauline perspective is established by the narrative of Christ Jesus.[14]

---

8. Diogenes Laertius *Lives of Eminent Philosophers* 7.121; Plutarch *Old Men in Public Affairs* 791c–d; *Stoicorum Veterum Fragmenta* 1.11.20-26; Dio Chrysostom *Discourses* 22.3, 47.2–3; Epictetus *Discourses* 3.22.83–85, 3.7. Summarizing centuries of debate among the philosophers is the rhetorical exercise found in Theon *Progymnasmata* 123.

9. Inscriptions provide further evidence that the manner of political engagement was an important issue. See D. Whitehead, "Samian Autonomy," in Rosen and Farrell, *Nomodeiktes*, 321-29.

10. See, e.g., Plato *Gorgias* 500c; Dio Chrysostom *Discourse* 44.11; Clement of Alexandria *Paedagogus* 3.11.81.2.2; *Stromateis* 4.4.15.4–6.

11. For the Platonic view of metaphor, see Plato *Republic* 590cff. ἠνχῶετ, which emphasizes political engagement. For a first-century c.e. example of Platonic political engagement, see D. Konstan and P. Mitsis, "Chion of Heraclea: A Philosophical Novel in Letters," in M. Nussbaum, ed., *The Poetics of Therapy: Hellenistic Ethics in Its Rhetorical and Literary Context* (Edmonton: Academic Printing and Publishing, 1990), 257-79.

12. Pseudo-Crates *Epistle* 5.

13. Aalders, *Political Thought*, 39-50, 75-77.

14. Something comparable occurs in 1 Clement 3.4. Yet there is an instructive difference: Paul uses a narrative term, the gospel of Christ, to designate the character of the action he exhorts the community to adopt, whereas 1 Clement uses a moral category drawn from Stoicism. Interpreting the meaning of political engagement in the light of the narrative of Christ — his voluntary enslavement to humanity for the sake of extending freedom — is Paul's aim.

Before we consider what this evaluative point of view might be, an earlier passage in the letter (Phil. 1:9-11) deserves our attention, one that also speaks of the character of communal interaction. In 1:10, Paul designates the community's central activity as "testing the things that really matter" (cf. 1 Thess. 5:21; Rom. 12:2). All participants are free to raise questions, offer objections, and make alternative recommendations that are themselves subject to the testing of the other members. Paul does not portray the moral life of the community as an imitation of a preexisting universal order, or as conformity to a particular historical tradition. Rather, people take part in a participatory process of discovery and consensual approval through testing.[15] Furthermore, testing is a privilege and is the responsibility of each member of the community rather than the possession of only an elite group.[16] The language of testing thus points to a highly participatory form of communal relations reminiscent of democratic procedures. As such it anticipates the term *politeuesthai* in Philippians 1:27.[17]

So far we have located Paul's language in the ancient world's discourse of democracy. I do not mean to suggest that Paul simply wishes his audience to form itself in imitation of the democratic assembly, or view itself as the inheritor of the Athenian heritage. However, I am proposing that Paul commends to his audience a community based on mutual openness to persuasion. His genius is to link this form of community, which is certainly present also in the theoretical accounts of ancient democracy, with the narrative of Jesus Christ. We turn now to a consideration of what that linkage involves. What does it mean for the members of the community to interact politically with one another in a manner worthy of the gospel of Christ?

The Divine Community

Paul holds the church's internal interaction up to the gospel of Christ as its measure of worth. This means that there is a political dimension to the

15. Here I need to recognize my debt to the moral theory of Jürgen Habermas. For the notion of "testing" in Habermas, see W. Rehg, *Insight and Solidarity: A Study in the Discourse Ethics of Jürgen Habermas* (Berkeley: University of California Press, 1994), 56-83.
16. Paul is aware of the dangers of placing "testing" in the hands of an elite group (see Rom. 2:18). For the ideology of mass decision-making, see Ober, *Mass and Elite*, 163-65.
17. See Engberg-Pedersen, "Stoicism in Philippians," 261, n. 9.

gospel itself. I do not mean merely that the gospel, essentially apolitical, has political consequences through a process of application of changeless truth to changing circumstances. Rather, for the term "worthily" to make any sense at all, there must be a political aspect to the gospel itself. This leads us to look for a narrative of Jesus Christ in which he becomes a political actor so that the good news about him is from the beginning cast in the language of politics. Where in the Epistle to the Philippians are Jesus Christ's actions portrayed in political language? The obvious answer is Philippians 2:5-8, the first half of the Christ Hymn.

Confirmation of my claim can be found in 2:5. Christ's action embodies the virtue of practical reasoning commonly recommended to those who intended to engage in political action. With the phrase "think this among you which is also in Christ Jesus," Paul introduces the Christ Hymn by exhorting the community to adopt the same form of practical reasoning that exists in Christ Jesus. The specific nature of this reasoning will be made clear in the account of his action in 2:6-8. The narrative begins in 2:6 with an original political community composed of God and Christ Jesus. We are justified in speaking of God and Christ Jesus in political community if we interpret the phrase "to be equal with God" in an adverbial rather than adjectival sense. Equality in the Christ Hymn refers to the character of interaction rather than the identity of some quality, in this case often described as "divinity."

Most commentators erroneously assume that when Paul wrote in 2:6 "to exist equally with God" *(to einai isa theō),* he really meant that Jesus was "equal to God" *(isos theō).*[18] The kind of equality implied by the latter phrase has a long history in Greek political thought, and it was quite unfriendly to democracy. We might call it the "substance version of equality," since the underlying idea is the equal distribution of limited goods (e.g., land, food, money, power, or prestige).[19] Assuming this version of equality, recent investigators have suggested that Paul is ironically opposing Christ Jesus to Hellenistic and Roman leaders, who were declared to be equal to god in the propaganda of the day. These rulers, because of their benefactions to the people, deserved honors equal to those paid to the gods.

---

18. See P. O'Brien, *The Epistle to the Philippians: A Commentary on the Greek Text* (Grand Rapids: Eerdmans, 1991), 216.

19. D. F. Harvey, "Two Kinds of Equality," *Classica et Mediaevalia* 26 (1965): 101-46.

The honorific title, which was usually applied to the political or military figure at the *end* of his career in recognition of his accomplishments, did not describe the relationship between the exalted leader and the gods; rather, it described only the high estimation in which he was held by the masses.[20] Therefore, the problem with reading *isos theō* into the Christ Hymn is obvious. Equality with God in the hymn is mentioned as a preexisting state of affairs for Christ Jesus, and this fact makes any comparison with the title, even if ironic, strained. The phrase speaks instead about Christ's *way of being with God,* and this relationship exists prior to and independent of any world in which humans become gods through popular acclamation.

A reconceptualization of the Christ Hymn from the perspective of equality in the discourse of democracy is in order. There was, in distinction to the substance version described above, another way of thinking about equality in ancient political theory. This was equality as equal participation in the governance of the community, or, as Aristotle called it, "reciprocal equality."[21] Equality in this sense was the cornerstone of democracy. It consisted not simply in the right to vote but also to make juridical decisions and to influence public opinion through speech. We frequently read about "equal access to political participation" and "equal access to public speech."[22] By thinking about equality in terms of the history of democracy, we are able to hear Philippians 2:6 as a description of an original political community, whose members — God and Christ Jesus — enjoy complete equality.

We should not be timid about reading Paul against the backdrop of Greek democracy on the assumption that, because he wrote in the first century, he could not use the language that had its home in the political

---

20. See K. S. Sacks, *Diodorus Siculus and the First Century* (Princeton, NJ: Princeton University Press, 1990), 69-82. See also Plato *Republic* 360c, 568a-b; *Vaticanum Gnomologium* 53, 545.

21. Aristotle *Politics* 2.1.5.

22. See K. Raaflaub, "Democracy, Oligarchy, and the Concept of 'Free Citizen' in Late Fifth-Century Athens," *Political Theory* 11: 517-44; *Die Entdekung der Freiheit: Zur historischen Semantik und Gesellschaftsgeschichte eines politischen Grundbegriffes der Griechen,* Vestigian 37 (Munich: C. H. Beck, 1985); "Des freien Bürgers Recht der freien Rede: Ein Beitrag zur Begriffs- und Sozialgeschichte der athenischen Demokratie," in W. Eck, ed., *Studien zur Antiken Sozialgeschichte: Festschrift F. Vittinghoff,* Kölner historische Abhandlung 28 (Cologne: Bohlau, 1980), 7-57; Ober, *Mass and Elite,* 74-75.

discourse of an earlier era. In spite of the arguments of antidemocratic theorists and the actuality of dominating rule in the wake of Alexander's conquest and the increase of Roman power, the extension of democratic participation was a theme in political thought in classical, Hellenistic times, and even during the Roman period.[23] At a bare minimum, it may be said that the notion of equality in its political sense did not die out with the diminution of the city-state, and thus it was available to Paul and his audiences.

Extending Equality

Faintly reminiscent of the popular praise of Alexander's world-unifying campaign, the Christ Hymn moves to the middle of the story of Christ Jesus (Phil. 2:6b-8) and narrates his decision not to keep his equality with God to himself as something to be grasped.[24] Rather, he regards the equality in participation with God as something that must be extended to others. This decision is striking as an innovation and as a leadership initiative. Christ Jesus opens the limits on equality with God. Notice what is not said: the pattern of the Father *sending* the Son, which plays such an important role in Paul's other letters (e.g., Rom. 8:3), is not the underlying idea here. For reasons that will become even more pressing below, it is important, when we interpret Christ's voluntary slavery, to see that there is no notion of a divine will that must be obeyed in Philippians 2:6-8. Instead, the emphasis falls on Christ's refusal to limit the political community to himself and God. The story here is not about conformity to God's will; rather, it tells of the extension to others of Christ Jesus' own equality with God. The original political community is about to grow through Christ's initiative. Significantly, God does not become an actor in this narrative until he responds to Christ's career in 2:9.

So far, I have argued for a political conception in 2:6 of Christ Jesus' equality with God. We have also seen that Christ did not rest content with an exclusive claim to this equality, but rather sought to extend it to others.

23. See C. Crowther, "The Decline of Greek Democracy?" *Journal of Ancient Civilization* 7 (1992): 13-48; E. Gruen, "The Polis in the Hellenistic World," in Rosen and Farrell, *Nomodeiktes,* 339-54; A. Lintott, *Imperium Romanum: Politics and Administration* (London: Routledge, 1993), 129-53.

24. Plutarch *On the Fortune of Alexander* 330d; cf. Plutarch *Alexander* 27–28.

But how exactly did he accomplish this? This is the question that 2:7-8 seeks to answer. The way it is answered has a profound effect on our understanding of Paul's ecclesiology, since the narrative of Christ Jesus defines the kind of political engagement Paul exhorts the congregation itself to embrace.

In order to extend equality with God, Christ Jesus takes on the form of a slave. How is his slavery able to communicate equality in participation with God? The dependence of equality with God on Christ's slavery is impossible to grasp if we assume, as many interpreters have, that Christ's slavery is to God as master. These interpreters drive home their point by claiming that Christ's obedience mentioned in 2:8 is given to God. However, there is another interpretation of 2:7-8 that makes better overall sense of the narrative and avoids the necessity of importing the concept of divine will where it has not been named.

Christ's obedience, even to the point of death and crucifixion, is given to humans, not to God; similarly, his voluntary slavery is directed to humanity. To help explain the connection between Christ's slavery and the extension of participation in the divine community, we first refer to the idea of freedom in ancient political philosophy. Freedom for civic activity was understood to depend on freedom from daily necessities. Aristotle emphasized the dependence of one person's freedom on another's labor, the master on the body of the slave: "Therefore all people rich enough to be able to avoid personal trouble have a steward who takes this office, while they themselves engage in politics *[politeuontai]* or philosophy."[25] Paul does not enter into a debate concerning the justice of basing the master's freedom on the slave's labor or whether this is an adequate theory of the relationship between the social and political realms.[26] He simply presumes this ideology for the purpose of narrating the way Christ Jesus extends equality with God to humanity. Christ becomes humanity's obedient slave and thus creates freedom for his masters at the expense of his own body. He empties himself for their freedom.

Another way of explaining the liberating power of Christ's slavery is

25. Aristotle *Politics* 1.2.23; cf. 2.6.2, 2.8.5–6, 4.5.2-6, 6.2.1, 7.8.2-3; Plutarch *Lycurgus* 24.2; *Comparison of Aristides and Cato* 3–4; Philo *Special Laws* 2.123

26. For a critique of the Aristotelian subordination of the social to the political — e.g., what one finds in Hannah Arendt — see R. Bernstein, *Beyond Objectivism and Relativism: Science, Hermeneutics, and Praxis* (Philadelphia: University of Pennsylvania Press, 1983), 238-59.

to think in terms of the rhetorical function of slavery language in political discourse. Paul relies on his audience's familiarity with the figure of the popular leader who extended democratic participation in the life of the city, but who was frequently derided by aristocrats as a slave to the masses.[27] Famous examples abound in the history of the expansion of democratic rights in Athens. Cleon and Themistocles, for example, were remembered for their slave-like behavior toward the people as they sought to place more power in their hands — to the dismay of the aristocracy.[28]

Our description of Christ Jesus' action in Philippians 2:6-8 as a popular leader whose goal is the extension of his own equality with God is supported in 2:8 by the overtones of the verb "he lowered himself." By treating it as a personal virtue, solely a matter of self-estimation, the various English translations (e.g., "he humbled himself") obscure the way this term sits on the line between social and political life. The adjectival form *tapeinos* should be understood as a derisive term used by the elite to define lower-class humans as "unrecognized and without public power."[29] Although not necessarily slaves, such persons were the lowly obscure who were occupied with daily necessities and never able to participate in the affairs of the city.[30] It was precisely this meaning of the term that made it attractive to aristocrats or oligarchs deriding the popular leader. When the people are glorified and power resides in their hands, it undermines leadership that is based on high birth or wealth. Dionysius of Halicarnassus frequently identifies the leaders who are *tapeinoi* and democratic.[31] Plutarch's account of Publicola, even though it betrays the author's own unease with popular leaders and his preference for moderation in his theory

---

27. For this *topos*, see D. Martin, *Slavery as Salvation: The Metaphor of Slavery in Pauline Christianity* (New Haven: Yale University Press, 1990), 86-116.

28. See Aristotle *Athenian Constitution* 3–4; Philo *On Joseph* 34–36; Plutarch *Theseus* 24–25; *Comparison of Theseus and Romulus* 2; *Themistocles* 23.4; *Cimon* 15.2; *Pericles* 9–15, 39; *Nicias* 5.3–4; *Aemelius Paulus* 2.6; *Comparison of Agis and Cleomenes* 1.1–2, 2.1–6; *Caius Gracchus* 1.5–6, 6.3, 9.1, 12.1; *Aratus* 26.3–4; *Precepts of Statecraft* 807a; *On Monarchy, Democracy, and Oligarchy* 827c; 816f–817c; Pseudo-Themistocles *Epistle* 6.

29. Isocrates *To Nicocles* 34.5; *Nicocles* 56.3; *Archidamus* 89.10; *Panegyricus* 151–152; *To Philip* 89; *Areopagiticus* 4–7; Dionysius of Halicarnassus, *Roman Antiquities* 1.4.1, 4.72.3, 5.75.1, 6.54.1, 77.1. See also Plutarch *Demosthenes* 1.1–3; *Old Men in Public Affairs* 785c; *Themistocles* 22; *Sulla* 3.5; Epictetus *Discourse* 4.1.55; Dio Chrysostom *Discourses* 2.7, 44.12, 47.4, 65.3.

30. Lucian *Dream* 9; *Nigrinus* 21.

31. Dionysius of Halicarnassus *Roman Antiquities* 2.8.1, 9.1.3.

of leadership,[32] illustrates the way this term functioned in the relationship between leader and democratic community:

> Wishing now to make not only himself but also the government, instead of formidable, submissive, and agreeable to the multitude, he removed the axes from the lictors' rods, and when he came into the assembly, inclined and lowered the rods themselves to the people, emphasizing the majesty of the democracy. . . . And before the multitude were aware of it, he had succeeded, not by humbling himself, as they thought, but by checking and removing their envious feelings through such moderation on his part, in addition to his real influence over them just as much as he had seemed to take away from his authority, and the people submitted to him with pleasure and bore his yoke willingly. They therefore called him Publicola, which signifies *people-cherisher*.[33]

This passage reflects the view that the popular leader magnifies the people by lowering himself in terms of glory and power. Living in a society in which the rhetoric about popular leaders was still heard, Paul's audience in Philippi might well have been expected to see the Christ Jesus of the hymn as a popular leader who voluntarily enslaved himself in order to extend to others freedom in participation with God. To accomplish this end, he had to lower himself in order that they might be empowered.

Political Action in the Church

The reason for exploring the first half of the Christ Hymn is that it promised to help us understand what it means for the church to "engage in political action worthily of the gospel of Christ" (Phil. 1:27). Our investigation of Christ's action leads to the conclusion that he is portrayed as a popular leader whose goal is to extend democratic participation in the divine community. The means to this end is his own voluntary enslavement to those he wishes to free. Therefore, in order to engage in the affairs of the community worthily of the gospel, every member, with respect to every

32. Plutarch *Camillus* 1.3.

33. Plutarch *Publicola* 10.5; cf. *Demosthenes* 24.1; *Cato the Elder* 12.4–13.3; *Demetrius* 45.3; *Tiberius Gracchus* 16.2; Dionysius of Halicarnassus *Roman Antiquities* 7.45.4–5.

other member, must take up the same goal — *extending freedom to the other* — and each will appropriate the same means to this end: *voluntary slavery to the other.* In other words, each member of the community will, in his or her own relationships with all other members, adopt the role of popular leader whose task is to enable others to participate in political community with God.

There is ample evidence in the hortatory material surrounding the Christ Hymn (Phil. 2:1-4 and 2:12) that Paul seeks to persuade the church to conceptualize its action as the innovative, freedom-extending action of Christ. The most obvious parallel between exhortation and hymn is the term "lowly-mindedness" in 2:3, which anticipates Christ's practical wisdom (2:5) and his action of self-lowering (2:8). Words formed on the *tapein* root characterized the popular leader who sought to put greater power into the hands of the people by reducing his own public recognition in order that the people might be magnified. Paul's exhortation to do this fits in well with this political background. The contrast with "vainglory" prepares the hearer to think in terms of public recognition.[34] The exhortation for all individually to regard others as surpassing themselves clearly has social status rather than moral connotations.[35]

The terminology of "slavery," commonly attached to popular leaders and central to the hymn, is echoed in the exhortation. Furthermore, the phrase "each not looking out for his own interests but also for the interests of the others" is a definition of what slaves do. Moving ahead to the transition from the end of the Christ Hymn back to the exhortation, we hear a phrase denoting mutual slavery: "Just as you have always obeyed." This phrase clearly picks up on the notion of Christ's obedience in 2:8. Since there is no direct object for the verb, there is some ambiguity about the person or persons to whom obedience is given. But there are compelling reasons to understand 2:12a as a reference to mutual obedience among congregation members. First, if there is to be a parallel with Christ's obedience, it must be rendered to humans. Second, the notion of mutual obedience is an interpretation suggested by the unmistakable mutuality in 2:3-4. In this way of thinking, 2:12a is a continuation of the exhortations contained in 2:3-4. Finally, we know from Galatians 5:13 that Paul, in at least

34. For vainglory as a political vice, see Philo *On Dreams* 2.46–155, esp. 2.78.
35. Plutarch *Themistocles* 22.3; *Coriolanus* 18.2; Dionysius of Halicarnassus *Roman Antiquities* 4.72.3, 11.22.7, 19.18.7; Dio Chrysostom *Discourse* 57.7.

one other setting, has conceptualized the internal action of the church as mutual slavery.

But what significance would this notion of mutual slavery have had for Paul's hearers? The key to answering this question is the paradoxical character of the communal relationships implied by mutual obedience. Each person in the community is simultaneously master and slave — or, to express it in another way, ruler and ruled. This paradox has an antecedent in the understanding of shared power in ancient democracies. Aristotle pointed out that the distinguishing mark of political rule, as opposed to the rule of master over slave or male over household, was an exchange of ruling and being ruled. Citizens must learn both to exercise authority over others and to obey the authority of those whom they once ruled or would rule.[36]

In democratic arrangements of power, a citizen could expect to be both ruler and ruled in temporal succession. Paul introduces a new factor by removing the temporal succession. But there is enough similarity between his understanding of the community on this point and the notion of power sharing in democracies to make a comparison meaningful. By removing temporal succession, Paul makes the relationships between the members of the community more complex. While each is a master, a full participant in the divine community (having been freed by the slavery of Christ Jesus), each is also a slave to the others. But since this slavery is mutual, the slave is again made a master.

We are now in a position to go deeper into the meaning of the exhortation to "engage politically in a manner worthy of the gospel of Christ." If we focus on the verb, this phrase exhorts each member of the community to play an active role in the formation of the group's plans, policies, and objectives. What is remarkable about this exhortation is the predominance of a process to discover a mutually acceptable form of life over assimilation to an already determined form of life. There is an openness that is to be limited by the participants themselves through speech and persuasion.

Nevertheless, modifying — but not retracting! — the high degree of individual participation and initiative is the adverbial phrase "worthily of the gospel of Christ." *In, with,* and *under* the interchanges of community members, interchanges that presume their freedom, each individual ex-

---

36. Plutarch *Themistocles* 22.3; *Coriolanus* 18.2; Dionysius of Halicarnassus *Roman Antiquities* 4.72.3, 11.22.7, 19.18.7; Dio Chrysostom *Discourse* 57.7.

tends freedom for participation to the other. We must admit that this activity, initiated by and modeled on the voluntary slavery of Christ to humanity and his self-lowering in obscurity, is in tension with the verb *politeuesthai*. How can I assert my freedom in challenging, proposing, and defending alternative schemes and simultaneously empty myself for the other in slave-like obedience with no public recognition? Taking this tension seriously, instead of rejecting it as a Pauline blunder or mystification through paradox, could be the beginning of fruitful reflection on the character of local Christian congregations. What concretely does it mean to extend freedom to the other? What kind of community presumes individual initiative and mutual obedience? What kind of self is implied as the one who carries out the imperative to engage politically in the affairs of the community worthily of the gospel of Christ?

Community for the Gospel

Critics both ancient and modern have condemned democratic communities as far too susceptible to dissolution owing to the freedom of the individual.[37] In opposition to democracy's emphasis on consensus through speech, rival political theories have asserted the need to begin with the unity that community members share prior to conversation. The primary value in this case is *homonoia* ("one-mindedness") rather than freedom of speech.[38] To this way of thinking, the task for the community as a whole and leaders in particular is to socialize individuals into a recognition and acceptance of a preexisting unity.

A rapid reading of Philippians 1:27–2:18 might suggest that Paul here calls the church to its preexisting unity. This would severely curtail the openness to innovation through moral conversation that we have so far

---

37. See D. Kagan, *The Great Dialogue: History of Greek Political Thought from Homer to Polybius* (New York: Free Press, 1965).

38. For the *homonoia* theme in political philosophy, see C. Farrar, *The Origins of Democratic Thinking: The Invention of Politics in Classical Athens* (Cambridge, UK: Cambridge University Press, 1988); C. H. Kahn, *The Art and Thought of Heraclitus: An Edition of the Fragments with Translation and Commentary* (Cambridge, UK: Cambridge University Press, 1979); see also Farrar, "The Origins of Social Contract Theory in the Fifth Century B.C.," in G. Kerford, ed., *The Sophists and Their Legacy* (Wiesbaden, 1981), 92-108; J. Ober, *Mass and Elite*, 295-99.

emphasized. Note the presence of *homonoia*-related language in 1:27 ("standing firm in one spirit . . . with one mind") and 2:2 ("be of the same mind, having the same love, being in full accord and of one mind"). The theme of *homonoia* culminates in the unity envisioned in the Christ Hymn (2:11), when every tongue confesses that Jesus Christ is Lord to the glory of God the Father.

However, it would be a mistake to conclude that Paul's emphasis on unity is designed to restrict the open participation of all members implied in the imperative of 1:27. First of all, we should observe that the consensus envisioned by Paul is both the *result* of political engagement, not a substitute for it, and a *future state of affairs,* which God brings about through the exaltation of the crucified Christ. Second, the envisioned consensus does not serve the maintenance of a system, as it always does in ancient political theory, but is directly related to mission, the expansion of faith in the gospel.[39] To put it another way, one-mindedness in the community has an external teleology, persuasion to the gospel, rather than the internal purpose of stabilization through uniformity. Members of the community struggle together for others to come to faith in the gospel.

The final reason not to regard one-mindedness as a retreat from individual initiative is that the specific content of the one mind is the mind of Christ, whose practical reasoning is narrated in Philippians 2:6-8 and, as we have already discussed, modifies the kind of activity denoted by *politeuesthai.* Indeed, there is an ethos that preexists for the members of the community and into which Paul is seeking to socialize them. But it is the ethos of extending freedom in the divine community through voluntary slavery to the other. This ethos requires that there not be an underlying sameness within the community, for unity of this kind would obviate the need for slavery to the other.

The issue we are dealing with here is the relationship between *is* and *ought to be* in moral exhortation. Most ancient political theorists grounded exhortations for political unity in the overarching unity of the cosmos or in the *homonoia* between the gods.[40] Paul also moves from *is* to *ought to be,* but instead of a preexisting unity, he points in 2:1 to the preexisting reality

---

39. Aalders, *Political Thought,* 16, n. 47; E. Kearns, "Saving the City," in *The Greek City: From Homer to Alexander,* 323-44.

40. See M. Mitchell, *Paul and the Rhetoric of Reconciliation: An Exegetical Investigation of the Language and Composition of 1 Corinthians* (Louisville: Westminster John Knox, 1993), 76-80.

of Christ, love, the Spirit, and compassion and mercy. Especially in the last two words do we see that the ethos of the community, the character of its action, is a matter of perspective-taking. These two affections have in common the idea of experiencing the world from the position of the other (cf. Phil. 1:7; 2 Cor. 6:11),[41] and both had a role to play in the social psychology of democratic communities.[42]

We have seen that the theme of one-mindedness in Philippians does not undercut the participatory character of the community's internal interactions but actually inscribes the freedom-extending action of Christ into the practical reasoning of each member. Of course, this could not have been our interpretation had we not observed Paul's subversive use of "one-mindedness," a key doctrine in the legitimation of regimes characterized by nonparticipatory power. The theme of "community" *(koinōnia)* presents us with a similar challenge. With the notable exception of Aristotle, ancient political philosophers used the notion of community in such a way as to negate democratic interaction.[43]

Community was conceptualized as a preexisting commonality of interests into which the individual must be socialized. Alternatively, the human being was posited as deficient as an individual, so that community was a goal to be accomplished, justified by human needs, and these needs and interests were already predetermined and not susceptible to debate.[44] Aristotle's treatment of political community puts a different twist on the issue and prepares us to understand what Paul may be up to in his repeated use of the term in Philippians. As Bernard Yack has emphasized, *koinōnia* was not an end in itself for Aristotle, but a means to an end — the happy life.[45] The exact nature of the end is not of primary concern to us in the comparison of Paul's usage with Aristotle's, though joy is a very important

41. The spleen was thought to be the center of compassion, pity, and forgiveness.

42. See T. Cole, *Democritus and the Sources of Greek Anthropology* (Cleveland: Western Reserve University Press, 1967), 121.

43. Yet, as a rare exception, see Andocides *Against Alcibiades* 13: "More than any other form of government, democracy seeks to make *koinōnia* its end." This imagines community as the result of mutual persuasion rather than a preexisting condition.

44. For *koinōnia* as a political term, see A. Saxonhouse, *Fear of Diversity: The Birth of Political Science in Ancient Greek Thought* (Chicago: University of Chicago Press, 1992), 9-15; Aalders, *Political Thought*, 33.

45. B. Yack, *The Problems of a Political Animal: Community, Justice, and Conflict in Aristotelian Political Thought* (Berkeley: University of California Press, 1993), 51-71; see also Aristotle *Politics* 1.1.6, 1.1.8–12, 3.5.13–14.

theme in Philippians and is present in Paul to the extent that the church fulfills its missionary function through the character of its internal relations. The main point for our investigation is that community in the Epistle to the Philippians is neither a preexisting unity nor a goal; rather, it is conceptualized as a means to an end.

This teleological perspective on community may help us appreciate Paul's treatment of the theme within the argumentation of the letter. First of all, notice that the initial and defining occurrence of the term in 1:5 emphasizes its teleological character, as a "community for the gospel." If we assume that "the gospel" here refers to the gospel as it is proclaimed, then the entire phrase must mean that the community's common interest and reason for existing is to promote wider belief in Jesus as Lord. The connection between community and making the faith persuasive to the world is repeated in 1:7. Here, Paul's audience of grace — and thus of his rhetorical point — is included as "my co-participants" in the activity of the "defense and confirmation of the gospel." Thus the theme of community in Philippians works very much as does Paul's emphasis on one-mindedness.

Conclusion: God's Action for the World in Congregations

The analysis I have offered so far may strike the reader as a-theological in the sense of saying nothing about God as an actor. There is an important reason for saving this discussion until now. As the story in Philippians 2:6-11 unfolds, God's action comes *after* Christ's. This fact, along with the "wherefore" of verse 9, implies that God's action in exalting Jesus and giving him the name beyond every name is God's *response* to Christ Jesus' innovative extension of participation in the divine community. There is a dramatic pause in the narrative between verses 8 and 9. How will God respond to this imaginative, popular leader whose action brings equality to those beyond the limits of the original community? Has Christ, like Prometheus, gone too far? Can the boundary of the divine community be expanded to include humanity?

God's response can be understood from two perspectives. First, from the perspective of Christ's story, the crucified one is exalted and his voluntary obscurity is reversed. He also receives "the name which is beyond every name," which we soon find out is "Lord," God's name. But if we shift perspective to God's action — and this should be considered the primary perspective of the argument, since the two aorist verbs of verse 9 have God as their subject — the doxological relationship God develops with Jesus Christ comes to the fore. One might even say that it is a confessional relationship, since both the verb "exalt" and the phrase "he freely gave to him the name which is beyond every name" can be understood as the action of giving praise, and both anticipate the confessional activity of every tongue in 2:11. Therefore, the Christ Hymn does not tell the story of a New Adam, who this time around is perfectly obedient to the divine will and is rewarded accordingly. Rather, it narrates the formation of God's will as a response in time to the political agency of Jesus Christ. The divine will is expressed in the *ina* clause of verse 10: it consists of all creatures coming to make the same confession that God makes concerning Jesus Christ as Lord. God exalts Christ and gives him the name Lord, and now works in order that all creatures might make the same confession. God's agency in the world is formed by this goal.

We can now attempt to explain how the church's agency in the world is simultaneously God's action. Through grace the church is God's means to God's end, the universal confession of Jesus as Lord to God's glory as Father.[46] Two key words capture God's mode of activity in Philippians, which are "work" and "grace." To grasp this formulation, we must analyze the two terms as they occur in the argument.

First, in examining God's work, we note initially that this theme forms an *inclusio* by appearing at the beginning (1:6) and toward the end (2:13) of the first half of Philippians. In 1:6 we learn that "the one who initiated among you a good work will continue to complete it until the day of Jesus Christ." The specific content of God's end emerges only in the course of the argument; but in 1:6 the reader is introduced to the end as a general concept, and to God as an actor with an end in mind. It is important to note the contrast between the aorist participle ("who initiated") and the future tense of the main verb ("he will continue to bring to completion"). The future tense suggests that between the present time of the text and the day of Jesus Christ, God repeatedly brings about God's desired end, even though its culmination is in the future. The end itself is named "a good work," a phrase that would have significant connotations for the first-century Greek speaker: it refers to the activity for the public good carried out by persons of

---

46. For the notion that God's glory is at stake in mission, see Rom. 2:23-24; 3:5, 7, 24-25; 9:23; 1 Cor. 10:31; 2 Cor. 1:11; 4:15; 9:12-13.

means. The good work won for its doer the enhancement of his or her reputation among the people.[47] We see the dual teleological nature of God's action, where God (a) repeatedly brings a good work to completion, and (b) in this way will obtain public recognition (1:11).

Explicit naming of the community as the means to God's end occurs in 1:5. The hearers of the letter discover that they are God's means to accomplish God's end. Paul makes the same point at the other end of the argument in 2:13. He again identifies God as the agent: "[F]or God is the one who is working among you both the wishing and the working for the sake of good will." The work of God goes on "among you" and is equated with the internal relations of the community, which, we have argued above, consist of mutual extension of freedom. God's good work is the public recognition of Jesus as Lord. This work is concretely carried out in the "wishing and working" of the community in each member's struggle to extend freedom to others.

47. Isocrates *To Philip* 35; Andocides *On His Return* 10, 16, 18; Lysias *Orations* 6.6, 14.37; Dionysius of Halicarnassus *Roman Antiquities* 9.33.3.1; Plutarch *Theseus* 7.2; *Romulus* 13.3.

God, Civil Society, and Congregations as Public Moral Companions

Gary Simpson

World War II ended more than fifty years ago, but the rage of nations did not. Since the fall of the Berlin Wall in 1989, rage now tends to erupt less often between nations, more often within a single national border. Today, in the midst of the culture wars,[1] the rage of nations can be found internally in the United States, even in our heartland, which was demonstrated in the Oklahoma City bombing in the mid-1990s. The metaphors that saturate our daily discourse signal this raging: "the disuniting of America," "the melting pot at boiling point," "drive-by politics," "hate radio."

Some fifty years after America's victory abroad, will we suffer defeat at home? Will the noble American experiment of trying to be one nation simply overheat and explode? Something deeply moral is at stake in our nation's current rage. Conceivably, this rage, as a moral thermometer, measures both the thwarted hopes of the marginalized and the decreasing possibility for the good life of an increasing number of ordinary residents.[2]

In the midst of this morally charged situation, how can Christian congregations hear again the call to serve in a *public vocation?* As we consider this prospect, three questions will guide our inquiry. First, where

1. James Davison Hunter, *Culture Wars: The Struggle to Define America* (New York: Basic Books, 1990).

2. See, e.g., Robert D. Kaplan's widely read "The Coming Anarchy," *The Atlantic Monthly,* February 1994, 44-76, which also appeared in newspapers across the country. See also Barbara Ehrenreich, *Fear of Falling: The Inner Life of the Middle Class* (New York: Pantheon Books, 1989).

might Christian congregations find a space in which they might attend to the public moral meaning of everyday rage? Such a public space is what we will refer to as *civil society*. Second, how can this public space of civil society be accessed so that its moral possibilities can be maximized? We will investigate *communicative moral practice* as the best model for accessing the moral possibilities of civil society. Third, on what basis are Christian congregations free to engage in communicative moral practice within civil society. Here we will probe the Trinitarian doctrine of the crucified God whose freeing agency empowers Christian vocation. What a communicative civil society needs, as it struggles with the moral meaning of our nation's rage, is the congregational vocation of *public moral companion*.[3]

Civil Society: Enriching Our Impoverished Public Spaces

Already before the 1989 collapse of the Soviet Union, Central and Eastern European dissidents were focusing on the renewal of civil society. They did so even in the highly restricted areas that were dominated by Soviet control. Here we refer to civil society as "the space of un-coerced human association and also the set of relational networks — formed for the sake of family, faith, interest, and ideology, that fill this space." These dissidents cultivated their fledgling democracies by nurturing their diverse social networks of churches, unions, neighborhoods, movements, and societies "for promoting and preventing this and that."[4]

---

3. The congregational vocation of public moral companion does not, of course, preclude other possible vocations. Furthermore, all congregational vocations stand intimately and distinguishably coupled with the congregation's fundamental missional identity as public witness to salvation through Jesus Christ (see Marc Kolden, "Creation and Redemption; Ministry and Vocation," *Currents in Theology and Mission* 14 [February 1987]: 31-37). The mission statement of my own institution, Luther Seminary, strives in a similar way to claim a distinguishable togetherness between ministry and vocation: "Luther Seminary educates leaders for Christian communities called and sent by the Holy Spirit to witness to salvation through Jesus Christ and to serve in God's world." My purpose in this chapter is to particularize the last phrase, "to serve in God's world," with a morally reflective and sociologically viable congregational strategy for the United States. For an especially winsome explication of the clause "to witness to salvation through Jesus Christ," see Patrick Keifert, *Welcoming the Stranger: A Public Theology of Worship and Evangelism* (Minneapolis: Fortress, 1992).

4. Michael Walzer, "The Idea of Civil Society," *Dissent* (Spring 1991): 293. A more thorough investigation that draws on the seminal thinking of Jürgen Habermas is in Jean

We have lived in the United States with such an approach to civil society for numerous generations, especially in the years since World War II. Most citizens have come to take it for granted in their everyday lives. But this neglect of attending to the dynamics of civil society has led to the impoverishment of public space. Our current increasing rage stands as a sign of the times of a diminished civil society.

The United States' emergence as a world leader during the twentieth century necessitated the cooperation of the two megasystems of modern life in our country: the democratic state and the market economy. Our victory in World War II had much to do — not everything, but much — with the successful cooperation of these two great systems. The success of these great systems in the war effort progressively drew, even seduced, large numbers of ordinary Americans to shift their focus: they began to fixate their attention and energies on the so-called "real world" of these great systems to the detriment of maintaining a public space of civil society.

This growing fixation by ordinary American people on the market economy and the democratic state draws on two rival Western heritages that were formulated over the last two centuries. Each of these intellectual heritages reveals something true about the pursuit of the good life in the modern era, but each does so by being too one-sided. The first heritage is the neoclassical republican tradition that was first proposed by Rousseau. He highlighted the moral agency of the *citizen,* and this has been the key for promoting democratic idealism ever since. In the republican heritage, the democratic political *state* is the public space of highest worth, and citizenship is the goal that all other moral agencies must serve.

The telling criticism of this heritage is not that democratic politics aren't good, for they surely are. Indeed, I would argue vigorously for the

Cohen and Andrew Arato, "Politics and the Reconstruction of the Concept of Civil Society," in Axel Honneth, Thomas McCarty, Claus Offe, and Albrecht Wellmer, eds., *Cultural-Political Interventions in the Unfinished Project of Enlightenment* (Cambridge, MA: MIT Press, 1992), 121-42. Habermas's own investigation appears in *Between Facts and Norms: Contributions to a Discourse Theory of Law and Democracy* (Cambridge, MA: MIT Press, 1996), 329-87. Peter Drucker, in a widely read article, has recently turned his attention to the significance of civil society, which he refers to as "the social sector," and to the contributions that religious communities can make in it ("The Age of Social Transformation," *The Atlantic Monthly,* November 1994, 53-80). The concept of a communicative civil society would add more depth to William Dean's focus on "the third sector" as his recommended location for religious critics (*The Religious Critic in American Culture* [Albany, NY: State University of New York Press, 1994]).

democratic state as the best possible state in the modern era. Nonetheless, a problem remains. Paradoxically, even though the democratic state significantly touches the breadth of ordinary living, and for the larger part does so beneficially, it is not the everyday life of very many ordinary people. The attention, time, and energy of ordinary people is focused instead on earning a living.

Earning a living awakens the other great Western heritage, that of the market capitalist tradition. This heritage spurns the citizen's fixation on the democratic state and focuses it instead on the *economy* as the place where moral agency can bring about the good life. The marketplace becomes the space of highest worth. With *market* as the root metaphor, even the moral agency of economic production plays second fiddle to the consumerism that provides the good life. The controlling orthodoxy is that autonomous, personal, private choice is what drives the market for the benefit of all. Entrepreneurs cater to the choosing appetite of consumers, and they are esteemed as "much the best thing to be," as Michael Walzer puts it.[5] It is to be a laissez-faire economy where, according to classic liberalism, economic production, consumption, and entrepreneurship must remain liberated from the state. Even the democratic state must keep its hands off the economy, thus the minimal state.

This one-sidedness of the market capitalist heritage shows up in several ways. Some come to the marketplace with far too few resources of their own to purchase the goods needed in order to participate effectively in our modern society. As a result, they feel left out and marginalized by the market economy. Many who come to the economic marketplace with enough resources to participate often do not sufficiently experience the good life in this space that they were looking for. Instead, they commonly experience a secular meaningless, even a heartless world. Many in this latter group search for a haven from the heartlessness of the marketplace, and they often end up in some cocooning space of private intimacy, such as the nuclear family or the familial-fashioned congregation. Disturbingly, far too many of them also find these private spaces to be just as heartless as the world of the economic marketplace or the democratic state. These encounters with heartlessness reveal that our private intimate spheres can be quite fragile. This is because they cannot flourish without being rooted in and accountable to the broader moral networks that constitute civil soci-

5. Walzer, "The Idea of Civil Society."

ety.[6] Furthermore, our private spaces too easily become colonized, whether under the consumptive strategies of the economic marketplace, or under the administrative necessities of the democratic state.

Tragically, neither of these two great heritages promotes an understanding of civil society, and thus each remains within its one-sidedness. This reality continues to contribute to the neglect and impoverishment of a morally significant public space. We revel in the cultural heritages of our everyday life-world. We coordinate our actions as groups according to perceived shared norms around them, and through them we develop individual and social identities. These are the key features of our everyday life-world: (a) our cultural embodiment, (b) our social integration, and (c) our socialization into citizenship and consumerism. These features have both an institutional dimension and a symbolic-metaphorical-linguistic dimension. Civil society as a public space corresponds to the institutional dimension of our everyday life-world.[7] However, we have the potential, by enriching civil society, to diminish the colonizing effects of both the marketplace, with its medium of money, and the state, with its medium of administrative power. At the same time, enriching civil society could also provide the more private spaces of our everyday life-world with a richer moral milieu. This would stand in contrast to the most common pattern of today, in which each solitary individual or family is trying to stitch together its own moral spaces.

Congregations have traditionally exercised great influence regarding

6. Christopher Lasch's account of the family, *Haven in a Heartless World* (New York: Basic Books, 1977), remains flawed precisely because he does not account for the heartlessness of the family "haven" itself, leaving Lasch unable to locate and access the moral resources that families themselves desperately need today. See Keifert, *Welcoming the Stranger*, for a trenchant account of the ideology of familial intimacy that infects much congregational life today.

7. See Wolfhart Pannenberg's theological analysis of "institutions" as an approach to the Reformation teaching about the "orders of creation" in *Anthropology in Theological Perspective* (Philadelphia: Westminster, 1985), 397-416. See also Carl Braaten, "God in Public Life: Rehabilitating the 'Orders of Creation,'" *First Things*, December 1990, 32-38. Robert Bellah and his associates correctly portray the difficulty that many Americans have in understanding how much of our everyday lives is lived in and through institutions; see Bellah, *The Good Society* (New York: Alfred A. Knopf, 1991), 3-18. Though much is good in this book, Bellah et al. also do not make "civil society" a theme. This remains a major flaw in their conceptualization of "the public church," where "God Goes to Washington" is the beginning of their analysis.

the symbolic-metaphorical-linguistic dimension in addressing the three basic tasks noted above that are associated with the everyday life-world. Still, in our contemporary situation, the ongoing survival of the life-world needs the institutional dimension that we have called "civil society." Here is where a plurality of institutional embodiments can come together for the mutual enrichment and recreation of a lively moral milieu. The multiplicity of struggling — and often isolated — institutions that are native to civil society are beginning to cry out to one another for help. Given a morally rich enough texture to civil society, even economic and government institutions could enter this space without dominating it. This would help bring valuable moral assistance to these institutions and their systemic worlds. By giving ear to these cries for help in developing a civil society, Christian congregations are recognizing a renewed calling, a public moral vocation. What kind of access is available to congregations for engaging the moral possibilities of civil society as they serve as *public moral companions* to the institutions of civil society?

Models of Moral Access to Civil Society

During those times when Americans have attended to civil society, three models have functioned to give institutions and Christian congregations access to its moral possibilities: the *agonistic,* the *liberal,* and the *communicative.*[8] Historically, the first two have dominated the American imagination and practice; unfortunately, as we shall see, this has also contributed to the current impoverishment of civil society. In the *agonistic* model, the dominant practices of civil society revolve around a competitive struggle among rival versions of personal moral virtue. In this model each rival tradition presents itself as a pure, self-sufficient, and cohesive totality of virtue. A tradition vies for preeminence over other traditions by displaying its moral ideals as publicly as possible. Each strives to gain the support of the majority of citizens who begin as passive onlookers, continue as active imitators, and finish as admired moral masters. These agonistic practices tend to lead to the dominance of a single agenda of personal virtue, which, in turn, downplays those of rival traditions.

8. Seyla Benhabib, "Models of Public Space," in Craig Calhoun, ed., *Habermas and the Public Sphere* (Cambridge, MA: MIT Press, 1992), 73-98.

With the agonistic model, civil society remains particularly susceptible to the technological temptations of the now ever-present sound bite.
Conventional clichés, simplistic stereotyping, and either/or scenarios fill
the airwaves with simplistic moral assertions. Communitarian heritages
often promote this model, as do certain Christian movements with a more
sectarian slant.[9] The advantage of the agonistic model is that personal vir-
tues for practical face-to-face living are cultivated via the economy and
politics; but these systems are themselves shielded from moral consideration. The social costs remain steep.

The *liberal* model of civil society originated in order to squelch the
moral totalitarian consequences of the agonistic civil society. In the liberal
model, moral discourse is subject to the constraint of neutrality whenever a
single moral tradition asserts that its moral conception of the good life is
superior to others. The constraint of neutrality prohibits three things:
(a) agonistic trumping; (b) translating moral disagreements into a suppos-
edly neutral framework; and (c) transcending moral disagreements by imagining some hypothetical circumstance. Instead of these approaches, moral
traditions must agree not to disagree in public; rather, they must confine
their moral disagreements to private spheres. Not only does this model pri-
vatize the act of disagreeing; it also privatizes the very terrain of controversial
subject matters. The result is that liberal civil society accedes more and more
relevant moral issues to the private-sector economy, or to lifestyle intimacy,
or to the religious conscience. Along the way, the liberal model also
privatizes the congregation. Paradoxically, the practices of the liberal model
contribute to the withering away of the very space of civil society.

In the midst of these two traditional models of civil society, a new
model — the *communicative* model — is emerging.[10] A communicative
civil society shares certain features with the other dominant models. Like
the agonistic model and unlike the liberal model of neutrality, it welcomes
questions of moral truth that have practical import for the everyday life-

9. The most influential contemporary version is Stanley Hauerwas and William H.
Willimon, *Resident Aliens: Life in the Christian Colony* (Nashville: Abingdon, 1989). My proposal of the congregational vocation of public moral companion contrasts sharply with the
Hauerwas-Willimon "colony" proposal and with other solely "contrast community" visions
of the congregation.

10. See Gary Simpson, "Human Nature and Communicative Ethics," *dialog* 33 (Fall
1994): 280-87, for an introductory essay on communicative ethics and for a more complete
bibliography of this emerging trajectory of moral reflection.

world. Unlike the agonistic model, with its characteristic practices of elitist moral display and purist moral trumping, the communicative civil society's hallmark is that its claims to practical moral truth must be redeemed critically through participatory practices. Participatory practices empower institutions that are affected by a moral claim to have a say in the formulation and adoption of moral norms. Boldly stated, the communicative civil society "comes into existence whenever and wherever all affected by general social and political norms of action engage in a practical discourse, evaluating their validity."[11]

By elevating participatory aspects, the communicative model eschews the totalizing and colonizing tendencies of the agonistic model, but without succumbing to the liberal model of public moral neutrality. The communicative civil society develops the capacity for creative moral possibilities through communicative practices; it also focuses on the systematic distortions that often accompany the self-interested bias of any single moral tradition.[12] Furthermore, the communicative model helps to overcome the rigid boundaries that have been built between the public and private by promoting their overlapping terrains.[13]

The Crucified God and Creative Agency

Behind this proposal for a *communicative* civil society breathes a Trinitarian doctrine of the crucified God and a communicative mode of creative agency. This represents our third line of inquiry toward a congregational vocation of serving as a public moral companion. The Christian doctrine of God historically has recognized a close connection between creation and God; Christian history also testifies to the fateful confusion — indeed, fusion — between the two precisely because of their close connection. When creation and God are confused, creative moral agency becomes

11. Benhabib, "Models of Public Space," 87.

12. Communicative ethics, such as Reinhold Niebuhr's, exercises a sharply double focus on both human moral resources and self-interested limitations. See esp. his *Moral Man and Immoral Society* (New York: Charles Scribner's Sons, 1932), xxiv. Niebuhr's subtitle, *A Study in Ethics and Politics,* manifests the weakness of his account that overlooks the public space of civil society as well as the communicative access to that space.

13. See Nancy Fraser, "Talking about Needs: Interpretive Contests as Political Conflicts in Welfare-State Societies," *Ethics* 99 (January 1989): 291-313.

instrumentalized: it becomes a mode of moral soteriology in which the fundamental human relationship with God is fashioned on human moral agency. Such an outcome would subvert our proposal for the public moral companionship of Christian congregations. Therefore, we need a preliminary critical inquiry into the Christian doctrine of God. Two classic times of confessing will fund our exploration: the Trinitarian creed of Nicaea and Martin Luther's theology of the cross.

The Trinitarian Creed of Nicaea

The first confession to speak of the proper relationship between the doctrine of God and creation arrived with the Creed of Nicaea in 325 C.E. It was immediately defended by Athanasius, who was in disputation with the Arian doctrine of God and its soteriological significance of Jesus. The debate that ensued provided the down payment for a more thoroughgoing critique of a moral soteriology that was based in a creation-mediated doctrine of God. Such a critical perspective is helpful precisely because we propose that congregations have a public moral vocation for the sake of the created world.

Of course, Athanasius offers substantial and lengthy theological contributions toward the doctrine of God, and yet he establishes in a mere two paragraphs several lasting insights.[14] We will concentrate on four points: (a) the logic in the doctrine of God; (b) the soteriological difference in the contesting logics of God; (c) the bitter root of the Arian logic of God; and (d) the soteriologically sweet fruit of the Trinitarian logic of God.

The primary identifying attribute of the Arian doctrine of God is "one God, alone un-originate."[15] Athanasius notes that the meaning of "un-originate" is thereby logically indicated by its relationship to things originated, to things created. That is, the identity and name of God come by way of created reality. "[F]rom the fruit is the tree known."[16] The Arians

---

14. Book 1, paragraphs 33–34 of *Orations against the Arians* (hereafter cited as *Ar.*) Unless otherwise indicated, we will follow the accessible translation in *The Trinitarian Controversy*, ed. and trans. William Rusch (Philadelphia: Fortress, 1980). These paragraphs include key sections written years earlier by Athanasius in *De Decretis*, 30–31.

15. See Arius's Letter to Alexander of Alexandria in Rusch, *The Trinitarian Controversy*, 31.

16. Here, in *Ar.* 1.35, as in other places, Athanasius cites Matt. 12:33.

agree. That is why, in their logic of God, they count Jesus as among things originated, a creature. He is the primordial, perfect creature through whom the rest of creation has its origin; but, as they emphasize repeatedly, he is most assuredly a creature and only a creature.[17] The Arians will ascribe any biblical attribute to Jesus so long as Jesus remains always and only on the creature side of the Creator/creation divide.

When teaching this controversy regarding Jesus and the divinity of the Son, we theologians usually assume we are preaching to the choir, and that the choir already knows how bad it is to place the Son on the creation side of the divide. Fortunately, Athanasius does not hold such faulty assumptions. He realizes how seductive it is to name God as "the un-originate," since true Christian piety recognizes God as Creator and also ascribes to God other attributes, such as "Almighty" and "Lord of the Powers." To expose the Arians' bait and switch of their doctrine of God for the Trinitarian doctrine, he must enter more deeply into the bitter logic of the Arian teaching.[18]

Athanasius's first step is simply to place the two logics side by side. Arians name God "un-originate" because they know and identify the deity only from God's originated works, with Jesus being the foremost of God's created works. A Christian Trinitarian view names God as "Father" because it knows and identifies the deity of this God from the Son. Athanasius sees this Trinitarian logic of God present in such classical Scripture passages as Matthew 11:27 and John 14:9. The bitterness of the Arian "one God, alone un-originate" remains closely bound up with the soteriological implications of God being so named. "Soteriology is pitted against soteriology, and neither adversary thinks otherwise."[19] Athanasius and the Arians also agree that the Arian creature-centered soteriology is emphatically a moral soteriology.

17. For a succinct summary of the Arian doctrine of God and the role of Jesus, see J. N. D. Kelly, *Early Christian Doctrines* (New York: Harper & Row, 1960), 226-31.

18. *Ar.* 1.1.

19. Robert C. Gregg and Dennis E. Groh, *Early Arianism: A View of Salvation* (Philadelphia: Fortress, 1981), 54. Athanasius also notices the moral character of Arian soteriology, e.g., in *Ar.* 1.39–40. Only recently, through the work of Gregg and Groh, has the Arian investment in soteriology been investigated, while Athanasius's soteriological investiture has long been acknowledged right up to the contemporary classics, e.g., Justo Gonzalez, *A History of Christian Thought,* vol. 2 (Nashville: Abingdon, 1970), 299-310; Kelly, *Early Christian Doctrines;* Bernhard Lohse, *A Short History of Christian Doctrine* (Philadelphia: Fortress, 1985), 56-61; Jaroslav Pelikan, *The Christian Tradition,* vol. 1 (Chicago: University of Chicago Press, 1971), 193-207.

The soteriological difference in the contesting logics of God manifests itself in the phenomenon of "praise and honor." These are Athanasius's soteriological code words in our two paragraphs. Here Athanasius is at his best. "For if they [the Arians] cared at all about praise and honor for the Father, it was necessary — and this was better and greater — that they know and say 'God the Father' rather than to name him thus [the un-originated]." For, as he continues, "the more the Word differs from originated things, so much more would the statement that God is 'Father' differ from the statement that he is 'un-originated.'"[20] Following John 5:23, Athanasius comprehends deeply what the Arians ignore, namely, that whoever dishonors the Son will inevitably end up dishonoring the Father. "Praise and honor" are the anvil on which a creation-centered soteriology gets hammered out. He pursues the crux of his critique by canceling out the genetic source for the Arian logic of God. He wants to maintain a creature-centered soteriology and its warrant in a creation-mediated doctrine of God.

Athanasius never tires of pointing out that it is the Greeks who discovered the un-originated and who bequeathed their logic of God to the Arians. Not only is this identification of God unscriptural, but it is also suspect, "suspicious" in Cardinal Newman's famous translation,[21] for it has "variegated meaning" by which our thoughts are "carried in many directions" (*Ar.* 1.34). It is no wonder that if one would waver with the Un-originate-mediated-through-the-originate, that one would also wobble in one's "praise and honor." It's also no wonder that the Arians have so little "confidence" in their discourse of their doctrine of God (*Ar.* 1.33).

In the paragraphs that follow our two key ones, Athanasius continues to press the Arians about the *indeterminate* character of their soteriology and doctrine of God. The Arian logic leaves its followers trapped in the same cul-de-sac in which Greek religion had always dead-ended, that is, its fate, its fickleness, and the dishonoring of God that it engenders.[22] Athanasius credits Paul in Rom. 1–2 for exposing this trap. Jesus as the incarnated divine Son of the Father is a "better and greater" story altogether, constituting the very trustworthiness of the deity and culminat-

20. *Ar.* 1.33.

21. See *Nicene and Post-Nicene Fathers*, vol. 4, ed. Philip Schaff and Henry Wace (Grand Rapids: Eerdmans, 1953).

22. Paul Tillich's analysis of the Greek preoccupation with fate remains one of the most salient; see Tillich, *The Protestant Era* (Chicago: University of Chicago Press, 1948), 3-15.

ing in everlasting praise and honor of God. Taken together, Athanasius's defense of the Trinitarian logic of God offers us a substantial critique of a creation-centered doctrine of God. It also provides a budding hermeneutic of the trustworthiness of the Trinitarian God that is rooted in the logic of the reciprocal dependence of the Father and the Son (*Ar.* 2.64-72).

Luther's Theology of the Cross

Luther's theology of the cross picks up on this. First of all, it offers us an intensified and expanded critique of the confusion of creation and God, thus preparing for their proper relationship. Second, it provides a more fully developed hermeneutic of divine trustworthiness that freely empowers congregations for the vocation of public moral companion with the creative agency of "the crucified God."[23]

Luther's retrieval of the biblically inscribed theology of the cross flowers in his twenty-eight theological theses known as the *Heidelberg Disputation.* And it flourished as the thoroughgoing criterion of his theology throughout his career.[24] Luther contrasts the theology of the cross with the full-blown theology of glory that was officially enthroned in medieval scholasticism. However, he emphasizes, as his interpreters often do not, that the source of the theology of glory lies within the sinful human condition. Strictly speaking, then, his critique focuses less on the "theology" of glory than on "theologians" of glory, every old Adam and old Eve included.[25] Not until Theses 19-21 of the *Heidelberg Disputation* does Luther forthrightly name the disputing modes of theology — of glory and cross. He carefully readies us for the conflict in the theses by criticizing the moral

23. See *Luther's Works,* American ed., vol. 31 (Philadelphia: Muhlenberg, 1957), 225 (hereafter *LW*).

24. *Heidelberg Disputation, LW* 31: 39-70. That the theology of the cross is the distinguishing mark of Luther's theology throughout is Walter von Loewenich's influential thesis in *Luther's Theology of the Cross* (Minneapolis: Augsburg, 1976), 12-13.

25. For an investigation of the sinful human condition as the "source" of the theology of glory, see Robert W. Bertram, "How Scripture Is 'Traditioned' in the Lutheran Confessions," in Kenneth Hagen, ed., *The Quadrilog: Tradition and the Future of Ecumenism* (Collegeville, MN: Liturgical Press, 1994), 82-87. That "theologians," more than "theology," are the subject of Luther's inquiry is a point made by both Jürgen Moltmann in *The Crucified God* (New York: Harper & Row, 1974), 208, and Gerhard Forde in *On Being a Theologian of the Cross* (Grand Rapids: Eerdmans, 1997).

soteriology of good works (1-12) and free will (13-18). In fact, his break-through is to notice the connection of a moral soteriology with the logic of the doctrine of God in the theology of glory.[26]

The theologian of glory, Thesis 19 declares, is that person "who looks upon the invisible things [being] of God as though they were clearly perceptible in those things which have actually happened [in those things which have been made, created]."[27] These invisible things of God *(invisibilia Dei)* are, following Paul in Romans 1:19-20, God's power and divinity, wisdom, righteousness, goodness, and so forth. Here, in the glory theologian's logic of God, we hear the once-waning echo of the Arians' creation-mediated logic of God waxing eloquent again.

In the centuries following Nicaea, medieval scholastic theology had returned to and even perfected the logic of a creation-mediated doctrine of God. They did so by returning to the auspices of Aristotelian philosophical assumptions. As Peter Lombard says authoritatively in the *Sentences,* "The human creature perceives the Creator in what is created in the world by virtue of the excellence through which the human towers above all other creatures and by virtue of the human creature's accord with all creation."[28] This inductive reasoning from the effects to the cause, from the creation to the Creator, lies behind all cosmological arguments for the existence of God. It is a perspective that is available to the gentiles in their efforts to develop a logic of God. But the problem, as Paul notes, is that humanity, following such a logic, does not end up honoring God. As Luther acknowledges in Theses 19 and 20, honoring God comprises the truth of a "wise and worthy" humanity. So far, Luther's critique of a creation-mediated doctrine of God corresponds to Athanasius's.

Indeed, Luther enlarges Athanasius's critique of the creation-mediated logic of God. He notes that the creation-mediated logic of God inevitably eventuates in a moral soteriology that instrumentalizes creation, God, and creative agency. This connection becomes explicit in Theses 22-24. Here he focuses on the use — or rather, the misuse — by hu-

---

26. Von Loewenich makes this point in *Luther's Theology of the Cross,* 19-20.

27. The bracketed translation comes from Moltmann, *The Crucified God,* 208, and offers a better understanding of Luther than does the standard English-language American edition. See von Loewenich's valuable insights regarding the translation and interpretation of this thesis.

28. Cited by Moltmann, *The Crucified God,* 209. Moltmann's explication of the assumptions and logic of the theology of glory is still one of the best available in English.

mans of the knowledge of and relationship with God available through the creation-mediated logic of God. First, that logic of God is not of itself evil. It is a wisdom that sees the invisible things of God in God's created works as perceived by humans. This is true for Luther as it is for Paul, because God is the one who makes himself available through creation in order to be praised and honored. However, people misuse this knowledge of God and the accompanying moral knowledge of God's law in the worst manner. Along with the innate capacities of "excellence" and "accord" that Lombard perceived in human nature, Luther targets the relational realities of "the old Adam" vis-à-vis God (Theses 18 and 21).

Luther notes that sinful humans usually take the credit for their goodness of creaturely life, and for the basic trustworthiness on which the created world appears to rest. Furthermore, being "so presumptuous" (Thesis 18), humans take credit for establishing their fundamental relationship with God based on the righteousness of their own moral agency. As a result, people become "increasingly blinded and hardened," and eventually they end up "completely" so (Thesis 22). Creation-mediated knowledge of God and of the moral law is never pure. It is always woven tightly together with one's own interest. In the case of sinners, their interests tend toward exalting the trustworthiness of human moral agency in establishing, maintaining, and completing the relationship with God. Thereby sinners instrumentalize God's good created world, and, in effect, they even try to instrumentalize God's own creative agency. Creation ends up suffering under such instrumentalization.

God's creative and life-preserving "civil use of the law" can never be severed from what Luther and the Reformation call God's "theological use of the law," for "through the law comes knowledge of sin" (Rom. 3:20).[29] Luther incorporates this interpretive breakthrough regarding the law into Thesis 23: "The law brings the wrath of God, kills, reviles, accuses, judges, and condemns everything that is not in Christ." It is at the end of the line of the theology of glory, of the creation-mediated knowledge of God. Here is where sinners encounter "the alien work of God" (Thesis 4) — *deus absconditus* ("the hidden God"), as Luther often puts it. Even Christ on the cross executes the judgment of God as "works are dethroned and the old Adam . . . is crucified" (Thesis 21). With this under-

---

29. For a classic discussion by Luther of the double use of the law, see his commentary on Gal. 3:19 (*LW* 26: 306-16).

standing, Luther intensifies Athanasius's critique of the creation-mediated logic of God.

Any proposal that extols the notion of the creational vocation of public moral companion, we believe, must first take this detour through a systematic critique of the creation-mediated logic of God. But our critical detour, while salutary, does not seem by itself to warrant our positive proposal. On the contrary, such a critique might be construed to warrant just the opposite, that is, congregational disengagement from the created world's public moral spaces. This has often been the case in the history of Christian theology. It is important that we keep the diagnostic seriousness of the critique coupled with the hermeneutic of the trustworthiness of the crucified God (Theses 4 and 7).[30]

The theology of the cross does not culminate with the crucified Christ as God's alien work of crucifying sinners. Rather, notes Luther, "an action which is alien [*opus alienum*] to God's nature results in a deed belonging to his very nature [*opus proprium*]: he makes a person a sinner so that he may make him righteous" (Thesis 16). As Scripture often testifies, God works against appearances (Theses 4-6), "under the opposite" *(sub contrario).*[31] Despite the sinful misuse of the knowledge of God mediated through creation, God "willed again to be recognized in suffering . . . so that those who did not honor God as manifested in his works should honor him as he is hidden in his suffering" (Thesis 20). We have in the crucified Christ a second hiddenness of God that constitutes God's righteousness-creating, and thus God's trustworthiness.[32]

30. As Pelikan notes, "To a considerable degree, the definition of sin in church doctrine appears to have developed a posteriori, by a process which, proceeding from the salvation in Christ and from infant baptism, made the diagnosis fit the cure" (*The Christian Tradition*, 1: 204).

31. Perhaps Luther's most famous statement in this regard comes from *The Bondage of the Will.* Summarizing "the nature of Christian faith itself," he says: "[F]aith has to do with things not seen [Heb. 11:1]. Hence in order that there may be room for faith, it is necessary that everything which is believed should be hidden. It cannot be more deeply hidden than under an object, perception, or experience which is contrary to it [*sub contrario*]. . . . This is not the place to speak at length on this subject, but those who have read my books have had it quite plainly set forth for them" (*LW* 33: 62).

32. Brian Gerrish speaks of the hiddenness of God I and the hiddenness of God II in "'To the Unknown God': Luther and Calvin on the Hiddenness of God," in his *The Old Protestantism and the New: Essays on the Reformation Heritage* (Chicago: University of Chicago Press, 1982), 140ff.

Luther vividly describes the trustworthiness of God's righteousness-creating through the image of "the happy exchange." Commenting on the power of faith, Luther says:

> [F]aith unites the soul with Christ as a bride is united with her bridegroom. By this mystery, as the Apostle teaches, Christ and the soul become one flesh [Eph. 5:31-32]. And if they are one flesh and there is between them a true marriage — indeed the most perfect of all marriages, since human marriages are but poor examples of this one true marriage — it follows that everything they have they hold in common, the good as well as the evil. Accordingly the believing soul can boast of and glory in whatever Christ has as though it were its own, and whatever the soul has Christ claims as his own.[33]

With or without the phrase "the happy exchange," and with or without the marriage imagery, the redemptive dynamic of the happy exchange remains central in Luther's writing, especially in his sermons, lectures, and pastoral advice. For instance, in a 1516 letter to his fellow Augustinian monk George Spenlein, Luther urges him to "learn Christ and him crucified. Learn to praise him and, despairing of yourself, say, 'Lord Jesus, you are my righteousness, just as I am your sin. You have taken upon yourself what is mine and have given to me what is yours. You have taken upon yourself what you were not and have given to me what I was not.'"[34]

A few months after the *Heidelberg Disputation*, Luther preached his famous sermon entitled "Two Kinds of Righteousness," based on

33. The phrase "the happy exchange" (in German, *der froehliche Wechsel*) appears in the German-language version of *The Freedom of a Christian*. Because the translation of *The Freedom of a Christian* in the standard English-language American edition was made from Luther's Latin original, the precise phrase "happy exchange" does not appear in the American edition, though the marriage imagery does. The "happy exchange" phrase does appear in Bertram Lee Woolf's English translation of *The Freedom of a Christian* because he translated from Luther's German version (*Reformation Writings of Martin Luther*, vol. 1 [London: Lutterworth Press, 1952], 363).

34. *LW* 48: 12. On the power of faith, see Luther's famous commentary on Gal. 3:6 (*LW* 26: 226-36). Robert W. Bertram offers the most insightful close reading of Luther's redemptive dynamic as it appears in Luther's famous 1535 *Lectures on Galatians* ("Luther on the Unique Mediatorship of Christ," in H. George Anderson, J. Francis Stafford, Joseph A. Burgess, eds., *The One Mediator, the Saints, and Mary* [Minneapolis: Augsburg, 1992] 249-62). Bertram also notes how the "happy exchange" redemptive dynamic appears in Luther's explanation of the second article of the Apostles' Creed in *The Small Catechism*.

Philippians 2:5-6. Here he uses the redemptive dynamic of the happy exchange to explicate "alien righteousness, that is the righteousness of another, instilled from without." "Just as a bridegroom possesses all that is his bride's and she all that is his, for the two have all things in common because they are one flesh, so Christ and the church are one spirit."[35] Later in the sermon, Luther highlights the bearing and extending character of the crucified Christ by contrasting him with that self-sufficient form of God that Christ "relinquished to the Father."[36]

We now stand at the precipice of another, often overlooked, aspect of Luther's theology of the cross. This is the basis of soteriology in his understanding of the Trinitarian being of God. Luther extols the dependence of the Father's mercy on the persuasive mediation of the crucified Son. He knows that the soteriological effects of the happy exchange between Christ and church believers are anchored in what the Crucified effects in the very life of God.[37] By bearing with sinners, Jesus extends to his Father the char-

---

35. *LW* 31: 297.

36. *LW* 31: 301. See also Luther's interpretations of Gal. 2:20 and 3:13, which are classic discussions of Christ's bearing and extending (*LW* 26: 172-79, 276-88). See how David Fredrickson exploits the bearing and extending dynamic adhering in Paul's slavery metaphor in Philippians 2 (in his essay in this volume).

37. *LW* 51: 277-80; *LW* 24: 252. One of Luther's most famous discussions in this regard takes place in his interpretation of Gal. 1:3. "But why," Luther inquires, "does the apostle add 'and from our Lord Jesus Christ'? Did it not suffice to say '[Grace to you and peace] from God the Father'? Why does he link Jesus Christ with the Father?" (*LW* 26: 28ff.) Robert Bertram follows this line of inquiry by focusing on "that singular dependence of the divine Child upon the Parent, so powerful in its effect that in the process the Parent, indeed the whole Trinity, takes on a new identity and new associations. To ask for less god than that — but now the Christian answer is obviously shaping the question — not only risks moralism but risks underasking" (Bertram, "Putting the Nature of God into Language: Naming the Trinity," in Carl Braaten, ed., *Our Naming of God: Problems and Prospects of God-Talk Today* [Minneapolis: Fortress, 1989], 97). Jürgen Moltmann follows a similar line of inquiry: "I turned the question around, and instead of asking just *what God means for us human beings* in the cross of Christ, I asked too *what this human cross of Christ means for God*" (*The Crucified God*, x). Indeed, David Fredrickson finds this rhythm within the famous Christ Hymn of Philippians 2. Or again: "It is crucial to note that as the story unfolds God's action comes after Christ's. This fact, along with the 'wherefore (διό)' of verse 9, implies that God's action in exalting Jesus and giving him the name beyond every name is God's *response* to Christ Jesus' innovative extension of participation in the divine community. . . . The Christ Hymn therefore . . . narrates the actual formation of God's will in response to the political agency of Jesus Christ" (64-65). See also Eberhard Jüngel's explanation of the "twofold interruption" of the Crucified: "God interrupts the continuity of our life as the one who allows our sin and death to interrupt his

acter and shape of his trustworthy, bodily communion with sinners. The Father's sending of the Spirit to raise the forsaken Jesus testifies to — indeed, constitutes — the Father's favorable reception of the Son's cruciform character as the Father's own. Ultimately, Christian soteriology rests in the reality of the crucified God. It rests in the reciprocal dependence of the Father and the Son through the Spirit, as Athanasius emphasized long ago.[38]

Luther probes the connection between soteriology and the doctrine of God while explicating the communication or sharing of attributes, the so-called *communicatio idiomatum*. These lie at the heart of the Trinitarian and Christological theology of the first four ecumenical councils. Luther's explanation of the critique of Nestorianism by the Council of Ephesus in 431 C.E. is particularly pithy:

> Now if I were to preach, "Jesus, the carpenter of Nazareth (for the gospels call him 'carpenter's son' [Matt. 13:55]) is walking over there down the street, fetching his mother a jug of water and a penny's worth of bread so that he might eat and drink with his mother, and the same carpenter, Jesus is the very true God in one person," Nestorius would grant me that and say that this is true. But if I were to say, "There goes God down the street, fetching water and bread so that he might eat and drink with his mother," Nestorius would not grant me this, but says, "To fetch water, to buy bread, to have a mother, to eat and drink with her, are *idiomata* or attributes of human and not of divine nature." And again, if I say, "The carpenter Jesus was crucified by the Jews and the same Jesus is the true God," Nestorius would agree that this is true. But if I say, "God

own life.... That is, man is defined by the eternal Father who allows himself to be interrupted by the crucifixion of his Son and, in this way, interrupts the continuity of our life; and, at the same time, in the loving unity of the Spirit with his Son, he enhances his life and ours" ("The Truth of Life: Observations on Truth as the Interruption of the Continuity of Life," in R. W. A. McKinney, ed., *Creation, Christ and Culture: Studies in Honour of T. F. Torrance* (Edinburgh: T & T Clark, 1976), 236. I am grateful to Jonathan Case for this reference and for the importance of this notion in Jüngel.

38. Wolfhart Pannenberg has undertaken the most thorough investigation of the nature and implications of the reciprocal dependence of the Father and the Son and especially the notion, largely undeveloped in the entire history of Trinitarian theology, of the Father's dependence on the Son mediated in the history of Jesus. The underdevelopment of the reciprocity of the persons discloses "a defect which plagues the Trinitarian theological language of both East and West, namely, that of seeing the relations among Father, Son, and Spirit exclusively as relations of origin" (*Systematic Theology* [Grand Rapids: Eerdmans, 1991], 1: 319; see 308-19).

was crucified by the Jews," he says, "No! For crucifixion and death are *idomata* or attributes not of divine but of human nature."[39]

Nestorius could not quite bring himself to Luther's conclusion, that is, to the bold Christian confession of a crucified God. This is because, as Luther notes, he held too deeply to the Greco-Roman basic assumption "that God and death are irreconcilable. It seemed terrible to him to hear that God should die."[40] Luther even chastises the Council of Ephesus for its "far too little" confession in this regard.[41] Therefore, Luther emphasizes that "only . . . if God's death and a dead God lie in the balance" is our salvation accomplished.[42]

The person and work of the Holy Spirit now come into the foreground, as Luther emphasizes in *The Large Catechism*. The salvation accomplished by the crucified God would "remain hidden," even "vain" and "all lost," if it were not for the agency of the Holy Spirit, who puts the accomplished salvation to "use" in us that it might be "enjoyed" by us and by God.[43] Word and Sacrament are, of course, the publicly available media of the Holy Spirit's agency in this regard.

The idea that through Word and Sacrament believers are incorporated into the communion of the Son with the Father finds its basis in the

---

39. *LW* 41: 101. Whenever Luther richly maximizes the communication of attributes, he is in essence beginning to burst the old Trinitarian wineskins with the fixation on the relations of origin to the neglect of the full reciprocity of the persons. Nevertheless, when Luther consciously turns to the doctrine of the Trinity, he remains largely within the strictures of the trajectory charted by Augustine (e.g., *LW* 15: 300-12). This situation warrants a more thorough exploitation, one that I hope to undertake in the future in the context of the connection between contemporary Trinitarian theology and the doctrine of the atonement.

40. *LW* 41: 102.

41. *LW* 41: 104.

42. *LW* 41: 103. Robert Jenson has a pithy way of putting Luther's point: "Christology is, or should be, the thinking involved in *getting over* the self-evidencies about God that antecedent religion will in each case of the gospel's missionary penetration have hidden in the minds of this new sort of believers. A Christological proposition is adequate just insofar as it outrages something comprehensively and radically that everybody at a time and place supposes 'of course' to be true of anything worthy to be called God" (Jenson, *Unbaptized God: The Basic Flaw in Ecumenical Theology* [Minneapolis: Fortress, 1992], 120). Jenson rightly notes — though I differ with his analysis of "the basic flaw" — that for Luther the traditional interpretations of and conclusions regarding the communication of attributes were "too puny" (129).

43. *The Large Catechism*, in *The Book of Concord: The Confessions of the Evangelical Lutheran Church*, ed. Theodore Tappert (Philadelphia: Fortress, 1959), 415.

personhood of the Holy Spirit as the very "condition and medium" of the personal communion of the Son and the Father.[44] Furthermore, "free agreement" marks the very mode of the personal communion at the heart of the Triune life of God.[45] Finally, this communion of free agreement of the Father and the Son with and through the Holy Spirit exists as a "communicative" free agreement, because in Scripture and for the Reformation, there is "no spirit that is not word."[46] In the beginning was the "conversation" and the "conversation" was with God and the "conversation" was God. So Luther![47] Not surprisingly, this communicative free agreement of the triune God constitutes the source and mode of God's creative agency as well.[48]

The Trinitarian life of the crucified God forms the basis for the communicative mode of God's own creative agency. So also, it forms our vocational participation in this mode of creative moral agency. We are now coming full circle. Christian vocation is freedom from our sinful instrumentalization of the created world that is effected by the trustworthiness of the alien righteousness of the Crucified and received by faith. In this vocational freedom, the entire created world remains the media and "masks" *(larvae dei)* of the triune God's creative agency.[49] Furthermore, Christian vocation is freedom for our "proper righteousness," which always retains its "basis," "cause," and "source" in Christ's alien righteousness.[50] In this vocational freedom we remain cooperators with God's creative agency *(cooperatio dei)* to bring temporal life into existence, to nurture that life, and to extend that life to all others.[51]

---

44. Pannenberg, *Systematic Theology,* 1: 316, 330.

45. Pannenberg, *Systematic Theology,* vol. 2 (Grand Rapids: Eerdmans, 1994), 30-31.

46. Robert W. Jenson, "The Holy Spirit," in Carl Braaten and Robert Jenson, eds., *Christian Dogmatics,* vol. 2 (Philadelphia: Fortress, 1984), 156.

47. *LW* 22: 7-13.

48. See Werner Elert's fruitful notion of the communicative mode of God's creative agency in *The Christian Faith* (Columbus, OH: Trinity Seminary Bookstore, 1974), 167-68; see also his *The Christian Ethos* (Philadelphia: Fortress, 1957), 23-27.

49. *LW* 26: 94-96. See Gustav Wingren's investigation of Luther's notion of the masks of God (*Luther on Vocation* [Philadelphia: Muhlenberg Press, 1957], 137-43). This book still remains the best interpretation of Luther's understanding of vocation. Recalling Brian Gerrish's notion of a hiddenness of God I and a hiddenness of God II, might not Luther's understanding of Christian vocation warrant a hiddenness of God III?

50. *LW* 31: 298.

51. *LW* 31: 55-56. One of Luther's most penetrating analyses of vocational cooperation appears in *The Bondage of the Will* (*LW* 33: 241-43).

On this point *The Large Catechism* is striking:

> Although much that is good comes to us from men, we receive it all from God through his command and ordinance. Our parents and all authorities — in short, all people placed in the position of neighbors — have received the command to do us all kinds of good. So we receive our blessings not from them, but from God through them. Creatures are only the hands, channels, and means through which God bestows all blessings. . . . Therefore, this way of receiving good through God's creatures is not to be disdained, nor are we arrogantly to seek other ways and means than God has commanded, for that would be not receiving our blessings from God but seeking them from ourselves.[52]

Might there not also be emerging in our time and place, by God's own bestowal, a newly created and creative "good," that is, a communicative civil society? This imaginative possibility, of course, lies behind the proposal for the vocation of congregations as public moral companions. Such a vocation is, indeed, to the "praise and honor" of God.

The Vocation of Congregations as Public Moral Companions

Vocations are the places and ways that one and all participate in God's ongoing creative work. Through their vocations, people nurture and sustain temporal life in the world. In trusting the gospel of Jesus Christ, we acknowledge these locations as God's creative work on behalf of our neighbors and ourselves as God's creative companions. Like an individual, a congregation also has a variety of vocations to bring God's creative work to bear on the life of our neighbors and our neighborhoods. Congregations that build up a moral milieu that makes life in our public communities possible are living out just such a calling. Civil society is the location for serving out this vocation of being a public moral companion. And communicative moral practice is the best model for nurturing the modern moral milieu.

Vocationally, congregations participate in the moral life of civil society in two ways, one more internal and the other more external. Internally, congregations have often assisted families in the task of the moral formation of its members, particularly of the young, and this will continue as a

52. Tappert, ed., *The Book of Concord*, 368.

prime moral vocation of the congregation. However, as they engage in this vocation of moral formation, congregations sometimes fall prey to the temptation to view themselves as private Christian enclaves where they can protect themselves from the truth claims of other moral traditions. However, in our increasingly pluralistic public environment, multiple traditions now make claims on congregations. They bid congregations to offer justification, in the sense of ethical grounding, for the truth character of the moral formation imparted through congregational life. In this way a congregation exists, by default if not be design, as a meeting place of private and public life.[53]

It is in the meeting of the private and public that congregations respond to their more external moral vocation as public moral companions. Today an increasing number of the institutions of civil society need moral companions who will accompany them in addressing the problems of contemporary life. Of course, this is a risky vocation, because Christian congregations do not have a corner on the moral wisdom needed in many conflicted situations. As a public moral companion, a congregation becomes an encumbered community, encumbered with the moral predicaments of the other institutions of civil society. However, Christian congregations are no strangers to an encumbered life, to a life of the cross. Herein lies the redemptive moment that characterizes every vocation, when the encumbered companionship puts a congregation's efforts of self-protection to death.[54]

In summary, consider certain marks that characterize the congregational vocation of serving as a public moral companion. As public moral companions, congregations acknowledge a *conviction* that they participate in God's ongoing creative work. In a communicative civil society, congregations exhibit a *compassionate commitment* to other institutions and their moral predicaments. The commitment of moral companions always yields a *critical* and *self-critical* — and thus a fully *communicative* — procedure for moral engagement. Finally, as public moral companions, congregations participate with other institutions of communicative civil society to help create and strengthen the moral fabric that fashion a life-giving contemporary society.

---

53. See Martin E. Marty, "Public and Private: Congregation as Meeting Place," in James P. Wind and James W. Lewis, eds., *American Congregations,* vol. 2: *New Perspectives in the Study of Congregations* (Chicago: University of Chicago Press, 1994), 133-66.

54. Kolden, "Creation and Redemption," 36.

PART II

DEVELOPING A THEOLOGICAL APPROACH FOR CONGREGATIONAL MORAL DISCERNMENT

The essays in the first section sought to break down the walls created and sustained by the artificial gap that was created during the Enlightenment between theory and practice. They breached the walls, at least, between ecclesiology and the practice of leading in a congregation. They did so through engaging in critical biblical interpretation and through reframing the use of the Bible in local congregations and the use of the Bible in theological discourse. And they offered an alternative for imagining congregations as public moral companions within the breached wall between the public and private spheres of modern life.

The essays in this second section occupy the space within these breached walls through engaging in the practice of Christian wisdom and imagination within the artificial gap between theory and practice. A linear reading of these essays would suggest that the theoretical discourse precedes the practical. But the experience of the authors was that the practices of Christian wisdom and imagination explored in the essays of this second section actually are the practices that make possible the more reflective discourse of the first section. In other words, the order of the sections does not suggest some sort of foundational assumptions that are fairly typical in most theological education. Neither the theoretical nor the empirical alone are able to establish this conversation; neither theory nor practice alone make the other possible. Rather, both theory and practice are integrated through two other human capacities or faculties: wisdom *(phronēsis)* and imagination *(poiēsis)*.

In the first chapter in this section, Pat Taylor Ellison describes the practice of text-dwelling and deep listening that leads to faith-based moral conversations in congregations. Within a rhetorical theory of public conversation, this is what Wayne Booth calls "listening rhetoric." In the case of the Christian community, a community created by listening to the Word of God, this chapter describes in concrete terms what such a listening rhetoric practice looks like.

In the second and third chapters, Ronald W. Duty explores the space between theory and practice by taking seriously the stories gathered in a number of the congregations that agreed to partner within the field study in doing theology together in the midst of tough conversations regarding morally disputed topics. Many subjects arose, some more bitter, difficult, dividing, and heated than others. The one subject that arose most often in the partner congregations concerned human sexuality. In his first essay Duty explores how some of the congregations used Scripture in their moral conversation regarding human sexuality. It examines how these congregations sought to understand God truly through seeking to discern the will of God in the midst of this heated and often terribly divisive conversation. Duty's second essay reflects on the role of the Christian imagination and practical reasoning regarding how members of the congregation read and engage the Bible. The conversation presented in this chapter illustrates the challenges associated with doing Christian theology in the space and time between theory and practice, but also introduces the helpful role of the Christian imagination and wisdom in doing so.

In the final chapter in this section, Pat Taylor Ellison explores and identifies the metaphors that frame the congregations' sense of themselves and their leaders in the midst of conversations on morally disputed topics. The essay begins by presenting an applied ethnographic methodology for engaging congregations as primary actors in their own quest to understand themselves and God truly. From the data that was collected, Ellison provides critical reflections regarding the implications for theological leadership in such circumstances.

Word-Dwelling, Deep Listening, and
Faith-Based Moral Conversation in Congregations:
A Nested Vision for Learning New Habits

Pat Taylor Ellison

How do congregations articulate and nurture faith? How do they come to terms with tough issues, strangers, and one another as they wrestle through their daily lives? What do congregations do when they must face the unexpected, the unjust, the shocking, the perilous? What habits do they have and what habits should they grow? These are questions facing every congregation, though many congregations may never actually confront them. In this chapter I propose a set of theological assumptions about congregations and the world they serve. I also propose a vision for nurturing the best conditions for faith-based moral conversation that takes on issues, comes to terms with strangers, and nurtures faith.

All of creation dwells within the Word of God, the Word who creates us, the Word who redeems us. The Holy Spirit, through words that speak to our spirits, keeps us mindful of whose we are. The Word of God is our beginning, our safety, and our identity. As creatures of the Creator, we have been given the Word within which we are to move, breathe, live, and talk together. Dwelling in God's Word is a naturally coherent, aesthetic, even synergistic process within which all things are possible and nothing is impossible.

Yet in creation there is sin — discord, ugliness, and pain. These forces work at cross-purposes to God's intent and often obscure the truth in our search for it. God and God's Word are ever present, yet we often do not remember to hear, to see, or to claim the promise that all things are possible. We seek to be shaped by God's Word, yet we fail adequately to wrestle with one another over the tough issues. We fail adequately to build our conversation and discernment from the biblical passages and the leading of the Spirit. Instead, we often choose to remain in isolation from one another. Or when we do come together, we often remain stranded in our individual understandings of truth, coloring them with our anxieties and our hopes. And then we wonder why we are all so different, especially as people who claim to be one in faith. We have forgotten, or have failed to develop, the skills for dwelling in the Word together. We still think about God, but we have lost the language for sharing those thoughts aloud. If we do dwell in the Word or produce theology, we tend do it quietly and alone.

Those of us who live and work primarily in congregations, among the long-time churched as well as new believers, know that local congregations do, in fact, produce theologies as they come and work together. They do it all the time. Individuals claim certain calls, they use certain gifts, they experience conflicts and joys, and they make sense of these things by drawing on their understanding of God. The congregation as a whole is apt to behave in ways that reflect their tacit picture of God. However, congregation members usually refuse to claim that they are doing theology. They leave theologizing to the pastors, because they have been taught to leave that sophisticated activity to others. Pastors, in turn, often leave it to the professionals in the seminaries and universities. Making statements about God and what God might be up to in their congregation's life does not feel like their job. They are fairly sure that doing theology would be too abstract and far too much work. And they fear that, even if they could do so, they might disagree with one another about their pictures of God. What would they do if they did disagree? How could they worship and work together? Disagreement is the enemy. Other viewpoints on questions of meaning and truth, especially about God, represent disaster in the making.

The result is simply this: there is almost no out-loud talk about who God really is, or about what God is really doing. And there is little discourse about how God speaks through Scripture, and what the mission of the congregation should be in its community. There is little, if any, dwelling in the Word and engaging in a mutual testing of ideas about the interpretation of that Word. Of course, Bible studies are taught in congregations, but too often these are activities in which laypeople come to hear professional pastor-theologian-scholars translate and open up new possibilities for thinking through texts. There may be some group Bible studies, but these are usually among laypeople who have known each other a long time, who have few doubts about each other's depth of Christian commitment, and who have created an unspoken set of norms. In such settings they are able to dwell together within the Word, reading it, discussing it, and allowing it to frame their talk about other matters, even risking disagreement about what it means and how it works on them. For the most part, however, we have forgotten the Word and dwelling within it, and we have disconnected ourselves from speaking and hearing it with one another.

Yet congregation members act on theological assumptions all the time. They use these assumptions to make sense of and respond to the world, periodically adjusting their pictures of God. Knowing our theological assumptions and being able to talk aloud about them is not just a vocation for seminary-trained intellectuals. In fact, if Luther had it right about the church being the priesthood of all believers, then one of the believers' primary tasks is to test all things. If theological education is to take life seriously as it is lived in congregations, then it is crucial that academics and congregation members teach and learn from each other. Together they must determine how theology is shaping and should be shaping the life and ministry of the congregation. Therefore, the guild and the congregation must make some connections in which mutual teaching and learning can take place. But even prior to that, congregational members must be cordially invited into dwelling in the Word. They need to be allowed to converse, make decisions, and take actions that are shaped by the living Word of God as they hear one another speaking it. They must be welcomed into dwelling in the creative Word of God and claiming their vocation of doing theology.

So how can congregation members grow the habit of dwelling in the Word? How can they discover the synergistic, right relationship with their Creator? There are many barriers. One is their lack of familiarity with the Bible; another is their diminished capacity to listen to one another beyond their biases; another is their fear of conflict and further splintering. Yet another is their reluctance to claim their capacity as theologians, no matter what their professions; and still another is their utter lack of disciplined habits for engaging in Word-dwelling, for having clean fights, and for doing theology. It seems to be too difficult to return to the habit of dwelling in the Word: it looks like a lot of work, more work than they want. "Perhaps we could if we had a qualified leader," they say. But who might step forward to lead this kind of work? The stakes are so high, and credentials seem almost unattainable.

This job is big enough that pastors cannot be the only leaders who engage in Bible study and Word-dwelling. There must also be lay leaders who lead Bible study and mentor others to do so. These lay leaders need to spread the habit through the congregation, and they also need to see that it passes out through the permeable boundaries of the congregation into the larger community. That is the way dwelling in the Word will move from being a private reserve to becoming a public wellspring, and it is the way congregations will make disciples.

But how? And, more importantly for lay leaders in today's congregations, why? What could motivate them to engage in changing their focus, in learning new habits of Word-dwelling, and in planting those habits, here and there, within the congregation's operating system? Why change? Change will bring discomfort and disagreement and conflict, and conflict will bring pain. No members of congregations need any more pain, so in the end they don't act.

Until they are face to face with the divine Other through the human other, when an apparent disaster arrives in some form either from without or within, it does not tend to really matter. But then the disaster arrives. It may be a social controversy or an internal political matter; it may be a scandal or even a windfall of money waiting to be spent. It may come suddenly or it may loom on the horizon for years. But there comes a point when everyone knows this Other must be engaged; yet they have few resources to help them do so. Instead, they are often more keenly aware than ever of their diminished capacity to listen to one another beyond their biases. They become paralyzed by their fear of conflict and further splintering, their reluctance to claim their capacity as theologians, their unfamiliarity with the Word, and their utter lack of the discipline for the activities of Word-dwelling, clean fighting, and doing theology.

So there they sit, aware of the approaching disaster and being unprepared. They want a conflict resolution activity that will solve the problem. They wait, desperately wishing for a single button to press, or even to have some sandbags to fill in order to hold the crisis at bay so that they can survive a while longer. But there is no one button, and not even a thousand sandbags will help them. For the Other is coming, and they must meet the Other. They must begin to see their lives as congregations within God's larger Word. They must begin to understand their Christian work as listening to God and to one another. They must meet conflict head on in order to discover and claim the truth that will unite them. They must be theologians with one another and to the world, and they must dwell within God's Word and God's life.

In this chapter I make the argument that a really good model for public moral conversation is but a single tool. But this tool is not the much sought-after "conflict resolution" intervention that so many congregations are using today. Instead, it is a set of habits that accomplishes its ends rightly by being nested within the larger work of free speaking and deep listening. This approach requires worshiping and doing theology together, and it requires dwelling together in the creating Word of God. This chapter is the story of a group of congregations who were eager for a tool to handle a looming disaster and who developed a different approach to increase their larger capacities to worship God, to do theology, to speak and listen freely, and to dwell in the Word.

The Setting and the Process

Imagine your local community declining before your eyes. Imagine the disappearance of one neighborhood landmark after another, the physical ones such as businesses or parks, and the intangible ones such as friendships. You see them either vanishing or being reduced to a shadow of what you remember. Imagine yourself standing in this neighborhood: you want to ask why, but your neighbors pass you by in cars or on foot, unable to talk with you.

It was this climate of isolation that made members of the Board for Church in Society of the Southwestern Minnesota Synod of the Evangelical Lutheran Church in America decide to act. They built a task force of pastors, synod staff, and laypeople who set out to do something about this simultaneous need for conversation and the inability to converse publicly about tough issues, especially issues that were morally divisive. The task force secured outside consulting services to assist some of their congregations in learning new practices for engaging in a faith-based model for public moral conversation.[1] The task force also introduced to these congregations an approach that has shown promise in other settings.

---

1. The consulting firm was Church Innovations, Inc., and the consultants were Patrick Keifert and Pat Taylor Ellison. The study process that was used, and the congregations that became involved, later served as a case study for the Congregational Study Research Team (CSRT).

Ten congregations, one from each of the ten geographical conferences in the synod, accepted invitations into the project: some were urban, some were small-town congregations, and several were rural. The task force recruited a pastor and three to five laypeople from each congregation to engage in the task of first becoming participant observers, and then later to serve as participant interpreters of their communities.

Learning to Become Participant Interpreters

Congregational leaders of the ten congregations were invited to attend the opening workshop of this project; about fifty appeared, and they were eager to get right down to the business of learning to do moral conversation. They expected to take home a tool that they could put to work right away. However, they were surprised that we spent our entire morning together in worship, Bible study, and theological discussion about God's revealed and hidden presence in the world. Some were simply surprised; the rest were disappointed. Even some on the task force and training team did not fully understand at that point how crucial those activities would be to the unfolding of meaningful moral conversation in these congregations. We did know that people needed tools for talking about profound social and economic community change from God's perspective. So we worshiped together, we talked, and we listened to their conversations about God. We also knew that, from the start, we wanted some record of the habits of these communities; therefore, we designed questions for interviews about past and present moral conversation and decision-making.

The interview process they learned was fairly simple. All lay participants in the training workshop were asked to set up three interviews. They could select interviewees purely on their own, or they could work as a team to select members of their congregation to interview. During each forty-minute interview, the interviewers were to assure the interviewees of anonymity. Then the interviewers were to ask a set of eight open-ended questions about past and present moral conversation and action in the parish, and about the interviewees' fears and hopes for the future. Finally, they were to summarize the interviewees' response to each question on a 3″ by 4″ block of space on a single page of paper. When the interview was finished, the interviewees were asked to approve the summaries of their responses and seal the interview in an envelope. Each interviewer then placed all the interview envelopes in a congregational envelope and was asked to convey it to the next gathering, which was set for sixty days later. During the training workshop, interviewers had a chance to practice asking and answering one of the eight questions.

At the end of that workshop, people went home without the tool they had expected for moral conversation and conflict resolution. Instead, they had spent the day in Word-dwelling, theological discussion, and interview training. When they left, the task force believed that those who had come hoping for the familiar button to press or even the sandbags to fill would probably not do the deep listening and connecting for which they had been trained. Our expectations were that one or two persons from each of the ten congregations would actually do an interview or two, and that only some of them would return to the next gathering to turn them in.

However, we were astonished to find what we did two months later: not only did almost everyone return for the second gathering, but, instead of the fifty or sixty interviews we had dared hope for, they returned with 108. We discussed in lively ways what they had learned during this process of deep listening and storytelling: What did this mean, given the divisive times their congregations faced? Together we planned the next major training workshop for the following autumn, when they would learn the model for moral conversation. We ended this gathering once again in theological conversation and worship.

Over the following months we formed reading teams that would be responsible for reading each congregation's interview responses. They were to look for emerging patterns in the answers and to construct summaries of the responses for each of the eight questions. They were to add recommendations about the patterns and expectations of the congregational moral conversation, and then they were to send the summary reports back to each congregation. Feedback from the interviewers told us that the reports provided rich and surprisingly accurate pictures of each congregation, even from a limited number of interviews. The interviewers had further opportunities to co-interpret these pictures of congregational patterns in the training workshop that followed. There they spent part of the morning describing what had been happening in their congregations on both controversial and mundane issues since the process of listening had begun.

We now know something about congregations that nest the process of moral conversation training and practice within a larger deliberate process of theological conversation. We have since learned how important it is to dwell together in both worship and the Word, and to engage in a process of deep listening and free speaking that helps participants study their congregation's habits. We have learned that congregation members who are trained to do moral conversation in workshops that unfold in God-centered worship and Word-dwelling are better prepared to conduct interviews in their congregations. They also stand a better chance of generating and supporting an ongoing practice of moral conversation than are congregations who simply learn the model and use it on a particular issue. Of the hundreds of congregations who have used this moral conversation process, which we call "Growing Healthier Congregations," when there was no training workshop and prior commitment to do interviews, only a few have put the process to regular use. However, at least half the congregations who have attended a training workshop and completed at least a moderate number of interviews about congregational decision-making have planted the faith-based model into the regular decision-making patterns in their congregations. Why should this be so?

The value of worshipful, theologically significant, and Word-filled training seems fairly clear. First, engaging in corporate, meaningful worship with strangers from many congregations brings these people into a shared identity around Christ. They see and acknowledge their differences, their own otherness, while recognizing their oneness in the Lord. Second, engaging in Word-dwelling and conversation about God's ongoing action in creating, redeeming, and making the creation holy sparks their Christian imagination. Together, they long to find ways to have the mind of Christ, and they are motivated to do so. They begin thinking in new and renewed ways about divergent views, about the kind of attending and asserting that is necessary for meaningful conversation, and about the work of God in the body of Christ. Third, the shared experience of these first two activities begins to create for participants a shared sense of purpose and a willingness to take risks for the sake of their faith.

The value of the training in applied ethnography might seem less apparent. However, three benefits of interviewing can be claimed. First, lay leaders become participant observers and interpreters in their congregations as interviewers. They see, hear, and reflect on congregational life in a whole new way. They are suddenly much more aware of what aids and hinders moral conversation and decision-making. They become more aware of the various communities within the congregation, and they also see their congregation as a community within several other communities. Some of these interviewers may never have considered themselves part of congregational leadership before this project. But as interviewers, they develop important skills that, not accidentally, often turn out to be very useful in leading moral conversations.

Second, congregation members who are interviewed are heard in a brand-new way. Since the aim of ethnographic interviewing is to get the insider perspective, the interviewer does everything possible to encourage depth and honesty in the responses. People who are perhaps not used to being heard in congregational conversation are suddenly being listened to in intense and respectful ways. A climate is developed for real attending and free speaking.

Third, as word spreads about leadership's interest in past and present practices of conversing and decision-making on moral matters, many people — even those not involved in the interviews — begin to think about those activities. Few people respond positively at first to the idea of doing moral conversation; our research tells us that the very words "moral conversation" are quite off-putting. However, by the end of this process of participant-interpretation of insider interviews, doors have been opened for the activity of moral conversation itself.

Learning to Do Faith-Based Moral Conversation

Our next training workshop, held a year after the first, invited the same group of ten congregations to participate along with leaders from six other congregations in the synod that had become interested in the project. The newcomers, like the veteran congregations, were asked to do interviewing and were given training for that purpose. While they practiced interviewing, the veterans spent time interpreting life in their congregations before and after the interviews had taken place. They discussed how congregational views had been changed by the congregational reports.

For the rest of the day the entire group of lay and clergy participants spent time together, beginning once again with worship and Word-dwelling. This large group discussion set the focus on God's activity in human communities. We placed a Bible passage at the center of their conversation in developing a theocentric, faith-based model for moral conversation. We began with the Word, revisited it in the midst of the training, and reconnected with it as the day ended. Then we turned to the work of learning and practicing a model for faith-based conversation.

This model consists of a set of ground rules and expectations, which we called the "Box," a ritual process for opening conversation, called the "Triangle," and then open conversation during which spiritual discernment can take place, which we referred to as the "Triangle-Pyramid." I describe the model below, showing how leaders can teach it to a group by beginning with dwelling in the Word. I also note some of the diverse circumstances in which congregations can use this approach.

The Box[2]

In public conversation about almost anything, we use an implicit system of behavior that is normative, behavior within which meaningful exchanges take place. The system handles all small talk quite well, as well as most matters of import in boardrooms or classrooms. It turns on our tacit agreement to keep touchy issues out of public discourse and our emotions to ourselves. However, public moral conversation on issues involving right and wrong looks much more difficult than typical boardroom or classroom conversation, because the touchy issues will arise — along with both reason and emotion — making for enormous risks of personal and communal injury. Since public moral conversation seems more difficult than more ordinary public discourse, we need to agree in advance to engage in four processes that will act as our safety net, as the ground rules within which we can exchange facts, values, ideas, opinions, and experiences. Because there are four processes, I illustrate them as the Box.

The Box

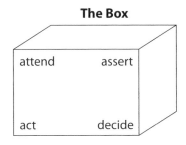

2. This discussion and illustration is based on Bernard Lonergan, *Method in Theology* (New York: Herder & Herder, 1972).

First, *attending* is profound listening. It is becoming so aware of the other that we seem momentarily to lose our own perspective. We attempt to listen without bias to what is being said, to what is gestured, and even to what is left out.

Second, *asserting* is speaking honestly about our thoughts, feelings, and intentions in order to further the discourse. We must do this without dominating. We assert to test our thinking, to find flaws, and to grow in mutual understanding.

Third, *deciding* is the purpose for our attending and asserting. We do not engage in moral conversation simply to talk; our public conversation forms our social awareness. This awareness helps us come to decisions as a community.

Fourth, *acting* is the ultimate result of our conversation. Acting is risky, but when we are called upon to act, especially as a group, it is better to act out of informed conversation and decision-making. Action is the fruit of this conversation.

The Triangle

Using attending and asserting in order to decide and act as purposeful ground rules, we begin the conversation. One of the challenges with discussing morally charged issues is knowing where to begin. Who will disclose first? Who will reveal a personal position and become vulnerable? It is helpful to think, along with Evelyn and James Whitehead, about looking at issues from three vantage points.[3]

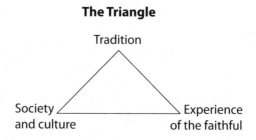

The Triangle

Tradition

Society
and culture

Experience
of the faithful

3. James D. Whitehead and Evelyn Eaton Whitehead, *Method in Ministry: Theological Reflection and Christian Ministry,* rev. ed. (New York: Sheed & Ward, 1995), 23-65.

Tradition, for those engaged in Christian moral conversation, begins with and gives pride of place to Scripture. But it also includes church history, confessions, hymnody, congregational history, and more. It includes whatever the participants want to include: the way things were when I was young, when George Washington was young, or when Moses was young. Any of these slants on tradition can work to get participants talking about the tradition regarding the difficult issue being discussed.

Society and Culture

Next, the leader explains from this model that *society* and *culture* refer to the influences of our society and our particular culture on the way we think about the issue in question. The human institutions of our society, as well as their deep underlying values and the habits of our culture, draw participants to think in particular directions about the issue. They may stand as a sort of contrast to tradition, and they also often overlap it.

SOCIETY: INSTITUTIONS

	Marriage	
The Family	Business	Politics
Government	Education	The Church

CULTURE: THE UNDERLYING VALUES OF SOCIETY

Caring	Reponsibility	Ownership
Freedom	Justice	Competition
	Inventiveness	

Finally, the leader defines *experience of the faithful* as what people hold to be true based on their own experience, as well as the experience their community has already had with the issue. This point of the Triangle is usually embodied in a set of memories and images held deep within each person or within each congregation. Because of the depth of these memories, people rarely share faith experience images in public conversation. Yet, people are informed by these experiences, and they make assumptions, take action, and sift information in their world. And it is often due to these memories that intense emotional reactions accompany participants' thinking and talking about various issues. It is important to get these images out in front of the group if it is to have an ideal speech situation. The difficulty of doing so is addressed through exercises of prayer, spiritual mind-clearing, and image-raising.

From Triangle to Pyramid: Theocentricity

Then the leader explains that there is a center point of the Triangle, a central faith-based image for reflection throughout the conversation. This usually emerges as an imaginative root metaphor in the conversation. One central faith image for Christian moral conversation using this model is the cross on which Jesus died, a most dramatic point of God's action in the world. Here the leader reminds participants that the model is theocentric, and she or he then asks the question: "What is God up to in this subject we are gathered to discuss?" Another faith image may arise from the Word-dwelling that surrounds the conversation: perhaps the image of the one who frees others, or of a group who, through their speech together, determine the future of their community with Christ as their model. In any case, when God's activity and example are seen as the center, the three vantage points of the Triangle become the base of a now three-dimensional figure, a Pyramid. Suddenly the issue at hand becomes richer, taller, fuller, deeper: it becomes a vehicle for God's activity to be seen by people who are willing to do public conversation with it.

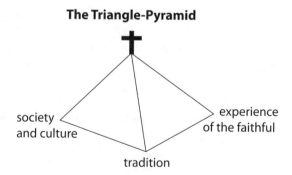

The Triangle-Pyramid

society and culture

experience of the faithful

tradition

What Does Such a Conversation Look Like?

In a real faith-based conversation, the conversation leader begins by dwelling in a passage that makes a case for people to speak freely in love and together work for their future. Then the leader explains the Box, and everyone agrees to work within it. The activities of the Box seem very basic: the actions represented by the verbs are what most people would agree to do. Their being readily understood is what makes them so easy to call on as the conversation unfolds. When people in the heat of the discussion either withdraw or aggress, a leader can remind the group of the Box and its importance to the outcome they have agreed to. The leader will usually find that the group provides almost universal support. The Box, then, provides the necessary safety net within which disagreement can be experienced and truth can be sought.

The leader then works through the categories of the Triangle for the participants. The group takes about twenty minutes to brainstorm about their ideas on the issue at hand, with the leader writing down their contributions onto newsprint or chalkboards labeled with the three categories of the Triangle. At the end of the process, the room's walls are covered with images, ideas, quotes, feelings, and descriptions. But there is a particular strategy for beginning the Triangle brainstorming.

The group begins with the *experience of the faithful* corner of the Triangle. The leader encourages the members to close their eyes and clear their minds, preparing to see some image (a picture, a word, a little movie) that will appear when the topic at hand is mentioned. When the group is ready, the leader names the topic or asks the question in as neutral a way as possible, and the people wait for images to appear. After a few seconds, they write down what they have seen and share that image with one or two people sitting near them. Then someone from their group reads these shared images and offers them as that group's brainstorm for the *experience of the faithful* portion of the Triangle. As the groups list images, statements, questions, and phrases, the leader records them on a board or on paper under the category of *experience of the faithful*. Then the group moves on to the categories of *tradition* and *society and culture*, with the leader recording all contributions to the brainstorm lists.

Of course, the three corners of this Triangle are somewhat arbitrary categories. They are overlapping labels that work as categories for eliciting remarks. Sometimes during a brainstorming session, it is difficult to know just what category a particular idea or remark fits into. But in the larger scheme of congregational conversation, the placement of an idea matters far less than the fact that it is finally spoken and added to the conversation. If we ask people to talk about a difficult issue from scratch, they do not quite know where to begin. But when a leader gives these three labels, people recognize and verbalize many ideas quickly, suggesting category placements for each idea.

The leader uses as much blackboard or newsprint space as is necessary to write down all participants' ideas, listing them under whichever of the Triangle's three headings the participant desires. This process of writing out bite-sized pieces of conversation and categorizing them as a starting point helps participants see how the diversity of experience, traditional perspectives, and sociocultural influences affect the issue at hand. Once people see their ideas in writing, placed on a public board or taped to the walls of a room, they seem better able to discuss their thinking, and they have less fear and pain than when the ideas remain wrapped inside the privatized values of their interior lives. Perhaps on the board the ideas look more factual, more publicly discussible, even the deeply private ideas categorized under *experience of the faithful.*

When the group has shared all of its brainstormed images without comments or discussion, then it is time for free-flowing conversation to begin. The leader asks the central question of the Pyramid: "What is God up to in this issue for us?" Or he or she brings back the Word, reads it aloud, and asks the group to consider God's active presence with them. Effective public conversation can begin from this starting point. Why? They become relational with one another as they discover their first position, both individually and within their community, look at that position critically, and then decide how they will function in light of that position. It is Ricoeur's move from first naïveté to the critical moment to second naïveté, done in community.[4]

The people hold their information and beliefs (first naïveté), and they gather to converse. They place those ideas and beliefs in the light of public conversation on a board or a piece of newsprint and start to discuss values as easily as they discuss facts (critical moment). They do this in the safe and engaging space bounded by the ground rules of attending and as-

4. Paul Ricoeur, *The Rule of Metaphor* (Toronto: University of Toronto Press, 1977), 318.

serting. After such conversation, they begin to realize that the diversity of their tradition, culture, and faith experiences does not relieve them of the responsibility to decide and act as a community. To do this, they must work out some process for living together (second naiveté). They also realize that it is in this diversity, in encountering views different from their own, that they become more able to face the Other that looms on their horizon, threatening to undo them.

In congregations, this model can be used in many different situations. Some governing boards or councils use it to conduct their business every month. Some congregation presidents use it to conduct annual meetings regarding mission and budget issues. Some adult education classes use it as a framework that helps them deal with sensitive subjects such as sexuality, marriage, and parenting troubles, social justice issues, and environmental concerns. It can also be used as an excellent framework for Bible-study discussions and the work of interpretation.

The Role of Leader

Leaders of this kind of conversation have several jobs. They encourage participants to explore where God is in the issue at hand, and where God is at work in the human community. Leaders also act as keepers of the ground rules. The aim, of course, is to get the conversation to take off with very little aid from the leader. This happens when participants lose self-consciousness about attending and asserting. They are no longer aware of who is saying what; they are simply participating as they feel moved to do so. The resulting conversation takes on an identity and a rhythm of its own, and people feel as though they have been a part of something greater than the sum of the participants and their ideas.

Public moral conversation of this kind can happen with as few as ten people or as many as a thousand, depending on the size and acoustics of the room, how well participants can see one another, and whether they can also converse in smaller groups of six to ten. Its effects in a large group setting can be quite dramatic. After all, we experience large groups as public spaces in which conversation has usually been restricted to safe topics. When a well-led public conversation takes place on a deeply divisive topic, and people have the chance to experience the development of a sense of community, especially within a larger experience of deep listening and

Word-dwelling, they do not forget it. They prefer it. In the Southwestern Minnesota synod project, since many of the moral conversation leaders had also been congregational studies participant-interpreters through the act of interviewing, they had an articulated sense of the climate they were entering for conversation. They knew that whatever loomed on the horizon would be threatening to their congregations. But they also knew that God would be at the edges and at the center of their conversation, and that the whole landscape was contained within the larger Word of God.

A Nested Vision of Faith-Based Moral Conversation

It is helpful to draw some conclusions about nesting moral conversation within a deeper layer of free speaking and listening. It is also helpful to place these conclusions within a deeper layer of worship, theology, and dwelling in the Word.

There are two important conclusions to be drawn regarding the placement of moral conversation within an activity of interviewing. First, the skills of *listening* and honest *assertion* are clearly modeled and encouraged from the beginning as the participants engage in workshop Word-dwelling and theological conversation. The participants then take these listening and asserting skills home and put them to work in one-on-one, open-ended interviewing. They practice those skills once again during mutual interpretation of the interview material. Finally, they put those skills to the most sophisticated test as a leader opens and invites others into faith-based public moral conversation.

Second, in highly practical terms, the knowledge that is gained through the interview process about congregation members' hopes and fears for their future together is invaluable for inviting and hosting faith-based conversations. Planners and leaders must understand the climate and the issues before they embark on this work; they must also anticipate the eventual harvest their congregation and community will reap from the seeds they are planting. They are inviting public moral conversation that crosses the permeable boundaries between the congregation and its civic community, between long-time churched and new believer, between thirsty public institutions and the faithful people of God who have been given living water.

Two important conclusions can also be drawn regarding the placement of both moral conversation and interviewing within the even more encompassing layer of worshiping, doing theology, and dwelling in the Word. First, speaking openly about moral conversation training as alive within a larger framework of dwelling in the Word helps facilitate ongoing public moral conversation. It causes us to claim the faith in our faith-based conversation, and it provides deep and rich metaphors that are given room to play themselves out within the believers' conversation and decision-making together as Christian community.

Second, the spirit of community, engendered in shared worship and work, requires and exudes trust of the kind that enriches the atmosphere, and that spirit in turn invites more and more people to participate in the life of God. It is built through the process of agreeing and disagreeing well in public moral conversation, and through communicating with others, the Other, even outsiders. It culminates in the congregation's coming to decisions and taking action together on tough issues.

Those who wish to lead public moral conversation need to first be nurtured and connected with strangers in dynamic public worship. Here they experience being included in an extended public conversation about God and a God-centered communal activity that is not that foreign to what they will eventually lead. When they are treated to intelligent conversation about their own faith traditions in Scripture — hymnody, foundational confessions, and basic theological questions — they find themselves doing theology.

When they learn to ask the hard questions, and really attend to the deep answers, they have begun a journey into the community mind that will help them map their eventual forays into community controversy. As they learn the community mind, they become more equipped to have that mind among themselves that is ours in Christ Jesus, inviting humans to participate freely in the life of God. The nested vision of faith-based conversation, even over conflicted issues, creates a congregational identity in which people do not fear the Other, but meet the Other, and welcome the Other as a gift. For the Word of God also often comes to us as the Other. Encountering, welcoming, and dwelling in it brings us into our natural state of a right relationship with God, whose Word makes us and saves us, and with whom nothing is impossible.

Discerning the Will of God: Congregational Use of Scripture through the Lens of the Cross

Ronald W. Duty

> *"All Scripture is inspired by God and is useful for teaching, for reproof, for correction, and for training in righteousness, so that everyone who belongs to God may be proficient, equipped for every good work."*
>
> 2 Tim. 3:16-17 (NRSV)

> *"Do not be conformed to this world, but be transformed by the renewing of your minds so that you may discern what is the will of God — what is good and acceptable and perfect."*
>
> Rom. 12:2 (NRSV)

> *"And this is my prayer, that your love may overflow more and more with knowledge and full insight to help you determine what is best, so that in the day of Jesus Christ you may be pure and blameless, having produced the harvest of righteousness that comes through Jesus Christ for the glory and praise of God."*
>
> Phil. 1:9-11 (NRSV)

Moral deliberation by the church is as old as the church itself. The first recorded incidents of faith-based moral conversation in the church appear in Paul's letters. There he responds to disturbing reports about the behavior of some members, and to the moral questions brought to him by members of the congregations in Asia Minor and Greece that he founded himself.[1] Moral decision-making and action were present in the church from the beginning. We see this in the appointment of Stephen and six others to assist the apostles in ministry when Hellenistic Jews complained that Hebrew-speaking Jews had neglected their widows in the daily distribution of food in the Christian community (Acts 6:1-7). We also see this at the First Jerusalem Council, which resolved a dispute over whether believing gentiles should be received into the Christian church (Acts 15:1-35).[2] In these accounts, neither Paul nor Peter was reluctant to use Scripture in his argument, nor was either one shy about reinterpreting it when new circumstances resulting from the actions of God warranted it.[3]

Thirty years ago, James M. Gustafson renewed the call for the church to be a moral decision-maker. He strove to clarify the use of Scripture in Christian ethics.[4] Gustafson's call was distinguished by the fact that he said

1. Studies of the ethical dimensions of Paul's letters are numerous. Examples include: Victor Paul Furnish, *Theology and Ethics in Paul* (Nashville: Abingdon Press, 1968); Nils Alstrup Dahl, "Paul and Possessions," and "The Doctrine of Justification: Its Social Functions and Implications," in his *Studies in Paul* (Minneapolis: Augsburg, 1977), 23-39 and 95-120, respectively; Wayne A. Meeks, "The Polyphonic Ethics of the Apostle Paul," in D. M. Yaeger, ed., *The Annals of the Society of Christian Ethics* (Knoxville, TN: Society of Christian Ethics and the Department of Religious Studies, University of Tennessee, Knoxville, 1988), 17-29; J. Paul Sampley, *Walking between the Times: Paul's Moral Reasoning* (Minneapolis: Fortress, 1991); and Brian S. Rosner, ed., *Understanding Paul's Ethics: Twentieth-Century Approaches* (Grand Rapids: Eerdmans, 1995).

2. Luke Timothy Johnson sees that council as the culmination of events that began with Peter's dealings with the gentile centurion Cornelius in Acts 10:1-48. See Johnson, *Scripture and Discernment: Decision Making in the Church* (Nashville: Abingdon, 1996), 61-132.

3. Paul's conversion demonstrates this along with his reference to the cross being a scandal to Jews and his subsequent reinterpretation of Hebrew Scripture in light of the cross. Regarding Peter, see Johnson, *Scripture and Discernment*, 90-106.

4. See James M. Gustafson, *The Church as Moral Decision-Maker* (Philadelphia: Pilgrim Press, 1970); Gustafson, "The Place of Scripture in Christian Ethics: A Methodological Study," in his *Theology and Christian Ethics* (Philadelphia: Pilgrim Press, 1974); *Protestant and Roman Catholic Ethics: Prospects for Rapprochement* (Chicago: University of Chicago Press, 1978), 21-29, 66-70, 97-101; *Ethics from a Theocentric Perspective*, vol. 1: 151-52, 339; vol. 2: 25, 86-87; "The Changing Use of the Bible in Christian Ethics," in Charles E. Curran and Richard A. McCormick, eds., *Readings in Moral Theology, No. 4: The Use of Scripture in Moral Theology* (New York: Paulist Press, 1984), 133-50.

that congregations, not just ecumenical bodies or denominations and their constituent judicatories, should be primary forums for public Christian moral deliberation.[5] More recently, a variety of Christian ethicists and theologians have joined Gustafson concerning the importance of moral conversation, decision-making, and action in congregations. Some have explored the complex theme, variations, and counterpoint of using Scripture in Christian ethics and in moral discernment in the church.[6]

Several denominations have encouraged faith-based moral deliberation in congregations in ways that incorporate the responsible use of Scripture. In this chapter I report on the use of Scripture by congregations participating in a pilot project on moral deliberation in the Southwestern Minnesota synod of the ELCA.[7] These congregations served as a major

---

5. Gustafson, "The Church: A Community of Moral Discourse," in *The Church as Moral Decision Maker*, 83-95 (article originally published in 1964); see also Gustafson, "The Voluntary Church: A Moral Appraisal," in *The Church as Moral Decision Maker*, 109-37 (article originally published in 1966).

6. See, for example, Edouard Hamel, "Scripture, the Soul of Moral Theology?" in Curran and McCormick, *Readings in Moral Theology, No. 4*, 105-32; Allen Verhey, "The Use of Scripture in Ethics," in Curran and McCormick, *Readings in Moral Theology, No. 4*, 213-41; Stanley Hauerwas, "The Moral Authority of Scripture: The Politics and Ethics of Remembering," in his *A Community of Character: Toward a Constructive Christian Social Ethic* (Notre Dame, IN: University of Notre Dame Press, 1981), 53-71; Bruce Birch and Larry L. Rasmussen, *The Bible and Ethics in Christian Life*, rev. and expanded ed. (Minneapolis: Augsburg, 1989); J. Philip Wogaman, *Christian Moral Judgment* (Louisville: Westminster John Knox Press, 1989); Charles E. Curran, *The Church and Morality: An Ecumenical and Catholic Approach*, Hein-Frey Lectures, 1991-92 (Minneapolis: Fortress, 1993), and "The Role and Function of the Scriptures in Moral Theology," in *Readings in Moral Theology, No. 4*, 178-212. See also Langdon Gilkey, "The Christian Congregation as a Religious Community," in his *American Congregations*, vol. 2, *New Perspectives in the Study of Congregations* (Chicago: University of Chicago Press, 1994), 120-24.

7. "Congregations in Moral Conversation" was a joint project of Church Innovations Institute, through the involvement of Patrick R. Keifert, director of research, and Pat Taylor Ellison, assistant director of research, and the synod's Task Force on Moral Deliberation, which I chaired. We would like to thank former Synod Minister, Rev. Barbara Knutson, former Bishop Charles Anderson, and Bishop Stan Olson for their support of this project. The experience of the rural crisis of the 1980s, which caused significant dislocation in many of the communities and congregations within the synod, contributed to my interest in having the synod initiate this project. While churches and church-related agencies were good at responding to the immediate needs of dislocated people, churches were at a loss as to how to serve as public forums to help people with visioning to identify goals and strategies for long-term community or congregational survival in order to decrease community vulnerability

case study for the Congregational Study Research Team (CSRT). The pilot project is one of a number of projects in the United States that have somewhat similar objectives.[8] The "Congregations in Moral Conversations Project" uses a *ritual model* for moral conversation, a model deriving from the work of Roman Catholic scholars James and Evelyn Whitehead that is a way of conversing about difficult subjects relying on certain rituals or etiquette of process.[9] Their approach encourages participants to draw on the sources of church tradition, the experience of the faithful, and common culture and society to address a substantive topic in the life of the congregation, the larger church, or community and social life outside the church. In this model, Scripture is primarily an aspect of church tradition.[10]

In our use of this model, we encouraged congregations to view material from these three sources through the lens of the cross (see preceding chapter), and we encouraged them to consider how the death and resurrection of Jesus speaks to their daily lives; further, they explore how this

---

and increase community resilience and regeneration. This was something a Rural Strategies Task Force that included religious groups identified as an important need, one in which rural churches had a stake as well as some possibilities of fulfilling. Cf. George Boody and Michael Rivard, "The Rural Crisis in Minnesota: Identifying Social and Economic Vulnerability and New Directions for the Future," *Agriculture and Human Values* 111, no. 4 (Fall 1986): 75-87.

8. See, e.g., Peggy Prevoznik Heins, *Salt and Light: A Leadership Training Manual* (Wilmington, DE: Catholic Charities, Inc., Diocese of Wilmington, 1995); Paul R. Peters, *Renewing Congregations through Education and Mission* (Cleveland: United Church Board of Home Missions, n.d.), which is designed to be used with Gil Dawes, *Renewing Rural Iowa Bible Studies* (Des Moines: PrairieFire Rural Action, 1994, 1995); Robin Peterson and Lou Ann Parsons, *See — Judge — Act: Pastoral Planning for a Prophetic Church* (Cleveland: United Church Board for World Ministries, United Church of Christ, n.d.). See also J. Philip Wogaman, *Making Moral Decisions* (Nashville: Abingdon, 1990), which, while it is not a denominationally sponsored training curriculum, is aimed at a distinctly congregational audience.

9. James D. Whitehead and Evelyn Eaton Whitehead, *Method in Ministry: Theological Reflection and Christian Ministry,* rev. ed. (New York: Sheed and Ward, 1995).

10. However, distinguishing the content of the three general kinds of sources is never absolute. Scripture, for example, can also be part of the experience of the faithful or even a commonplace of culture in some instances, such as a residual respect for the Bible or knowledge of certain well-known passages of Scripture such as Ps. 23, the Christmas narratives of Matthew and Luke, or 1 Cor. 13. Below I will discuss how Scripture functions implicitly as part of the experience of the faithful to inform moral conversation and to help form Christian imagination even when it does not function explicitly in spontaneous use by biblically competent Christians.

helps them discern what God is now doing in the matter they are considering, and how God may be calling them to respond. A dozen teams from the selected congregations, after an initial training session, were sent home to practice using the model on topics they selected themselves. The materials in these next two chapters are drawn from extensive interviews with teams from five participating congregation — after their initial experience with the process. When these teams left their initial training workshop, several of the participants wondered what they would talk about. Two weeks later, when press reports leaked information about the first draft of a proposed ELCA social statement on human sexuality, most of these teams not only knew what they *had* to discuss; they also felt *empowered* by their training to handle a very contentious and difficult subject.

So, while congregations chose to discuss various other topics, the common element in most of the experiences I am reporting on here is the discussion of this draft statement on sexuality. The range of other issues that congregations chose to discuss included a congregation's traditional senior banquet for youth, stewardship in the context of a church council retreat, congregational planning, and large-scale hog confinement practices, an issue that divided some members of one congregation from other members.

The use of Scripture in congregational life, whether in its worship, Bible study, devotional reading, or Christian education, significantly shapes the faith and piety members bring to public moral conversation in congregations.[11] Gustafson argues that it is piety that significantly distinguishes Christian moral deliberation from true Christian spiritual and moral discernment.[12] Elsewhere in this volume, David Fredrickson

---

11. See, for example, *The Journal of Religious Ethics* 7 (1979), where an entire issue is devoted to worship and ethics; see also Richard A. McCormick, S.J., "Scripture, Liturgy, Character, and Morality," in Curran and McCormick, *Readings in Moral Theology, No. 4,* 298-302; Michael G. Cartwright, "The Practice and Performance of Scripture: Grounding Christian Ethics in a Communal Hermeneutic," in D. M. Yaeger, ed., *The Annual of the Society of Christian Ethics, 1988,* 31-53; Vigen Guroian, "Bible and Ethics: An Ecclesial and Liturgical Interpretation," *The Journal of Religious Ethics* 18, no. 1 (Spring 1990): 129-57; Guroian, *Ethics after Christendom: Toward an Ecclesial Christian Ethic* (Grand Rapids: Eerdmans, 1994); and Harmon L. Smith, *Where Two or Three Are Gathered: Liturgy and the Moral Life* (Cleveland: Pilgrim, 1995).

12. James M. Gustafson, *Ethics from a Theocentric Perspective,* vol. 2, 10-11; and "Afterword," in Harlan R. Beckley and Charles M. Swezey, eds., *James M. Gustafson's Theocentric Ethics: Interpretations and Assessments* (Macon, GA: Mercer University Press, 1988), 243-44. Craig

refers to congregational life, broadly construed after the model of the Greek *politeuesthai,* as a forum for common discussion of the public issues of the community of faith, discussion that then forms the mind of Christ in the congregation.[13] In most congregations, members' familiarity with Scripture and their engagement of it varies widely. These differing levels of familiarity and skill in interpreting present both difficulties and opportunities to develop Christian imagination. To take advantage of the opportunities and to overcome the barriers, I will argue that those members who are gifted with a knowledge of Scripture, whatever their sophistication, need to take the lead in helping the congregation interpret relevant Scripture passages. Those members are pivotal in helping a congregation reimagine itself in light of Scripture, and in helping a congregation use Scripture creatively in the moral dilemmas and difficulties it faces.

Seeking to Discern God's Word

James M. Gustafson has said the following:

> God is present, and seeking to speak his word in the life of the church. Although one cannot claim full confidence that the moral consensus of the church is the voice of God, nevertheless his Spirit is present in human deliberation and action. The moral community is called into being by its Lord, nurtured by its participation in its life, and guided by its understanding of his present Living Word in and through the life of the congregation. He has witnessed in the prophets and in Jesus Christ, in the events of Israel's history, and in the history of the Church. Scripture points toward him, what he seeks to do and what he seeks to say. The moral community is a religious community gathered in faith, trusting in God and loyal to him. Its deliberation and action are expressions of its effort to discern God's will and way. The volun-

---

Dykstra also argues that congregational life and the public and private use of Scripture help shape Christian vision and character for moral discernment (*Vision and Character: A Christian Educator's Alternative to Kohlberg* [New York: Paulist Press, 1981], 86-87, 118, 124).

13. See also David Fredrickson, "Pauline Ethics: Congregations as Communities of Moral Deliberation," in Karen L. Bloomquist and John R. Stumme, eds., *The Promise of Lutheran Ethics* (Minneapolis: Fortress, 1998), 115-29.

tary congregation seeks to walk in the way of the Lord. It has a living Lord who leads it.[14]

Most Christian congregations, at least in theory, probably aspire to this vision about God's presence and being able to come to a human moral consensus in the church. One faithful team member of a pilot project congregation said, "Everything is based on Scripture." Implied in this simple statement is the faith that Scripture points to what Jesus Christ is saying to Christians as they seek to walk in the way of the Lord in their congregational life.

A more skeptical colleague of mine, who genuinely shares the vision Gustafson articulates, thinks that often congregations are simply paying Scripture a "metaphysical compliment," as he puts it, with such pious statements. He believes with Gustafson that they often hold a rather different view of God's presence and how to come to a human moral consensus in the church. It is one shaped by the aftermath of the Enlightenment, where "God is so remote, so silent that the life of the church is dependent upon the human cogitation and action that take place in the democratic process." Here, forming a moral Christian community is more like "a socially contracted group who agree on certain basic principles and seek the implications of these in areas that require moral decision."[15]

Certainly, the reality of congregational practice in the use of Scripture often falls short of its professed ideals. But this reality is also complex. The unspoken — and often unacknowledged — practical assumption of many congregations may be what Gustafson and my friend describe. But the ideal vision Gustafson presents to us is not just pious talk that rationalizes whatever individuals and congregations may want to read into Scripture in their own images; it also represents a genuine aspiration for many Christians and their congregations. The members of the Congregational Studies Research Team believe that the vision Gustafson voices also says something important about God. It conveys that, despite our captivity to these Enlightenment assumptions, God is active in Scripture and church tradition, in our personal and communal faith experience, and in our common secular culture.

God's active presence frees us to hear God's word and to discern

14. Gustafson, "The Voluntary Church: A Moral Appraisal," 132-33.
15. Gustafson, "The Voluntary Church," 132.

what God is calling us to decide together as we respond to the Good News of Jesus Christ. This takes place in our personal daily lives, in our vocations in the world, and in shared Christian ministries. The Holy Spirit is active in raising up attentive readers and hearers of Scripture through whom we can be led into spiritual discernment of the truth. By this I mean not only the truth of the gospel, but also the truth that God is freeing us from our captivity to Enlightenment assumptions about the remoteness of God. It also includes the truth of what God is calling us to decide and do together as we freely live out our faith in service to our neighbors.

Perhaps the idealistic illusions, as well as the skepticism, surrounding the use of Scripture in congregations need to be tempered. People do appreciate having a scriptural basis laid out on an issue. One man conveyed the following, after a church council planning retreat when his pastor presented a broad view of stewardship and provided a detailed scriptural basis for it:

> I belonged to First Lutheran for twenty years and I never heard this discussion! Why have I belonged twenty years and never really known what true stewardship was?

However, our earlier research in congregations showed little *spontaneous* mention of the use of the Bible in moral conversation and decision-making.[16] In fact, this man's excitement is the mirror image of this reality. Because there was, up to this point, evidently little use of Scripture in serious moral conversation and decision-making in his church, its judicious use in this case was a revelation in his experience and understanding of stewardship. As such, it became a cause for rejoicing and an implicit judgment. Clearly, the potential for an increased responsible use of Scripture to inform moral conversation is significant. There is, at least among some laity, a latent hunger for it.

Different Words, Different Readings, Different Hearings: Interpretation in Community

> [The Bible] must be read, heard, and interpreted, which will lead to different readings and hearings. "Creative" readings must be justified.

16. Patrick R. Keifert, "The Bible, Congregational Leaders, and Moral Conversation," *Word & World* XIII, no. 4 (Fall 1993): 392-97.

There are rules. . . . Rules and arguments and methods do not get us to the truth, however. For that we must rely on creative imagination, or to use a nice word, divination. If the Spirit is at work among us, we may trust there will be moments of illumination.

Determining what is a valid reading and where minds need to be changed is a community task. Conversation is not only a means of testing, however; it is the way communities are formed and grow. Disagreements are not a sign of community breakdown but of life. The possibility of edifying conversation in the face of differing opinions, however, requires a measure of trust and goodwill — the result, the church claims, of the presence and work of the Spirit. Here is why interpretation should not be divorced from the life of a worshiping community that engenders goodwill and trust.[17]

People sometimes disagree about how to interpret Scripture, or about which passages of Scripture pertain to a particular moral issue, or about their relative importance. In addition, there are times when passages of Scripture themselves seem to disagree with one another when they are brought to bear on moral matters; often this creates tension in congregations' conversations. When people assume that they basically think alike, the discovery that they do not think alike only disrupts their picture of basic agreement. And when the stakes of the issue are high, it also has the potential to disrupt relationships in the congregation. When people discover that the Bible says more than one thing on an issue, and may not always agree with itself, this often is an unexpected and disconcerting experience. People must then cope with these differences of opinion and differences of scriptural emphasis or its occasionally contradictory content.

In such cases, there are sometimes impulses to resolve the tension too easily without getting at the heart of the matter, either in Scripture itself or in the relationships among members of the congregation. But such tensions are, as Donald Juel recognizes, often opportunities to wrestle with the depths of Scripture and to grow personally and corporately through the struggle of conversation. Such situations are often when the Holy Spirit is most actively present, rather than absent, in the life of a congregation.

The wisdom of Juel's observations about the need for goodwill and

---

17. Donald H. Juel, "'Your Word is Truth': Some Reflections on a Hard Saying," *The Princeton Seminary Bulletin* XVII, no. 1 (new ser., Feb. 1996): 23-24.

trust in the face of inevitable disagreements that will result from interpreting Scripture in moral conversations is confirmed by our pilot project in congregations. Most of the participants in the conversations we led operated in just such an environment of goodwill and trust, where they had known each other in the congregations — in some cases for decades. When Scripture disagreed with their views, or when participants disagreed with each other, their trust and goodwill were put to the test. When Scripture was diverse and gave multiple perspectives, some wanted to explore this diversity, but it made others uncomfortable. The pastor of Holy Cross described the discomfort of his conversation partners this way:

> They weren't comfortable with [disagreement]. For the most part, they wanted [Scripture] to be clear and to state the way things were. . . . [These are the kinds of] people who want to have it black or white and clear-cut. And it just drives them crazy to take an idea and expand it. What they want to do is take it and melt it down.

St. Luke's drew on the prevailing cultural etiquette to initially *minimize* this discomfort:

> I think we were Minnesota Nice during that period. I think we just accepted both [arguments]. . . . We certainly didn't come to any conclusions or any agreements.

A team member from First Lutheran described how some members of Bible study groups in their congregation wanted to avoid such problems of biblical interpretation by appealing to a trusted expert, the pastor:

> It's confusing — who do we believe? . . . One time we were going to change the women's Bible study and have [it] as part of the Search Group, and Pastor Johnson wouldn't have been in charge. Well, these ladies all rebelled because they wanted a pastor who, they felt, could truly understand the Bible, could relate it to them the way it should be related, because . . . people do interpret it in different ways.

But sometimes the discomfort must be faced. The etiquette doesn't always help us finesse awkward contrasts, and the expert can't — or won't — always resolve the dissonance for us. At such times, there is little else to do but draw on the reserves of trust and goodwill. Here it is necessary to follow the Spirit's leading into the dissonance, the awkwardness, and the conflicts. But this can be an intense experience for a congregation. Tension is mentioned frequently in accounts of such experiences. A member of one congregation's team simply said, "It was tough!" A member of St. Luke's team describes some of the tension:

> I think [those were] maybe some of the most tense times. Folks did say that there are certain quotes you can pick out of the Bible on one side or the other. . . . And I think they were quoted almost back to back by kind of opposite sides. I think that led into . . . more intense discussion.

At Grace, the intern pastor was perceived to be the focus of the lack of consensus about interpreting Scripture:

> A lot of tension came in because Duane was an East Coast person [coming from an] East Coast seminary to boot, and he brought his values with him in that conversation to people who have lived their whole lives here in Minnesota in the Midwest, people who just say, "That's the way it is." Yes, there was a lot of challenge going on there.

The intern's perception and the recollection of other team members of the conversations confirms that:

> There were those who afterwards felt that it was difficult to be there because of the depth of the emotional tension. It was tense at times!

These disagreements, both in Scripture itself and among the interpreting members, challenged the presumed consensus of a congregation. When such challenges occur, people may avoid them altogether, or, to maintain the appearance of peace, take conflict underground. Both tactics indicate a deference to a key rural value of avoiding open conflict, which was the case at Grace:[18]

---

18. Rural sociologist Jim Krile of the Blandin Foundation identifies the avoidance of open conflict as a key value in rural life and culture, expressed for example in the old saw "Respectable people do not disagree in public." See Beth Russell, "Churches Play an Important Role in Crisis," *In Tense Times* (Montevideo, MN: University of Minnesota Extension Service for West Central Minnesota, 1993), 2.

The big problem there was the emotional. For instance, [the intern pastor] said, "There were those who felt afterwards it was difficult to be a part of that because of the definite emotional tension of the topic."

[Interviewer]: So, some people might have stayed away because they didn't know if they could handle. . . .

Yeah! Right! There was some tension in some of those groups. In some of those evening sessions we kind of got into it a little bit. And I think that's really hard in this congregation. I think that idea of keeping the waters calm — people getting along with each other — that is a big priority in this congregation. And if there is much conflict here, I tend to think it probably goes underground.

When people are predisposed by a key cultural value to avoid open conflicts, it is difficult to deal openly and constructively with controversial topics, or with apparent inconsistencies within Scripture, or different interpretations of biblical texts. It is to the credit of the congregational leadership teams that they took the risk of open conflict in spite of this cultural norm. They plunged ahead with conversations using a process one of whose implicit assumptions is precisely that respectable people *may* disagree in public — even about the Bible.

But not all this tension can be ascribed to cultural influences. Some of it, of course, may also be due to participants' self-consciousness or lack of confidence in their biblical knowledge. This became evident when they were confronted with passages or perspectives that apparently contradict their own understanding of what the Bible says on a particular topic. Or such experiences may make it appear that their biblical knowledge is incomplete. But even beyond their feelings of inadequacy or shame, the tension also comes because they realize that the Bible often says more than one thing about something. They discover that the Bible's own witness is sometimes complex rather than simple and straightforward, that it sometimes disagrees with itself. This experience can be frightening, and some people may want to back away from it. Such an experience may even make some people begin to doubt their faith. At those times, a knowledgeable reader of Scripture, such as a pastor, will be of crucial help in leading such persons to deal constructively with their doubt and discomfort.

But there are various ways to deal with this tension — even for those who plunge ahead. One way, which we have already observed, was to try to dismiss uncomfortable interpretations by dismissing the interpreter. Another way was to make the classic religious liberal move of appealing to general principles such as God's love. In one congregation, multiple perspectives on Scripture applied to homosexuality were apparently resolved in this way, at least for a time; even though the resolution was incomplete, it did include a sense of mystery. A team member from St. Luke's said:

> And that's mystery for them — that God loves people, all kinds of people of various kinds of sexual orientation. . . .

A third way is simply to deal with the complexity according to whatever intellectual equipment and knowledge of Scripture they come with. The associate pastor at Our Savior's, a very sensitive observer and a very astute pastoral theologian, said:

> In the conversations themselves, people being explicit [about] biblical metaphors or scriptural passages and how they actually shaped what they had to say or how they would listen, that was absent, even though I felt we made a fairly concerted effort to give some tools and orientation reminders about Scripture. I think obviously . . . that in doing moral deliberation, people will go with the tools they have, and it's simply a separate issue and a comprehensive one [to teach them new tools for interpreting Scripture].

Despite the tensions of different points of view and interpretations, most participants in these congregations went with what they had. But some responded differently. They did so regardless of any feelings of inadequacy about biblical knowledge, and they resisted the temptation to completely dismiss those whose perspectives were different. There were a few who left the conversation when they realized that the process really emphasized deep listening rather than presenting them with an opportunity to get on a soapbox and hold an audience captive to their biblical interpretations. However, some who had reputations for being out of the mainstream of their congregation stayed in the conversation when they realized people would give them a serious hearing. As Juel observed, deep reservoirs of trust in the communities in which they worshiped, along with trust in God's grace, enabled them to remain in the tension of difference and disagreement while they tried to work things through together on tough issues.

What are the tools people in the church use when they deal with a difficult moral matter in conversation? How does Scripture function for them? What tools do they bring into the process to help them make sense of what Scripture is saying? What language are they speaking when they try to discern the language of Scripture? And how do they use that language? In other words, how do they open themselves up for growth?

What Language Shall I Borrow?
The Function and Use of Scripture

> The Christian enterprise is utterly invested in changing minds. The gospel truth, for which the church has regarded the Bible as a reliable source and norm, matters only when it enters bound imaginations and frees people who have no hope and dare not dream of living abundantly. But if people are to hear a strange new word, someone will have to learn their language and speak with them. Genuine conversation is required, and conversation is risky. . . . A real question is whether there is a Spirit of truth who may be trusted with the future of these conversations.[19]

The role of the Bible in Christian moral conversation, decision-making, and action is complex. As we will see in the next chapter, the proportion of ELCA members who read Scripture regularly is modest. Although some stories or passages reside in their memories, many today are not exactly fluent in its language and imagery. They may not know many of its important stories, and they speak its dialect in a halting fashion. Therefore, it should surprise no one that the influence of the Bible in forming Christian imaginations among many ELCA members is sometimes relatively indirect. There is ample evidence of this in our interviews with conversation teams from the pilot project congregations.

Furthermore, to some it is a highly private and personalized language. The observation of Our Savior's church's associate pastor about how people use Scripture is this:

> I think that most people [go to] Scripture for personal comfort and devotion, but it is not [something] that necessarily norms or regulates

---

19. Juel, "'Your Word is Truth,'"15.

their views or thinking. . . . The practice of our time is to seek other sources, [those] having more to do with personal experience and the tenor of [the] times.

Even when used for devotional purposes, the Bible can help form a Christian imagination; but regular devotional reading is also at a modest level in the ELCA. And if the Bible and one's faith in Jesus are seen to be largely a private matter, a Christian imagination will not always readily enter the public realm in an explicit way. Nor will the language of the Christian imagination or that of the Bible be readily seen or used as an explicitly public language.

But perhaps it functions implicitly rather than explicitly. That is the opinion of St. Luke's pastor:

[T]here's a difference between [something being] directly tied to Scripture and . . . something that's inside of us, part of our life. Why do we believe the things we believe? Why do we value what we value? So [Scripture] may have been there a lot more than we're giving it credit [for], too. It may be just such a part of our belief . . . that without quoting Scripture, without chapter and verse, the Word can still be working, right?

If that is true, how might the Word be working? A St. Luke's team member described how Scripture played a role in its conversations:

Maybe just a couple times it was an actual passage. The rest of the time was maybe more in general, maybe asking rhetorically . . . "What would Jesus think of this?" or "What have we learned from Scripture?" Not too much direct reference.

One way that Scripture works in the moral conversation for some church members, those who are not highly biblically literate, is by way of an imaginative leap into the mind of Christ. Another is by way of coming to a generalized understanding of the Bible's depiction of the way faithful people live. However, neither of these is based on detailed knowledge of specific passages or stories that would give particular insight into Jesus' character.

There are also ways that Scripture might function implicitly in moral conversation. The liturgy and hymns, the sacraments and festivals of the church, and religious art can all shape our relationship to Jesus and our understanding of his story with respect to our own. The structure of the Lutheran liturgy begins with confession and absolution, moves to praise and thanksgiving to God, whose victory over sin and death in Christ is celebrated in the Eucharist, and continues with the reading of Scripture lessons that rehearse the story of the people of God and, most important, the story of Jesus. One or more of these lessons is often the focus of preaching, which strives to interpret our own stories and experience in relationship to Jesus. The hymns themselves express the relationship of faithful people to God the Creator, to Jesus Christ, or to the Holy Spirit. In the sacraments of baptism and Holy Communion, believers receive and experience the grace of God in Christ personally for themselves.

The major festivals of the liturgical year rehearse and interpret the major events in the life of Christ and the church in which believers' own life stories are now caught up by virtue of their faith and participation in Christian congregations. The language of the liturgy itself is often lifted directly or paraphrased from Scripture. Religious art, if only in the form of simple crosses, graces many sanctuaries or bulletin covers, sometimes graphically depicting Bible stories. In many cases, the cross itself, interpreted in various ways in a congregation's life, becomes a lens through which we see Scripture, our experience, our communities of faith, and our world. The way a community of faith lives outside of worship may itself be its way of interpreting the cross.

All of this happens without Christians necessarily being regular readers or students of Scripture. Indeed, it is only since the sixteenth century that there were significant numbers of readers of Scripture in vernacular languages at all. Prior to the Protestant Reformation, a Christian imagination and moral character, as well as the character of Christian communities, were formed in people who were incapable of reading Scripture. Why should we assume that this no longer happens, except among preliterate children?

In other words, the *experience* of the people of God, one of the corners of the triangle of sources in our model of Christian moral conversation, shapes Christian imaginations (see preceding chapter). The pastor of St. Luke's put it this way:

> Most of them have been . . . baptized, they've been in the church — part of this family — for their whole lives. So it helps . . . to shape their

lives and form who they are in ways that they don't even remember or realize. That's true for most of us.

If Scripture functions in connection with the experience of the faithful in this way, it can help make issues concrete and personal rather than leaving them in the abstract. The pastor of Holy Cross observed the following about the role of experience in that church's conversation:

> That was very helpful because it helped put a face on the issue, which I think led to a more compassionate discussion with more understanding. Because they would relate their experience, be it in their family, their community, in their education, how it's changed, questions that they had had. I think that impacted [the conversation].

They can then bring their personal and communal faith experience to bear in interesting and fruitful ways on their experience of everyday life in the common culture. In order for the Bible to function explicitly concerning our experience in the world, in order for it to shape imagination and behavior in daily life, not only is knowledge required — or as one pastor put it, "the distinctive language and voice of the church in the tradition of Scripture" — but also the ability to "speak the language of the world" in a way that relates the two. Luke Timothy Johnson refers to this as "a properly *ecclesial hermeneutic*," by which he means

> . . . one that places the writings in their proper canonical context and that involves the entire faith community in the interpretive process. For such a hermeneutic to work, there must be the active discernment of the work of God in the lives of believers today, raised to the level of a narrative of faith; there must be, at the same time, an active discernment of the canonical texts in the light of these experiences and narratives. This process must occur in a public context that enables discussion, debate, disagreement, and decision. In this creative if tension-filled context, the canonical witness can again shape the identity of the Christian community.[20]

One way to relate these two distinctive languages is to focus on eschatology, or, as the associate pastor of Our Savior's church put it, "How do we see ourselves in relationship to the end?" He elaborated on that:

20. Johnson, *Scripture and Discernment,* 38.

How we imagine our particular concrete existence in relationship to our life in Christ, our life in the world, our relationship to our own death, the coming of the kingdom of God. . . . What people imagine is their primary existence is their everyday life, work and family, and that that has some relationship [to their life in Christ]. One has a relationship to God and to Christ and to one's own salvation, which is a part of that [life in Christ].

This way of relating the world of the Bible to our everyday world through eschatology tends to approach that relationship through the images, persons, and events described in the Bible in connection with our ultimate destiny, if not in its peculiar language.

Paul Gerhardt uses a line from the old German Lenten chorale "O Sacred Head Now Wounded" to pose this question: "What language shall I borrow?" It is an effort to talk about the fitting human response to Christ's graciousness in suffering death on the cross. He answers his own question by appealing immediately to the human language of intimate, self-giving friendship. A way to relate the world of the Bible to our everyday world is to borrow language from the secular culture. The language many Christians may borrow to wrestle with moral dilemmas and difficulties in their Christian imaginations may often be the cultural language of American pragmatism. The associate pastor of Our Savior's church noted this; his comments are worth quoting at length:

> If you think about it, there is an American pragmatism, which is: You do whatever it is you [need to] do to make it work. But what happens if as a Christian your primary belief is in God's goodness and graciousness? And the power to forgive is a primary one that can overcome and kind of pull together the messy reality you must deal with? On the basis of that, or on top of that foundation, we say, "How am I going to respond to the sort of shifting moral landscape?" And most of us do not make responses in the vein of economic pragmatism, sort of like, "What's going to get me farthest ahead?"
>
> You do what it takes to maintain some network of some of those basic human commitments of caring and concern for one another. And Lord knows how one might reflect on this theologically or scripturally or traditionally. I don't know how it all fits together. God will take care of it, and we will all go forward and take communion. And that allowed some freedom to make those shifts in thinking. It is a dif-

ferent foundation to a different kind of pragmatism. I'm not sure if you'd call it that. So when we say that . . . experience and culture are what is normative for shaping how people view what is right and wrong, there is a way in which the tradition is viewed like that, [and] specifically witnesses to God's forgiveness and grace, which maybe gives some freedom to take some risks. And you're not quite sure how it all fits together.

The language of Christian pragmatism may be congruent with the risks required of faith. Such Christian pragmatism likely has the capacity to cope with the disagreement that Gustafson and Johnson presume are part of moral deliberation and discernment. And one can see how it could be open to the leadership of the living Lord and the Spirit, which both Gustafson's assumption and Juel's vision call for. But does it have any spiritual integrity that could qualify it as a language fit for the discernment of the work of God in the lives of Christian believers and their congregations? And how might it be connected with the discernment of those individual and corporate lives via an eschatological perspective?

The Word of the Cross: The Power and Wisdom of God

Since God calls us anew in every moment, the response of faith is never-ending. This hearing demands an asceticism of attentiveness. There is never a moment before death when faith can say, "Enough, it is finished," for the Word of God is not fully spoken to each individual until death. God's word unfolds with every breath we breathe. Faith moves constantly from death to life: death to our prior understanding, footholds, and securities; and life, given freely each moment by another. A perilous progress. For this reason, we can recognize Jesus as the pioneer and perfecter of our faith. He moved in obedience to the death of the cross, and when he wished to live on his own terms, he said "yes" to the one who called him.

Where the church exists as something more than institution or ethical society, it is marked by this kind of faith. The church is a paschal community, dying in order to live. In the lives of its individual members, faith seeks to discern the call of God in their particular circumstances. As a group, the community as well seeks to discern the Word spoken to this people in the challenges of the present. The identity of

127

the church is always being shaped by its response to God's call in the context of its worldly life.[21]

The role of Christian pragmatism in discernment, and what connection it may have to an eschatological perspective on life, seems to come from the focus of the cross in a congregation's imagination. In the model of moral conversation we used, we asked members to view whatever they could discern of the working of God through the lens of the cross. This included church tradition, the experience of the faithful, and the views of culture and society. Discussions of grace, sin, and Christian identity were all entry points into the cross serving as the lens to help participants see where the reality of God working in Christ affected the reality of their lives and the topic about which they were conversing.

The insight of the pastor of Our Savior's church about Christian pragmatism suggests that God's grace for Christians is seen primarily in Jesus Christ and the cross. If this is true, then Holy Communion can be a sacramental link between the cross and everyday life in the Christian imagination. This seems close to the mark for people of the Holy Cross congregation, where grace became specified in terms of the inclusiveness of sin and forgiveness and the sacrament of Holy Communion. Its pastor recalled:

> I think we talked about communion and the sacraments, and that Jesus died for all, and the inclusivity of this term. . . . Even regardless of where we stand on this issue, still, we are called as Christians to be church for everyone.

He added: "People could very much relate to that: 'Yes, we sin, too.' We all stand in need of confession and forgiveness." For this pastor, the cross is the major focal point:

> It all gathers at the foot of the cross. Everything ultimately is in the shadow [of the cross]. You can't get around it without going through it.

The Holy Cross congregants understood that everyone sins, and that through Holy Communion everyone gathered at the foot of the cross is offered forgiveness. At St. Luke's, the entry point — where the

21. Johnson, *Scripture and Discernment,* 24-25.

lens of the cross began to focus the conversation — was grace. Grace's pastor said:

> I think that we certainly talked about grace. In terms of the sexuality issues, we certainly said somewhere along the line that it's important to realize that one's sexual orientation is not a precondition for salvation. We don't want to make rules that ruin the gospel. That was said in relationship to the sexuality issues.

Invited to elaborate, he added:

> It's because of the Christ event that we can talk about grace. And hopefully grace informed everything we said and did in these conversations. That aspect of theology of the cross is certainly part of the life of this congregation. It's preached, it's taught, it's talked about.

At Our Savior's church, the cross is connected with the believer's identity in Christ. Someone recalled that Howard, a socially conservative interpreter of Scripture, said "that we should remember that the cross covers all of us." The associate pastor of Our Savior's told how he had talked about the cross on more than one occasion during their series of conversations on the ELCA's draft on sexuality:

> [T]here are some things thicker than this document, that our identity in Jesus Christ is what unites us and that we may have a difference of opinions on this, but that is not a ground [for destroying our unity in Christ]. . . . A few minutes [were spent] in framing the whole conversation so that we could understand what was primary and then what was of a secondary nature. . . . It was a good point, in terms of Jesus did die for us all.

At Our Savior's, believers' identities in Christ are understood in terms of the cross, which covers all for whom Christ died. The members of Grace saw the cross as transcending people's different agendas in the midst of conflict. Its intern pastor observed how its conversations took note of

> . . . where Christ is in the midst of this conflict . . . and what you do with that. And how . . . one way to deal with conflict is to look to the Bible as a way to find God's grace in all this . . . and for direction . . . where God, Christ, is leading the conflict.

At Grace, the cross shows Christ in the midst of their conflict but also as transcending people's differences. Recognition of the cross helps conflicting people look at issues and at each other differently; it also helps them look to where Christ is leading them in the conflict.

Each congregation, however, tends to imagine itself and the world through the lens of the cross somewhat differently. As each one does so, it begins to discern how God's victory on the cross speaks to the daily sufferings and victories of its members and neighbors. It begins to discover how its life is shaped by the shape of the cross, and how this cross-shaped life influences its conversation about moral matters in the congregation's common life.[22] They can also begin to discern, as Luke Timothy Johnson suggests above, how God may be calling them beyond their past life to new life in the future. Grace's pastor tells of one woman for whom this began to happen:

> [W]e had a woman in the group who is very well respected in this congregation . . . who has an open mind and is willing to listen. Her comment to me, which was really delightful to hear, was, "Pastor, I thought I had it all figured out and I knew exactly what I believed and exactly what was right and wrong. . . . Now I don't know what I believe anymore, and I don't know exactly what the answers are. I have more questions now than when I started." And I patted her on the back and said, "Good! That's what it was about!" The point . . . was to examine this and find out that there aren't necessarily black-and-white answers for us.

The theology of the cross was the imaginative center of Luther's theology. He regarded it as the source of our most trustworthy knowledge of God, both revealing and hiding the nature of God's love. In its hiddenness, faith contradicts the wisdom of the world. Requiring trust in God's Word, this faith points us away from God's glory and power and toward God's weakness and suffering. Yet Christ's work on the cross was, to Luther, the work of a victor, vanquishing sin, death, and the devil. Moreover, to him the cross was the ultimate image of God's liberating presence among God's people. Finally, Luther saw the cross as shaping the lives of Christians and Christian communities to be lives of service to others for the sake of the gospel, service that did not avoid suffering on their behalf.

22. Patrick R. Keifert, Pat Taylor Ellison, and Ronald W. Duty, *Thriving in Change: Talking, Deciding, and Acting as Christian Community: A Training Toolbox* (St. Paul: Church Innovations Institute, Inc., 1997), B-58–B-59.

Luther's understanding reflects a particular kind of hermeneutical circle. He begins to come to this understanding of the cross through the language of Scripture. He maintains that imparting this understanding is the primary purpose of the gospel as presented in Scripture.[23] But it is also clear that he comes to see Scripture through the image and experience of the cross.[24] Therefore, both Luther's understanding of Scripture and his Christian imagination are mutually dependent. Together, they shape how he understands Christian moral discernment and how Christians live the moral life together.

The challenge for biblically competent people in contributing to moral discernment, as it was for Luther, is to focus the imaginations of their fellow parishioners on the situations they face with the lens of the cross. The practical task of discernment is to help bring together whatever knowledge of Scripture they may have with the practical dilemma of living the Christian life. The cross helps them imaginatively focus on how Christ frees them so they might serve those around them, both individually and as congregations, without avoiding the suffering this may bring them in the process of that service. Becoming this kind of "paschal community," as Johnson calls it, is not always easy or certain. Even a congregation such as Grace, with an understanding of the cross that sees Christ as transcending their differences, may have great difficulty trusting where Christ may be leading them. It may also have difficulty discerning how it might serve neighbors who are radically different from themselves, whose way of life seems to threaten their identity or tradition as Christians.

For congregation members to fulfill their calling in serving as biblical guides to others seems to require that they work with both the implicit biblical imaginations that have formed in people, as well as people's experiences in everyday life. Both of these sources need to be focused through the lens of the cross so that people's Christian imaginations grow and are transformed as they decide how to serve in the situation at hand.

23. Luther, "A Brief Instruction on What to Look for and Expect in the Gospels," in Timothy F. Lull, ed., *Martin Luther's Basic Theological Writings* (Minneapolis: Fortress, 1989), 104-11.

24. Ibid., 104-05: "Thus the gospel is and should be nothing else than a chronicle, a story, a narrative about Christ, telling who he is, what he did, said, and suffered — a subject that one describes briefly, another more fully, one this way, another that way. For at its briefest, the gospel is a discourse about Christ, that he is the Son of God and became man for us, that he died and was raised, that he has been established as lord over all things."

Scripture, Christian Imagination, and the Testimony of Experience in Moral Conversation

Ronald W. Duty

> *[W]hen we discern together, our diversity is not about mere individualism, but about the necessary mediation of our constructed cultural and social worlds, which continue to interpret, and be interpreted by, the central narratives and symbols of Christianity.*[1]

The cross of Jesus Christ is the particular event that provides congregations with an image that makes intelligible their common life and the lives of their members.[2] It is the focus of their worship life. It is the focus of Scripture for Christians. Though variously interpreted, the cross shapes the imaginations of the common life shared by congregations; it also shapes the faith experience and imaginations of their members.

If this is true, then Scripture is the *penultimate* source of Christian imagination. The cross is the event that is the ultimate source of our most reliable knowledge about God. Scripture functions as the testimony to this

---

1. Ann O'Hara Graff, "Ecclesial Discernment: Women's Voices, New Voices, and the Revelatory Process," in Mary Ann Hinsdale and Phyllis H. Kaminski, eds., *Women and Theology,* The Annual Publication of the College Theology Society, vol. 40 (Maryknoll, NY: Orbis Books, 1995), 212.

2. H. Richard Niebuhr, *The Meaning of Revelation* (New York: The Macmillan Co., 1960), 69. Paul Ricoeur points out and ponders the significance of this observation in "The Bible and the Imagination," in his *Figuring the Sacred: Religion, Narrative, and Imagination,* trans. David Pellauer, ed. Mark I. Wallace (Minneapolis: Fortress, 1995), 146ff.

event and as a set of interpretations of its significance. In this sense, the cross is the source and Scripture the norm of the church's life. All aspects of that life — liturgy and sacraments, preaching, teaching, devotional practice, service to others, and advocacy for justice on their behalf — derive from and are accountable to the gospel narrative that focuses on the cross.

Reading and hearing the stories and other forms of Scripture, as Paul Ricoeur maintains, allows the imagination to guide interpretation of the text so that people can imagine what it means for their situation.[3] His work helps illuminate the way biblical texts shape the Christian imaginations of their readers and hearers. In this chapter I will first review Ricoeur's work in this area. Then I will look at how two of the congregations who participated in our study process, Grace and Our Savior's, dealt with the issue of homosexuality. These congregations were part of the case study for the work of the Congregational Study Research Team (CSRT). We will note how their experience with homosexuals — or lack of it — helped to influence how they interpreted biblical texts. It will become evident that both the texts and their experiences acted to shape their Christian imaginations in different ways. As we consider the complex interrelationship of Scripture and experience in such a discernment process, I will consider some barriers to using Scripture in moral discernment. I will seek to address the objection that testimony to experience should take precedence over appeals to Scripture in this kind of discernment. Finally, I will reflect on the role of this complex interaction of Scripture and experience in a polycentric and multicultural church. I will pay special attention to the gifts and callings of those who are knowledgeable about Scripture in the moral deliberation of congregations and groups of congregations in a multicultural, polycentric church.

Scripture and Imagination

Ricoeur, along with many of those influenced by him, has helped us better understand how Scripture works to shape Christian imaginations. Attending to the biblical text shows how the imagination is at work in the text to create analogies between those things described in the biblical

3. Ricoeur, "The Bible and the Imagination," 145.

text and things elsewhere in the world.[4] Ricoeur understands the imagination, as a process governed by metaphor, to be both a *rule-governed invention* and a *power of redescribing experience*.[5] Metaphors work by first violating existing rules about relationships between words, sentences, symbols, narratives, and so forth, as they are ordinarily used. Simultaneously, they establish new semantic relationships between them from which new meaning emerges. "Things or ideas which were remote appear now as close," he observes. "To see the like is to see it in spite of and through the different." This new relationship consequently redescribes conventional experiences. We come to *see* something as something different from what we previously saw. When ordinary references to things in language are abolished, we come to have a new and more radical way of looking at things.[6]

Ricoeur shows this metaphorical process at work in the Bible by analyzing the parables of the wicked husbandman and of the sower in his "The Bible and the Imagination."[7] When a parable and the narrative

---

4. Ricoeur, "The Bible and the Imagination," 146, 161; see also Ricoeur, "The Metaphorical Process as Cognition, Imagination, and Feeling," *Critical Inquiry* 5 (1978): 143-59. This insight is not unique to Ricoeur, though he has done the most technical work on how metaphor and analogy work in language and biblical texts. But William F. Lynch also noted the implications of this for theology: "[W]e may roughly and initially describe the analogical as that habit of perception which sees that different levels of being are somehow one and can therefore be associated in the same image, in the same and single act of perception. We lump together [in contrast to the analogical] under the word 'manichaean' all those habits of perception which instinctively dissociate, which dispose levels of being in a relationship of hostility or complete otherness." "Theology and Imagination," *Thought 29,* no. 12 (March 1954), 66, 82. Amos Wilder has also called for a Christian imagination. He insists that the imagination works with metaphors, symbols, and myths that have the ability to engage us at a deep level, though in his book *Theopoetic: Theology and the Religious Imagination* (Philadelphia: Fortress, 1976) he does not, as Ricoeur does, try to show how these function to enlarge or transform our understanding of God or reality. However, Wilder's purpose was to argue for a Christian reengagement with such features of Scripture in contrast to rationalized doctrinal statements and creeds so that a Christian imagination might more fruitfully engage secular experience, symbols, and myths in order to more effectively show how the Christian gospel responds to secular experience and dilemmas.

5. Ricoeur, "The Bible and the Imagination," 144. David Tracy has recognized this to be a key to Ricoeur's philosophical work on metaphor in *The Analogical Imagination: Christian Theology and the Culture of Pluralism* (New York: Crossroad, 1981), 199, n. 96.

6. Ricoeur, "The Metaphorical Process," 147-48, 149-50, 153-54.

7. Ricoeur, "The Bible and the Imagination," 152-160.

within which the parable is told intersect with each other, both become complex metaphors, even though they are not literally or strictly like one another. Although different, their similarities draw them closer together, so that we can then see that they interpret each other. The parable of the wicked husbandmen in Mark 12:1-12 is a case in point (pp. 152-56). The context in which Jesus delivered this parable is the Temple in Jerusalem. In Mark's narrative, the Jewish leaders have a problem concerning the authority by which Jesus is acting — that is, in what they consider a questionable way. The reader of Mark knows that this is occurring during the week of Jesus' crucifixion. The leaders perceive that Jesus' parable is being aimed at them, and Mark tacitly affirms that this is true. The parable both foreshadows Jesus' death on the cross at the instigation of these leaders, and it is interpreted by means of that death to confess Jesus as the Son of God (p. 162). The son in the parable, the heir of the landowner, is killed by the wicked husbandmen. The parable challenges the imagination to see the similarity between the world of the parable and the situation in the Temple: they are parallels of each other despite their obvious differences. This parallel, or likeness, reveals a deeper structure of the world both inside and outside the text: Jesus is the Son sent into the world on his Father's authority to reclaim it for his Father, but he dies on the cross carrying out his mission (pp. 156, 160).[8]

Mark's Gospel increasingly shows recognition of Jesus as the Christ, so that he is finally confessed as such by the centurion at the foot of the cross in the narrative (Mark 15:39). This gradual development helps the readers and hearers come to the same recognition, and then to become capable of the same confession.[9] Ricoeur insists that this happens because of the way the story is written or told, in other words, because of the text itself and the rules by which this kind of metaphorization works.[10] Because

8. See also Ricoeur, "The Metaphorical Process," 153.

9. Ricoeur, "The Bible and the Imagination," 152; see also Ricoeur, "Toward a Hermeneutic of the Idea of Revelation," trans. David Pellauer, in Lewis S. Mudge, ed., *Essays on Biblical Interpretation* (Philadelphia: Fortress, 1980), 108-17. Ricoeur argues that this happens when readers or hearers respond to the gospel's "non-violent appeal."

10. Ricoeur, "The Bible and the Imagination," 161. In his discussion of interpretive narratives using Mark's Gospel as one example, Ricoeur argues the following point extensively: ". . . that the juncture between exegesis and theology, before the work of interpretation applied *to* the text, already functions in the text if this text is a narrative with an interpretive function." "Interpretive Narrative," in Ricoeur, *Figuring the Sacred*, 181.

Scripture works this way in the imagination, Garrett Green argues that the imagination is "the point of divine-human contact," the point where revelation is given as an act of God's grace and where the act of imagination that takes revelation as grace is an act of faith.[11] William Spohn argues that Jesus functions as a paradigmatic figure in Scripture who embodies a moral pattern for Christians, who "move from his story to their new situation by analogical reasoning." Such reasoning helps them discern which features of their situation are religiously or morally significant, how they are to act, and who they are to become.[12]

Christian imagination does more than *see* the world of the text as a possible world.[13] It also *takes* that world as one with hopeful possibilities for the world in which one lives, possibilities on which one may act.[14] Feel-

---

11. Garrett Green, *Imagining God: Theology and the Religious Imagination* (San Francisco: Harper & Row, 1989), 40. Green also asserts that "the anknüpfungspunkt [point of contact] of revelation is therefore the faithful imagination, trust in the images of scripture in the absence of direct vision" (p. 145).

12. William C. Spohn, *What Are They Saying about Scripture and Ethics?* rev. ed. (New York: Paulist Press, 1995), 102.

13. The understanding of imagination as "seeing as" originates with Wittgenstein in his *Philosophical Investigations*, 11, xi. Ricoeur uses this insight in his work on metaphor; see his *The Rule of Metaphor* (Toronto: University of Toronto Press, 1977), 6, 61, 212, and "Metaphorical Process as Cognition, Imagination and Feeling." Wittgenstein's notion of imagination as "seeing as" is reformulated by philosopher Mary Warnock in her *Imagination* (Berkeley: University of California Press, 1976), 182-96.

14. David J. Bryant, *Faith and the Play of Imagination: On the Role of Imagination in Religion,* Studies in American Biblical Hermeneutics 5 (Macon, GA: Mercer University Press, 1989), 115, 118; see also Kathleen R. Fisher, *The Inner Rainbow: The Imagination in Christian Life* (Ramsey, NJ: Paulist Press, 1983), 131. Bryant takes imagination as an active and not merely a passive power: "In sum, imagination is the power of 'taking as' that enables one to be open to the play of dialogue (include the 'dialogue with ourselves' that is thought), whether this is a dialogue with a contemporary text, a tradition, or whatever. I prefer 'taking as' to 'understanding as' because the former more directly suggests the holistic nature of the imagination. Since it emphasizes the active nature of our imaginative encounter with the world, it also underscores the fact that understanding includes a facility, an ability to do something. Imagination could also be defined as attunement to the movement of play, by which we are taken into its movement" (p. 115). Elsewhere he says that ". . . imagination emerges out of the interplay of tradition, subject matter and subjectivity. It is, then, a complex reality containing both receptive and constructive dimensions. . . . In other words, the interplay of tradition, subject matter and subjectivity engages imagination in such a way as to open up, or to disclose, certain possibilities for life-in-the-world. And these disclosures are given support, or rendered questionable, through their concrete actualizations in life"

ing helps to enable this *taking as*. Ricoeur maintains that feeling accompanies and completes imagination in representing the new similarity. When what is imagined by a text is felt, as well as seen, by us readers or hearers, feeling makes this thought ours and includes us in the process as knowing subjects. Just as the imagination in the text depicts new relationships between and among things, it also structures a particular mood through which we feel. Ricoeur argues that the operation of poetic feeling elicited by the text involves: (a) a suspension of the emotions of everyday life about certain things, and (b) a transformation of them so that we find ourselves in the world attuned to aspects of reality not referred to by the way ordinary language is commonly used. We begin to see in a new way in accordance with the new reality disclosed by the text. This process, he maintains, has a structure analogous to that of the cognitive and imaginative aspects of the metaphorical process described above.[15] Spohn argues that this process also works to create moral feelings that engender dispositions to act. "Scripture, through a gradual reflection and assimilation in faith, can engender a distinctive set of affections correlative to its story, which disposes the agent to act in distinctive ways. . . ."[16]

At the same time that Mark's Gospel shows increasing recognition of Jesus as Christ, Ricoeur argues that puzzling "enigma expressions" in the text, such as "kingdom of God," are described in extravagant ways to imply a utopia beyond the workings that are characteristic of the ordinary world of the text.[17] This utopia is also reflected in elements of the parables, such as the landowner who sends his son after the servants were killed, or the sowing that yields thirty-, sixty-, or even a hundredfold. In presenting the world of the text, Scripture does not take for granted the world of either its original or its later audiences. Instead, it redescribes them by its metaphoric nature. Simultaneously, it also holds open a possible world we

---

(p. 118). Fisher emphasizes the hope that seeing the world as the text portrays it will lead to action: "Seeing alternatives to the present makes hope possible. Imagination opens up personal and communal possibilities for action" (p. 131). Ricoeur himself understands "'being-as' to be the correlate of 'seeing-as,'" and he seems to suggest that this is something like what Bryant refers to as "taking as" (*Time and Narrative*, vol. 1, trans. Kathleen McLaughlin and David Pellauer [Chicago: University of Chicago Press, 1984], 80).

15. Ricoeur, "Metaphorical Process as Cognition, Imagination, and Feeling," 153-54, 159.

16. Spohn, *What Are They Saying about Scripture and Ethics?* 110.

17. Ricoeur, "The Bible and the Imagination," 165.

might inhabit beyond the one we do inhabit.[18] It proposes a new world: a kingdom of God, a new covenant.

These figures of language express some of our deepest human hopes in the face of life's limits. They help generate our imagination about the text to wonder about how it is similar to, or dissimilar from, the world in which we live. They also help us think about the implications of that world of the text and the way it proposes for living the Christian life in the world today in our particular circumstances.[19] There are, of course, similar implications to ponder together about our common life together. Using Karl Mannheim's distinction between "ideology" and "utopia," Ricoeur argues that imagination may have two possible functions. On the one hand, it can serve as either an ideological or conservative function that aims at preserving or restoring an order that is passing (or at least adapting its essential features to new historical circumstances). On the other hand, the imagination may have a utopian function of projecting a world or a way of being in it that is beyond what is presently experienced but perhaps fervently hoped for.[20] Christians in their deliberations may decide together to act in such a

18. In his essay "The Language of Faith," Ricoeur argues for the use of the language of faith and the Bible precisely in order to give ourselves some distance from the everyday world we do inhabit so that we might have a language with which to question its problematic aspects, and to envision possibilities imagined by God in the word God speaks to humanity in Scripture. Charles E. Reagan and David Stewart, eds., *The Philosophy of Paul Ricoeur* (Boston: Beacon Press, 1978), 223-38.

19. Ricoeur, "The Bible and the Imagination," 165-66; "The Image of God and the Epic of Man," in Ricoeur, *History and Truth,* ed. and trans. Charles A. Kelbley (Evanston, IL: Northwestern University Press, 1965), 126-28; "Metaphorical Process as Cognition, Imagination, and Feeling," 154-55; and "Appropriation," in Ricoeur, *Hermeneutics and the Human Sciences: Essays on Language, Action and Interpretation,* ed. and trans. John B. Thompson (Cambridge, UK: Cambridge University Press, 1981), 185, 192. See also Ricoeur, *Time and Narrative,* vol. 1, 81.

20. Ricoeur, *Lectures on Ideology and Utopia,* ed. George H. Taylor (New York: Columbia University Press, 1986). Ricoeur even calls these two functions two kinds of imagination at one point: "My presupposition . . . is that imagination works in two different ways. On the one hand, imagination may function to preserve an order. In this case the function of imagination is to stage a process of identification that mirrors that order. Imagination has the appearance here of a picture. On the other hand, though, imagination may have a disruptive function; it may work as a breakthrough. Its image in this case is productive, an imagining of something else, the elsewhere. In each of its three roles ideology represents the first kind of imagination; it has the function of preservation, of conservation. Utopia, in contrast, represents the second kind of imagination; it is always the glance from no-

way as to approximate the world proposed by the text, to try to bring it into being in various ways.

Imagining Homosexuals as Christians: A Contrast of Two Congregations

It is not always Scripture alone that redescribes our reality so that we can reimagine it. Sometimes Scripture is aided in this task by the way we *experience reality*. Evidence suggests that the experience of homosexuals as Christians affects the imaginations of congregations about them and also about how Scripture pertains to them. Our two pilot-project congregations differed in their experiences with homosexuals and their stories. This difference in *experience* had a rather marked influence on how they reacted to what the ELCA draft statement on human sexuality said about homosexuals, as well as how they reacted to media reports of public conflict in ELCA congregations over the issue of homosexuality. More to our point here, this difference in experience affected their ability to imagine homosexuals as Christians and colored how they interpreted Scripture and church tradition with respect to homosexuals. When their experience helped them *imagine* homosexuals as Christians, Scripture was able to interact with that experience to redescribe that reality. It not only redefines who could be a child of God baptized in the name of Christ; it also frames both what it means to be a Lutheran in relationship to homosexuals and what it means to be a Lutheran congregation.

As the pastor of the Holy Cross congregation noted, rural culture does not feature open discussion of sexuality: this is because, simply by default, heterosexual experience heavily informs rural culture and rural people's exercise of judgment. Forms of sexuality other than heterosexual are seen to be threatening and are not openly tolerated. That pastor observed that rural congregants' lack of experience with homosexuals prevented many of them from being "able to put a face" on the subject: "Experience in these areas is very limited . . . out here."

---

where. . . . [It projects] itself aus — outside, nowhere — in this movement of transcendence . . ." (265-66). See also his comments in "Imagination in Discourse and Action," *Analecta Husserliana*, vol. 7 (1978): 15-22. Ricoeur's work on ideology and utopia is a further analysis and reflection on the topic of Karl Mannheim's classic sociological work *Ideology and Utopia: An Introduction to the Sociology of Knowledge*, trans. Louis Wirth and Edward Shils (New York: Harcourt, Brace & World, Inc., 1936).

In the Grace congregation, this inability to put a face on homosexuality, and the fact that personal relationships with homosexuals are — as a practical matter — unimaginable, markedly affects how Scripture informs their conversation. One younger member commented:

> In other words, they would have a very difficult time imagining or even dealing with [homosexuals]. And I think my in-laws are the same way. . . . In fact, there are people my age that are this way, that [if you asked them,] 'What would you do if your son was a homosexual?' well, the answer to that is, that would not happen . . . or that cannot happen.

Consequently, it was difficult for the members of Grace to imagine homosexuals as Christians and to consider a wide range of Scripture to be applicable to them as Christians. The Scripture that was usually brought into Grace's conversation came from people's own knowledge of the Bible. This included the knowledge of laypeople who were recognized as biblically skilled, and from the biblical sources used in the ELCA's sexuality draft, rather than from deliberate Bible study. Discussion focused on the familiar passages that are usually cited on this subject — those commonly interpreted to view homosexuality as sinful. Grace's intern pastor brought other passages of Scripture into the conversation, which tended to introduce other perspectives. But they also created tension.

Diverse biblical perspectives could not overcome the lack of experience with homosexuals as Christians. Neither did these other biblical perspectives immediately alter the Christian imaginations or views of most of Grace's members about homosexuality. Their views had been formed by Scripture passages with which they were more familiar. For many of them, personal experience and church tradition coincided.[21] Well-publicized homosexual challenges to church policy regarding homosexual clergy in California created what the pastor called "paranoia" at Grace about a movement "to change the world."[22] This sense of threat was intensely personal for some people at Grace. One member expressed it this way:

---

21. The intern observed: "The church tradition and people's personal faith experience in this church pretty well went together. . . . I mean, what goes on in the church tradition is probably pretty much the [same as] the personal. . . . They're not going to be too radically different at church."

22. In 1990, First United Lutheran and St. Francis Lutheran churches of San Francisco ordained three homosexuals to the ministry in violation of the ELCA policy barring practic-

And that affects the experience of the faithful, because my church is the center of my faith, where I worship, you know, and if something . . . like this might injure that place, then I look for a different place.

And Grace's pastor added:

They saw it as very threatening. Very threatening, because not only was it threatening to the church . . . but they saw it as a threat to the very social fabric that holds the church together. So it was a pretty explosive topic.

Because they did not have any firsthand experience with homosexuals or did not know that church experience and tradition they might have in common with them, many of the people of Grace were not able, at that time, to use their understanding of the cross as transcending people's differences.[23] They were unable to see how Christ might be leading them through the conflict, and they were experiencing a sense of threat about differences in sexual orientation and behavior. Neither were they able to use their understanding of the cross to see the relationship of those differences to church tradition. At the same time, they did know that listening to those with different experiences was important. Asked what makes for a safe place for moral conversation, the pastor responded thoughtfully. "Trust in a shared tradition [and] willingness to listen to different experiences." They had not had an opportunity to put a face on homosexuality and to listen to a homosexual person's experiences. Yet they could begin to imagine how they might be able to do so if they had

---

ing homosexuals from ordained ministry. On January 23, 1993, Jeff R. Johnson was installed as pastor of First United Lutheran after having served as assistant pastor since his ordination in 1990. Two lesbians, Ruth Frost and Phyllis Zillhart, were also ordained. Rev. Lyle G. Miller, Bishop of the Sierra Pacific Synod, refused to sign letters of call for them because the three would not agree to be celibate. Both congregations were expelled from the ELCA in 1996 after a five-year suspension during which they did not come into compliance with ELCA policy. See *The Lutheran* 42 (Mar. 1993: 38; Dec. 1995: 45; Jan. 1996: 34; Feb. 1996). Our research with the congregations in this study was conducted largely in 1994.

23. Of course, gay sons and lesbian daughters are born into rural families and grow up in rural churches and communities just as they do in urban ones. And some homosexual pastors serve rural congregations. The unimaginable actually does happen to rural people. But the cultural factors noted above make it far less likely that these persons would "come out" publicly to their families, congregations, or communities about their sexual orientations in the way that many of their urban counterparts eventually do.

enough common experience and church tradition with homosexuals. One member remarked:

> We would let anyone who was a homosexual come into this church and worship and do anything if they did not flaunt it. If they would not even say anything. If they did not make this the issue. [If] they're coming here to enrich their Christian faith and not to show off that they're homosexual, it wouldn't bother anyone in the congregation.

This comment surely reflects a rural culture's norm against making sexuality a public matter of discussion. It tends to affirm in practice the prevailing heterosexual assumptions of this culture, and it implicitly grants to homosexuals an acknowledgment that they might conceivably have a place at Grace. This member's comment seems to imply that a real, acknowledged experience with homosexuals who shared their own Christian tradition and personal faith experience at Grace might prepare them to listen to the experience of homosexuals. It prepared them for a change in their Christian imaginations about homosexuality, which the other passages of Scripture that the intern was bringing into the conversation might help them make:

> If we had seen those [who didn't want to flaunt it] first, we would have found that there are some out there who don't want to make this the issue, who want to make the fact that they're a child of God the issue. But it was . . . the protesters and the activists who we heard about. And so that [influenced our reaction].

Such experience of homosexuals as Christians might also enable them to see how the cross actually transcends their differences. It might help them discern how Christ could lead them all through the conflict over the differences that still might divide them. The experience of seeing homosexuals as Christians might open up a world that includes them all together as members of Grace Lutheran.

Personal and corporate experience with homosexuals, by contrast, did help to play this role at Our Savior's. Members there talked about how personal experiences had changed their view. Matters such as divorce, abuse, alcoholism, and the practice of elderly widows and widowers cohabiting for financial reasons had changed their attitudes and made them less judgmental. They also noted how these experiences had changed the way people affected by these things were ministered to in congregations. When they were able to put a face on homosexuality, they could open up to similar changes in views about homosexuals. One member expressed the following:

> The congregation was talking about homosexuality, and someone shared a very touching story about a young man who committed suicide, and it was thought it was because of [his] homosexuality. And that was a very quiet moment, and there was no way to continue the conversation at that point.

Some members of the congregation had a face-to-face encounter with a Lutheran pastor who is the father of a gay Christian man, and this provided another opportunity to reexamine attitudes and behavior.

> [1st member]: I think the people listened to the person who had the gay son, and there were some people [for whom] that really was quite an achievement, and very enlightening to a lot of people.
> [2nd member]: Very enlightening! Because all of a sudden the issue had a face and a name.

When the issue has a face and a name, and when congregation members remember how they have experienced various hard things in life or made the "wrong" choices, those at Our Savior's were less inclined to be summarily judgmental. They were also open to reexamining their own attitudes, wrestling with the variety and complexity of Scripture, and having their Christian imaginations changed by the interaction of experience and the reading of Scripture.

> Actually, if anything, in this case Scripture functioned as grace and forgiveness. So that, if Scripture [is normative], I suppose it would be that norm is that God is a forgiving and gracious God!

The people of Our Savior's were able to see their common identity in Christ regardless of sexual orientation through the cross.

> We had talked about our identity with Christ. The crucified and risen one is our primary [identity], and that is what we all share and that is the basis for which we gather. . . .

The Grace and Our Savior's congregations shared a common cultural and rural context. Both had biblically knowledgeable laypeople helping them wrestle with the issue of homosexuality and the church. Direct experience with homosexuals at Our Savior's — or being able to put a face and a name with a homosexual Christian — interacted with the richness of the biblical witness to elicit a different discernment about homosexuals than was the case at Grace. At the time of these deliberations, people at Grace heard the norm and promise of Scripture differently than did the congregation of Our Savior's. At the latter, passages expressing the accusation of the Law seemed far less important than such passages were at Grace.[24] Had the people of Grace had the opportunity to deliberate with those of Our Savior's and to hear about the latter group's experience with homosexuals, they might have discerned differently. Later, a member of the Grace congregation admitted as much: he observed that, had his congregation been aware that the issue for some homosexuals was simple acknowledgment and acceptance as a child of God, their discernment might have been closer to that of Our Savior's congregation.

Christian Imaginations for Deliberation: Scripture and Testimony to Experience

While experience may help people interpret Scripture, form Christian imaginations, and may aid moral deliberation, it is no substitute for Scripture. Scripture is the primary norm for forming Christian imaginations and informing Christian moral deliberation and discernment. But there are barriers to using Scripture in faith-based moral deliberation for which the formation of Christian imagination through Scripture prepares Christians in the ELCA. The first of these, as we have already noted, is the relative lack of reading of Scripture among ELCA laypeople, and the lack of intimate familiarity with Scripture. Contact with Scripture among ELCA laity outside of worship is spotty indeed. A "Lutherans Say" survey

---

24. The reluctance of some people at Our Savior's church to imagine that the accusation of the Law might actually apply to certain forms of homosexual behavior is, of course, as problematic as the inability of some people at Grace to imagine that homosexuals might actually be Christians who are given forgiveness of sins and salvation by grace through faith in Jesus Christ. In the Lutheran tradition, Christians are called upon to rightly discern both Law and Gospel.

in the 1990s, which dealt with the personal concerns of ELCA members, indicated that 24 percent of ELCA lay members *had not read the Bible at all* during the year before the survey; of the 76 percent who had read it, only about half of them had read it *at least once a week.*[25] In a similar survey about a year later, ELCA laity reported that only about one-third of them read the Bible *on their own* at least once a week, while only 28 percent had read or *discussed the Bible with friends or family* at least once a week.[26]

Little wonder, then, that our earlier research reported relatively low levels of the spontaneous use of Scripture in congregational discussions of moral matters. Only a modest number of ELCA laity are likely to be familiar enough with Scripture to be competent and spontaneous users of it in moral conversation, and they are more likely than others to have mature Christian moral imaginations formed by a knowledge of Scripture. Some others will be familiar with certain passages. This was the case at Holy Cross Lutheran regarding passages cited in the ELCA draft on sexuality, where the pastor observed:

> Most were familiar with particular passages and some were less familiar with the context and the connections between passages. They might have known the passage, but not the connections that were being made.

Often their familiarity with the Scripture passages was because the passages supported their own point of view on a moral matter. One team member from Grace Lutheran observed:

> [They are] familiar with the ones that support their view. I mean, everyone knows what Paul has to say about homosexuals in the Epistles and maybe about what the laws of Leviticus in the Old Testament say, but talk about some of the other [texts] in between. . . .

Furthermore, many people's confidence in the use of Scripture is not high. Often people cannot think of particular passages by themselves, and when

25. Kenneth W. Inskeep, "*LUTHERANS SAY . . . 3:* The Quality of Life, Religious Traditionalism and Concerns for the Decade" (Chicago: ELCA Office for Research, Planning and Evaluation, Mar. 1, 1990), Appendix 1, 6.

26. "*LUTHERANS SAY . . . 5*" (Chicago: ELCA Office for Research, Planning and Evaluation, June 1991), Frequencies, 2.

they can, they are generally unfamiliar with the context of those passages, or how they might be connected with others. Not surprisingly, participants in organized efforts to have moral conversation do not prepare in advance by reviewing relevant biblical passages or their contexts. They often come in cold, and thus they need to rely on either personal guides — that is, biblically knowledgeable people — or textual guides, such as a section on the scriptural background of an issue in the text of a social statement.

For these reasons, using Scripture in moral conversation often requires careful preparation. Congregations figured out various ways to do this. If prepared materials were available, leaders made the point that participants needed to review the Scripture passages cited in them. Or they invited people on various sides of an issue to make presentations in which they used biblical materials in support of an argument. One could also imagine that pastors or laity could research relevant biblical background for the group. The pastor of Holy Cross, for instance, told of how he attempted to broaden the scriptural perspective on a certain topic:

> I broadened the scriptural base . . . and [I] would use other passages, particularly to discuss how [Scripture could be used to broaden our] understanding, to discussions about [how it is] a living word . . . how interpretation and application have changed over the years. How passages that were once thought to be very self-evident have changed. Discussion, too, about . . . how you can take all sorts of laws from the Old Testament that people are willing . . . to quote and say, "This is a hierarchy of law. . . ." And yet they extract one verse regarding the [subject] from [its context] . . . . [We need] to point out that this verse that they're quoting is in the context of a whole bunch of other laws . . . in many cases that we don't adhere to anymore. And how does that impact how we look at that?

However, even when there is preparation, it is not necessarily sufficient to encourage people to use Scripture. The pastor of Our Savior's Lutheran reported that, even after a presentation on the use of Scripture and the theology of the cross, a later small-group discussion of the ELCA draft on human sexuality ignored Scripture:

> I would certainly say that in most of the small groups, Scripture was not referred to — wasn't mentioned. [The subject] was experience and culture.

146

Upon reflection, it seems clear that any preparation that pastors and laity may make to encourage the use of Scripture needs to be very carefully thought out. When laity lack confidence in their use of Scripture, some ways of preparing people to use it responsibly may actually backfire. This can discourage people from trying to use it by making them feel even more incompetent. Parenthetically, we should acknowledge that Scripture might not be directly relevant to all topics of moral conversation. It is difficult to imagine, for example, what passages one would bring to bear on a discussion of how fitting it would be for a congregation to continue its tradition of a banquet for graduating high school seniors without stretching the credibility of either Scripture or the conversation itself too far.[27] Some issues may also be of relatively little importance to a congregation to bother with Scripture. These matters may be more a question of good order.

When people do use Scripture in moral conversation, they use it in various ways. One way is to use it literally, quoting isolated passages for the plain sense of the text. This varied in style and purpose. One method was simple and straightforward, which the pastor of Holy Cross described in our interview.

> I think that, as we walked our way through the [sexuality] study, the study was using Scripture a great deal. So we used that as a reference.

However, another literal use of passages was more self-interested. This is the use of what might be called "Bible bullets": quoting passages backing the user's point of view. People use these "bullets" in exchanges with an intent to kill any reply from another perspective, and thus to cut off possible discussion involving different points of view. A team member of Our Savior's described it this way:

> Usually it was used in a line of defense. When they wanted to defend something they had said, they would quote Scripture.

27. Scripture is one *aspect* of church tradition in this model, but it is by no means all there is to church tradition. Besides Scripture, these traditions include the relevant ecumenical and denominational confessions, the tradition of Christian theology, as well as traditions of liturgical practices, hymnody, styles of piety, forms of preaching, denominational as well as congregational histories and practices (or particular segments of those histories and practices in the vivid memories of the living members). These aspects of tradition would carry varying weights on different issues, about which the participants in the moral conversation would have to make judgments in the particular matter under discussion.

And from Grace, a team member made this observation:

> . . . it's also obvious that some people in this group were not here to discuss the moral issue but to state their stand without any intention to change their thinking.

Some people, however, were able to give a nuanced discussion of passages in their context, which recognized the diversity of Scripture. These people could be either conservatives or liberals on an issue. Here is how members of Our Savior's described someone known to be conservative on an issue:

> Howard was using Scripture, of course!
>
> Actually, he used it very well.
>
> Yes, he did, very gently.
>
> If anyone, you would think he would use Scripture as a bazooka, and yet he used it quite well.
>
> And we had warned people not to get into it.
>
> But when he pulled it out, he gave a good reason and [a] fairly well-developed statement of his views using Scripture — and not just quoting laws, but using a more extended and metaphoric and fuller understanding of passages. Actually, I felt, shucks, of all the people gathered here, Howard is one person who had spent some time in saying, "How does Scripture inform?" He had done that fairly intelligently.
>
> [Interviewer]: So what would you say about your experience with him given the format of using the model to shape the discussion, or how he used Scripture?
>
> Yes, in the sense that he did not use it to blast somebody out of the water. I think it caused him to be a little more deliberative and reasoned in how he used Scripture, rather than just pulling out a quote to silence the group.

As people seek to discern God's Word in Scripture together, they bring with them various levels of familiarity with Scripture, differing levels of confidence in their ability to use Scripture, and different styles of sophistication in the practice of interpreting Scripture. This variance presents problems for seeking to discern through Scripture. Scholars do not understand these difficulties well, and the research just barely begins to clarify the issue. How, for example, can those with little exposure to the Bible be encouraged to begin to interpret it without being shamed by those whose familiarity is greater? How can the insights of the former be honored at the same time one honors those of the latter? How can those whose approach to Scripture is straightforward and literal be put in sustained fruitful conversation with the insights of those whose approach is more contextual?

In one important sense, rather than having merely a variety of difficulties, the church may also have a variety of gifts. Those having little familiarity with Scripture may be able to approach it with fresher eyes and thus see things that those who have built up layers of preconceptions over the years of their study may have trouble seeing. One who approaches a passage with a plain sense and one who has a nuanced contextual knowledge may each be able to enhance the discernment of the other. But learning to use these gifts for the common good in moral discernment is not easy.

People unfamiliar with Scripture are less likely to have Christian imaginations, in contrast to those whose imaginations are formed by the richness of the stories, poetry, symbolism, wisdom sayings, or imagery of Scripture.[28] They may be less able to participate in moral deliberation in which Scripture plays a prominent role. They may also find such deliberation to be either irrelevant or incomprehensible. Instead, they may prefer to appeal to the experience of the faithful, or to everyday American culture, as was common among some participants in our pilot-project congregations. Or they may lack confidence in the face of knowledgeable laity or clergy — at least those they perceive to be more competent. Finally, in the extreme, they may feel embarrassment or even shame for their lack of familiarity with Scripture.

Second, those unfamiliar with Scripture may feel shut out of those parts of a process of deliberation that are heavily reliant on biblical liter-

---

28. For a lament on this fact and a proposal for the Christian catechumenate to recover knowledge of Scripture, see L. Gregory Jones, "The Word That Journeys with Us: Bible, Character Formation, and Christian Community," *Theology Today* 55, no. 1 (Apr. 1998): 69-76. For discussions of how various genres of biblical texts shape Christian imaginations beyond the example of the Gospel narrative and parable discussed above, see Paul Ricoeur, "Toward a Hermeneutic of the Idea of Revelation," 73-118, and "Biblical Time," in *Figuring the Sacred*, 167-80.

acy. They may not think that they have something to contribute to the conversation out of their Christian imaginations formed from experiences other than reading Scripture. The other side of the coin is that more competent users of Scripture may tend to dismiss less competent users of Scripture from the conversation — or even assume that the latter lack a genuine Christian imagination.

Similar concerns about the requirements, rules, and expectations in secular processes of political deliberation in the United States have led political theorist Lynn Sanders to propose a moratorium on political deliberation.[29] She believes that political deliberation between unequals in the United States is, as a practical matter, now impossible. This is because marginalized people — that is, people from lower-middle-class or poor and minority backgrounds — lack the skills for upper-middle-class rules of deliberation requiring selfless, emotionally temperate, reasoned, universal arguments. Even when they are skilled in these forms and rules of deliberation, their lower "epistemological authority," as she calls it, makes them less likely to be listened to and taken seriously by others with more upper-middle-class backgrounds (pp. 348-49). Examples of this phenomenon in the deliberations between even upper-middle-class men and women are abundant in feminist discourse.

Sanders argues instead for diverse *testimony* to bring the experiences of marginalized people into public conversation. She argues that the exchange of testimony to these experiences would bring them to the attention of those who would otherwise not be exposed to these experiences — or who might otherwise dismiss them. Testimony, in her view, allows marginalized people to contribute important information and perspective to public conversation without necessarily being skilled in the practice of upper-middle-class political deliberation. Exchanging testimony, she argues, might be a model that allows for the expression of different perspectives rather than seeking what is common; and she advocates this model of exchanging testimony about differing experience as a better way to achieve mutual respect in democratic discussion. In her view, "the contrast between the pursuit of commonality, and the simpler aim to include and represent a fuller range of critical voices, is at the core of the difference between deliberation and testimony" (pp. 350, 371). She also assumes that

29. Lynn M. Sanders, "Against Deliberation," *Political Theory* 25, no. 3 (June 1997): 347-76.

those who are so skilled in deliberation and are accustomed to making policy should, from a moral point of view, be obligated to take such testimony into account:

> When the perspectives of some citizens are systematically suppressed in public discourse, then democratic politics should aim simply and first to ensure the expression of those excluded perspectives. Instead of aiming for a common discussion, democrats might adopt a more fundamental goal: to try to ensure that those who are usually left out of public discussion learn to speak whether their perspectives are common or not, and those who usually dominate learn to hear the perspectives of others (pp. 372-73).

While it is not my concern to evaluate Sanders's argument as it concerns politics, I want to assess its implications for a faith-based moral deliberation process such as the one used by congregations in this study. I am noting an analogy between middle-class rules of political deliberation and the process of faith-based moral deliberation used in this study, where the use of Scripture is one of the main sources from which conversation proceeds.[30] And I am asking whether a lack of familiarity with Scripture by many means that a process of faith-based moral deliberation that significantly involves Scripture is unworkable, and perhaps discriminatory, in the same way that Sanders believes democratic deliberation is discriminatory toward the socially marginalized, who are unskilled in upper-middle-class processes of political deliberation. Should a Scripture-based process of moral deliberation be replaced by one that places more emphasis on testimony to personal experience?

---

30. That this is not a trivial analogy is shown, perhaps, by the struggle that the other developers of this process and I went through in deciding how to refer to this process and what to call it. For our largely rural congregations (and with urban, blue-collar, poor, and multicultural congregations also in mind), we made a conscious decision to drop the term "moral deliberation" when advertising the process and when training leadership teams from congregations. We also tended not to use this term in the training material itself. We have come to believe that it reflects a class and cultural bias from which we wish to dissociate the process. Instead of referring to it as a process of "moral deliberation," we refer to it in less class- and culture-bound terms as a process for "talking, deciding, and acting as Christian community." Obviously, though, the discussion in this article involves more than names and descriptions. For what is at stake goes beyond the vocabulary describing this process to the very nature of the process itself.

In adopting the term "testimony" from evangelical Christian rhetoric, Sanders quite properly recognizes the importance of experience to community discussion and decision-making. The process of moral deliberation used by congregations in this study includes experience as one of the three main sources for conversation: that is, it has testimony to experience built into it. As we have seen, the natural tendency of people in most of these congregations was to speak from experience. Even so, one might argue that, because Scripture and church tradition together comprise one of the other three sources of conversation, testimony to experience might be *epistemologically disadvantaged* talk. In fact, this may sometimes be the case in Christian moral deliberation. But this is often not because upper-middle-class Christians impose ways of dealing with Scripture on the conversation. Instead, it may happen because people in general — of various classes or cultural background — often use Scripture texts as "Bible bullets." In effect, to mix metaphors, they play Scripture as if it were a trump card rather than allowing the diversity and richness of Scripture to open up the play of the discussion. Like the ladies of First Lutheran, people may prefer to appeal to their pastor as an expert on biblical interpretation rather than open interpretation up to the whole community of faith and wrestle with the diversity of interpretations that might result.

Testimony to experience is a valid source of conversation that can contribute to mutual respect and can enhance the range of information relevant to the conversation. However, testimony to experience, like references to the Bible, should not be used as a trump card to close off discussion.[31] Succumbing to the temptations to use experience as a trump card, or to accept experience uncritically, is making the sources of conversation other than experience epistemologically disadvantaged. Since people offer testimony to convince others of "facts" that they allege to be important — that is, to prove something — we should not accept that testimony uncritically. Testimony, including testimony to religious experience and testimony about God, needs to be interpreted and judged.[32] Testing appeals to experience is like using a reflective equilibrium in which one tries to fit various

---

31. Paul Lauritzen, "Ethics and Experience: The Case of the Curious Response," *The Hastings Center Report* 26, no. 1 (1996): 6-7. See also Paul Ricoeur, "The Hermeneutics of Testimony," in Lewis S. Mudge, ed., *Essays on Biblical Interpretation,* trans. David Stewart and Charles E. Reagan (Philadelphia: Fortress, 1980), 123-29.

32. Ricoeur, "The Hermeneutics of Testimony," 145-46; see also Lauritzen, "Ethics and Experience," 8-14.

convictions into a coherent scheme, granting each one an initial credibility. For example, one would look for narratives in the testimony that are consistent with credible understandings about people. If there is inconsistency there, one might judge a particular appeal to experience to be wrong.

In one critically important respect, Scripture is epistemologically advantaged in the church's life, including in its faith-based moral deliberation. It is the "authoritative source and norm of the Church's proclamation, faith and life."[33] We need to take Scripture into account in all aspects of its life for it to function as that source and norm. It cannot function in the church without also being a norm for the experience of its members' lives. This means that it is both a norm that is a standard of judgment of their experience, shaping their character and the character of their Christian communities, and a promise of God's vision of their preferred future.

To be the source of the church's life in the present, the story of grace and redemption through Jesus Christ needs to function as life-giving in the present. But it also needs to have an eye for the future of the church and the world. At the very least, we should not use it in such a way as to intimidate those faithful Christians less familiar with that story. Nor should we use it to make their experience epistemologically disadvantaged; it may, in fact, also be an experience of the Spirit's working in their midst. Scripture becomes a source of the church's life when it is used to cast light on the experience of the faithful, to interpret that experience, and in turn to be interpreted by it. Moreover, Scripture becomes a source of the church's life when it actually shapes the way our imaginations see our experience, and it shapes our ability to discern how God is active in our experience and our social and cultural world.

Therefore, the objection to using Scripture in faith-based moral deliberation cannot hold. Nor does an analogy hold between middle-class norms of deliberation and the use of Scripture in moral deliberation. The one is a set of rules for a process; the other is one source among others from which moral deliberation proceeds. Although one may insist that only trained experts are entitled to use Scripture, using Scripture should not be completely defined by these rules. To do so would, de facto, privi-

---

33. "This church accepts the canonical Scriptures of the Old and New Testaments as the inspired Word of God and the authoritative source and norm of its proclamation, faith, and life." *Constitution, Bylaws, and Continuing Resolutions of the Evangelical Lutheran Church in America,* 2.03 (Chicago: ELCA, rev. Aug. 20, 1997), 19.

lege the rules and processes for exegesis that pastors learn in seminary. Such exegetical rules may help inform the conversation, but interpretation according to other schemes is also allowed. One of these is to look at Scripture in light of the experience of those participating in the conversation.

Discernment through Scripture and Experience in a Polycentric, Multicultural Church

The experience of faithful Christians and Christian communities varies, precisely in terms of how Scripture casts light on experience, how it speaks a life-giving word, and how it is appropriated. It varies with respect to such factors as the setting of the audience, the social location of the hearers in that setting, and factors such as gender or sexual orientation, race, or ethnicity. The culture within which these settings and social locations occur also plays an important role and is another source from which one carries on conversation.

The experience of the faithful is also a major locus where God's action or Christian responsibility may be discerned in the present. Theologian Ann O'Hara Graff has explored the importance of experience for the discernment of the church. Indeed, for her, "experience is our necessary and best starting point for recognizing revelation and practicing discernment."[34] Experience, of course, is not experience in general, but is particular to individuals and groups in their own circumstances. Nor is experience only limited to empirical sensory experience.[35] God's word is heard as speaking to people in particular circumstances, "'in, with and under' its empirical elements," as Peter Berger says of God's presence in the world.[36]

---

34. Graff, "Ecclesial Discernment," 203.

35. It may also include, according to David Tracy, "the primordial, pervasive experience of the self as a self: active, in process, feeling, embodied, intrinsically social, radically related to all reality," as well as "feeling, mood, body awareness, time-space awareness," and relationships with others. And it may also include both negative limit experiences (such as anxiety, guilt, death) and positive limit experiences (fundamental trust in the whole of reality), or revelatory experiences of manifestation and proclamation within the church. See David Tracy, "The Particularity and Universality of Christian Revelation," in his *On Naming the Present: God, Hermeneutics, and the Church* (Maryknoll, NY: Orbis, 1994), 112-14.

36. Peter L. Berger, "Protestantism and the Quest for Certainty," *The Christian Century*, Aug. 20–Sept. 2, 1998, 793.

God's word to Israel through the prophet Elijah during the time of Ahab and Jezebel was different from God's word to Israel in exile in Babylon through Second Isaiah. Although God's intention by way of his promises to the patriarchs was for Israel to be a light to the nations, God's word in Hebrew Scripture was initially, though not exclusively, a word to Israel. The law of God concerning the eating of clean and unclean things was addressed to Israel as a people set apart. But when opportunity arose to share the gospel of Christ with the gentiles, God told Peter in a dream to kill and eat unclean things as a way of preparing him to receive the friends of the centurion Cornelius, so that they, in turn, might bring Peter to Cornelius to proclaim the gospel (Acts 10:1-48).[37]

"If the revelation of God is disclosed in and through our experience," Graff argues, "it must be within the specific experience we have as culturally, historically, socially located people."[38] Hearing and reading Scripture are common, or nearly so, to Christians. Even if they seldom read Scripture, Christians who worship at least occasionally hear the weekly lessons and the language and imagery of Scripture in liturgy, hymns, and prayers. They appropriate Scripture in light of their experience "in order to name the sacred in our midst" (p. 208). Christians in different circumstances may understand and appropriate that word differently — as a word spoken to them in their contexts. What we find is that Scripture gives life in setting after setting, but not always in the same way.

A process of discernment is required that is simultaneously communal and conversational. Such a discernment process, Graff suggests, "would start with conversation about the experience of the situations and the power of the symbol/narrative within them" (p. 209). As illustrated in her quote at the beginning of this essay, she observes that experience of the situations and the symbol or narrative would be *mutually interpreting*. Thus, for Graff, experience may be the best starting point, but it is not the only important element in the process of discernment. Nor is it the be-all and end-all of discernment. Scripture, as the source and norm of the church's life, needs to play a prominent role. The Christian imaginations of the participants in the discernment conversation will be formed or reformed by this interaction between their experience and Scripture:

37. For an interpretation of this passage, see Luke Timothy Johnson, *Scripture and Discernment*, 91-96.

38. Graff, "Ecclesial Discernment," 205.

through this interaction Scripture gives life in a new setting. And the participants are able to judge whether their witness "is in conformity with the original apostolic witness."[39]

The important issue that further interests Graff about discernment is how this diversity of Christian imagination and interpretation could be *mediated* in a mutually accountable way, that is, a way that is ultimately accountable to Scripture and common Christian confessions, "in order that we might affirm together the event of Jesus the Christ and his good news in our midst" (p. 208). One can catch a glimpse of why this may be both needed and helpful in the conversations at Grace and Our Savior's congregations about homosexuality and Christian faith. These congregations did not hold conversations with each other about the issue; thus they neither recognized the experience and insights of the other, nor were they accountable to each other for their views. It should be noted that this situation is fairly common throughout the ELCA on this issue, even though the written and phone response to the draft document received at the ELCA churchwide offices was huge by historical standards.

For Graff, the need for mediated, mutual accountability in interpretation entails a truly polycentric church. Such a church would have corresponding institutionalized practices for mutual discernment that would include as full participants all those who otherwise would be regarded as marginal (pp. 209-10).[40] Fleshing this vision out somewhat, she says:

> I would like to see the realization of the church as a Catholic church of diverse and authentic local churches, whose unity is incarnated in the common conversation to discern, affirm, and challenge multiple forms of evangelical praxis in local churches around the globe. My vision is that local churches might come together in regional areas to discern together, and that the Vatican might become a center of inter-

39. David Tracy, *The Analogical Imagination* (St. Louis, MO: Herder & Herder, 1998), 239.
40. Graff here cites Roberto Goizueta, "United States Hispanic Theology and the Challenge of Pluralism," in Allan Figueroa Deck, ed., *Frontiers of Hispanic Theology in the United States* (Maryknoll, NY: Orbis, 1992), 14. David Tracy has also picked up this polycentric theme: "There is a price to be paid for any genuine pluralism — that price many pluralists seem finally either unwilling to pay or unable to see. It is that there is no longer a center. There are many. . . . The others [of our polycentric present] must become genuine others for us — not projections of our fears and desires. The others are not marginal to our centers but centers of their own. Their conflicts and their liberationist self-namings demand the serious attention of our center on their own terms" (*On Naming the Present,* 4-5).

national ecclesial discernment, challenge and support. . . . [Such a discernment process of conversation among local churches] would allow us to name and practice the gospel differently, as our locations require, yet to mediate our diversity in the commerce of conversation about the narratives and symbols we all share (p. 208).

There has been a glimpse of what this might look like on a couple of occasions when my colleague Pat Taylor Ellison has led ELCA Synod assemblies in discussing specific items on their agendas using the same moral conversation process that the congregations in this study used. It is a qualitatively different kind of experience from the use of procedures defined by Robert's Rules of Order that are the usual fare for synod assembly business proceedings. Extended genuine conversation occurred among people from different congregations, and the moral conversation process enabled the discernment of both Scripture and experience.

Such a practice, as Graff points out, affords the participating churches "the opportunity to learn from beyond our own perspective, to meet our own limitations, and be challenged, as well as affirmed in our efforts to live out of Scripture and tradition in our own situations" (p. 209).[41] We are often aided in these opportunities by our own experiences of being able to shift perspectives between the various realities and settings in which we live. Through this, we learn the facility of seeing reality and reading biblical texts from the perspective of others when they are able to describe their reality and perspective to us in conversations.[42] But

41. Graff's vision of these discernment conversations is reflected in Fernando Segovia's vision of interpreting biblical texts in intercultural dialogue: "Out of this experience emerges a key element in the theology of mixture and otherness: a commitment to critical dialogue and exchange with the other, subjecting our respective views of one another and the world to critical exposure and analysis. Out of this experience emerges as well a key element in the hermeneutic of otherness and engagement: first, a commitment to critical dialogue and exchange with the text as other, subjecting our respective views of the world to critical exposure and analysis; second, a commitment to critical dialogue and exchange with other interpreters of the text, both historical and contemporary, again subjecting our respective views of the text and its world to critical exposure and analysis." Fernando F. Segovia, "Toward a Hermeneutics of the Diaspora: A Hermeneutics of Otherness and Engagement," in Segovia and Mary Ann Tolbert, eds., *Reading from this Place*, vol. 1: *Social Location and Interpretation in the United States* (Minneapolis: Fortress, 1995), 71.

42. See Segovia, "Toward a Hermeneutics of the Diaspora," 70; see also Mary Ann Tolbert, "Reading for Liberation," in *Reading from this Place*, vol. 1, 266, 275, and "The Politics and Poetics of Location," in *Reading from this Place*, vol. 1, 314.

for such processes of discernment to work well, whether in local congregations or in regional gatherings of congregations, members with a knowledge base and certain skills are required. There is a need both for those with the requisite range of experience and also those with some knowledge of Scripture and church tradition.

If Scripture is to play an important role in both forming and informing the Christian imaginations of the participants in these discernment conversations, both laypeople and clergy will need to participate as trustworthy guides to Scripture. Those knowledgeable and regular readers of Scripture in every congregation can be viewed as possessing a spiritual gift for the common good (see 1 Cor. 12:4-11). Their role would be not so much that of authoritative interpreters as it would be to open up the territory of Scripture. They would use the free play of their imaginations to explore how Scripture both interprets their experiences and is, in turn, interpreted by those experiences. They would be needed as much when individual congregations engage in moral conversation as they would when congregations engage in mutual discernment. One could argue that learning to discern within their own community is an important preparation for engaging in discernment with those from other communities of faith where the variety of biblical interpretations offered by various participants might be greater. However, we do not have to choose between the sheer inclusion of everyone and the work of open and trustworthy guides. Biblical guides as I have envisioned here can judiciously serve to enhance the Christian imaginations of everyone by helping to include them in the process of biblical interpretation and moral discernment.

Doing Faith-Based Conversation:
Metaphors for Congregations and Their Leaders

Pat Taylor Ellison

Years spent studying the process of faith-based moral conversation in congregations has revealed something about the nature of congregations and their leadership. For several years I led and trained others to lead faith-based moral conversations on tough subjects in congregational life.[1] In some places we worked amid deep conflict, and in other places we worked during more relaxed times of learning, storing up information, and practice for stormier days. At the end of that period, I spent another year interviewing and writing a phenomenological analysis of the responses of six people (three laypersons and three pastors) who had been trained to lead those conversations. The interviews were two-tiered, in-depth, and conversational in nature: the interviewees responded to open-ended questions that were formulated in a classic applied ethnographic style that was designed to gain emic perspective.[2]

In the years following, I have continued to train people to lead faith-based congregational conversations. I have studied the words, traditions, and self-portraits of congregations who have expressed the desire to be trained for such conversations, including both those who have come to be trained and those practicing conversations such as these in their faith communities. Patterns have been emerging, patterns that suggest some-

---

1. A summary of some of this work is available in my earlier essay in this volume.

2. Patricia Taylor Ellison, *Pioneer, Prophet, Servant-Leader: Metaphors for Leading Public Moral Conversation in Congregations* (Ph.D. diss., University of Minnesota, 1995).

thing about both the congregation as a whole and the individual leaders of conversation.

First, a minimum knowledge base, skills, attitudes and beliefs, and behaviors are usually present in the congregations in which hospitable conversation is encouraged and developed. Second, those who lead such conversation have a knowledge base, a particular set of skills, and attitudes and beliefs themselves. As we teach congregational leaders and as we think through places that could benefit from such conversation, we must consider these four Aristotelian elements, as displayed on the accompanying grid.[3]

"just enough" knowledge base	attitudes and beliefs
skills	behaviors

Congregational Knowledge Base, Skills, Attitudes and Beliefs, and Behaviors

Faith-based conversation brings Scripture and a set of traditions to bear on the tough issues people face. It also brings out the voices of a culture and a society, as well as the personal and communal experience of faithful people.[4] It requires a set of ground rules, along with expected outcomes: that people will attend to one another, assert with one another, come to a mutual decision, and take action together.

Congregations desiring to make this kind of conversation a habit already show at least five markers that characterize their shared life. First, they are *ready.* Usually, there is a crucial question before their congregation, and they are motivated to work it through. Second, they are *hope-filled.* They know that such questions can split congregations apart and cost them members and momentum in their ministry; yet they believe that, with God at the center of such a conversation, hope will abide. Third, they are also *active:* that is, they know the difference between being acted upon by a professional outside expert and training to do it themselves, and

3. Aristotle, *Nichomachean Ethics,* Books 1 and 6, trans. T. Irwin (Indianapolis: Hackett Publishing, 1985).

4. James D. Whitehead and Evelyn Eaton Whitehead, *Method in Ministry: Theological Reflection and Christian Ministry,* rev. ed. (New York: Sheed & Ward, 1995), 23-65.

they prefer the latter. Fourth, they are *inventive:* they are unafraid of altering not only their old habits and behaviors but also the conversation process itself, confident that a new way will work for their congregation and respond to their particular dilemma. Finally, they are *hospitable* — even to those conversation partners who may not share their values, their status in the dilemma, or their faith.

Who are these congregations that desire the habit of faith-based conversation? Some of them are large and resource-rich congregations, but most of them are small to middle-sized congregations that are filled with ordinary people trying to make sense of life, the world, and God. All of them face high-intensity, high-risk struggles. Most of them are led by pastors and laypeople who have little experience in doing faith-based conversation about tough issues. These leaders know that when talk starts, fire starts, and these flames have the power to destroy what seems like a peaceable kingdom. If they can just keep things battened down, they think, then they can go on living together and not be shaken to their core about matters that go deeper than they can handle.

The product of years of holding back controversy in a congregation often works like very fine, very strong piano wire that binds the members together as a community. Listen to the struggles in a composite of fourteen congregations in the following portrait.[5]

> We see perpetual quarrels over *resources.* ("We argue over money. Some fight about the use of volunteer time. We disagree about what the pastor should be doing. Fights center on the carpeting and the parking lot.")
>
> We see distress and rearrangement of the *structure* of ongoing work, governance, and decision-making. ("Whether we the members should be first on the daycare's waiting list. Our council decisions are countermanded or ignored. When a couple of church leaders decide something should get done, it does!")
>
> We see a misguided view of natural energy and *power* as evil or benevolent manipulation. ("Some lobby others. One person continually puts pressure on our young pastor to agree on a position. I am suspicious of how things are done because people with sway get what they want.")

5. The source of these quotations is a collection gleaned from fourteen congregations that we studied during 1997 while being engaged through the work of Church Innovations in a "Congregational Discovery" process over moral conversation and renewal questions.

Finally, we see an *inward-turning focus of mission* that understands the purpose of the congregation to be the perpetuation of the delicate balance of itself. ("How are we going to keep our congregation going when our young people keep leaving? I am sure in five years our doors will be shut. If the Lord wants this church to survive, it will be so. We need to follow our constitution. If we had a more attractive youth program, we'd have a future generation for our church.")[6]

The congregation rolls along, bumping through life month after month. Whenever a potential controversy occurs, the community — in order to weather the storm — tightens the piano wire around everything so that the resources, structure, and energy cannot be moved out of the pattern that holds everything in place.

Almost everyone knows that there is conflict.[7] Almost everyone says that Christians are called to dwell in the Word and the fellowship of believers to ground their communal spiritual life.[8] So they gather. They pray before meetings. They earnestly pray alone, desiring that some guiding word will be dropped into their midst that they will be able to pick up and nurture. That nurture, however, may take freedom of movement. They long for a place to drop the resistance, step out of those bonds, and speak freely, working through the stories of Scripture, stories of their parents and mentors in the faith actually living out their faith in their talking, deciding, and acting together. Listen to the longing in this composite summary of congregation members' responses to a question about how they fight together: "People disagree about everything, but not openly. We see quietness; problems are ignored, swept under the carpet; much behind-your-back maneuvering. Often we don't say anything for fear of making people mad. The

6. For more on struggles over resources, structure, power, and mission, see Robert W. Terry, *Authentic Leadership: Courage in Action* (San Francisco: Jossey-Bass, 1993).

7. Data from 186 congregations on Church Innovations' *Church FutureFinder,* an online interactive research database available at www.churchinnovations.org. When asked the question, "How does your congregation fight?" two-thirds of the respondents in most congregations describe healthy and unhealthy ways of dealing with conflict.

8. Most congregations, however, feel that it is the pastor or priest's job to lead conversations and even action on morally disputed topics, according to responses to our Congregational Discovery interviews on this subject. Over 80 percent of members believe that the pastor or priest leads by example, and should do so by means of teaching and preaching. At least half of that 80 percent are just as quick to point out that their clergyperson should not mandate the members' actions on such issues.

elected persons pass resolutions that are later allowed to fall away." People can name what is troubling and would love to find a better way; and they long to engage in a satisfying process of spiritual discernment. This longing is necessary, but it is not sufficient.

Congregational leaders know that they must seek what they feel is missing. In our Aristotelian grid, these missing pieces seem to be the bare-minimum knowledge base that will allow them to carry out such conversation over tough topics. They already possess the belief of God-centered hope, the attitude of or preference for action, the skill of adaptation and invention, and the behavior of hospitality. Thus equipped and moving ahead in faith, they encourage one another, each freeing the other into the kind of conversation that generates the future of the community.

"just enough" knowledge base	attitudes and beliefs God-centered hope preference for action longing for discernment
skills adaptation and invention	behaviors hospitality

What is missing in their knowledge base? Partly, an inventory of what they already know. Congregational leaders, both lay and clergy, understand from their experience in society at large that conflict can be a sign of deep trouble. They also know that they can and do encounter conflict in any number of ways every day of the week. They know that there are methods for dealing with conflict; indeed, many of these leaders have studied those methods and need to take stock of what they know in order to put that knowledge base to work.

Key leaders thus educated believe that conflict can be handled, managed, and/or resolved. But what if conflict, rather than being passive, is instead active, organic, a living part of the living organism of the congregation? What if conflict is an indicator of vivacity and diversity, a marker that the congregation is doing what it's called to be doing: encountering the divine Other in other people? In that case, the handling, managing, or resolving of conflict will kill what it is trying to bring forth — new ways of listening to, living with, and thriving in community with the other.

Some of what these leaders understand about conflict techniques will still work within this shifted conceptualization of conflict. Excellent listening, using "I messages," laying out the problem clearly, and so forth — all these will only enhance conversation.[9] Leaders must claim what they already know from the broadening field of conflict management and resolution to add to their accumulated knowledge base. However, they must ask themselves and their congregational conversation partners not only about the pain and distress the conflict is causing them, but also what God might be up to as they are pressed about particular issues. Is the conflict they are experiencing an example of evil thrust on them, or are they encountering this struggle as a way of being asked to empty themselves, taking the form of slave in order to free others into the communion of God (see David Fredrickson's essay earlier in this volume)?

Finally, we might add into the knowledge base a certain number of Bible stories and other writings from the congregation's traditions that call the members to be in conversation with one another. These words from the holy and honored tradition work to authorize and even mandate conversation, making it a sacred part of the life of the Christian community. For Lutherans, the lining up of the "mutual conversation and consolation of the brothers [and sisters] in Christ" from Luther's own voice is a serious encouragement to read more of his works.[10] Fredrickson's work in Philippians is certainly fresh and compelling for believers predisposed to action. As the Christ Hymn is unfolded around equality of participation in God's conversation, people's imaginations are opened to discover more and more conversation partners with whom to share the gospel and the work of God.

Now we see a more complete Aristotelian grid of the congregation and what its corporate knowledge base, attitudes and beliefs, skills, and behaviors present as a *nest* for any given conflict situation. We've added several things: (a) the claiming of known techniques; (b) a shifted conceptualization of conflict as a gift from God being set before them; and (c) calls from Scripture and tradition, especially from the Christ Hymn, to have "this mind among you" of the one who emptied himself into slavery to free us for participation together with God. When a congregation begins to

---

9. Roger Fisher and William L. Ury, *Getting to Yes: Negotiating Agreement Without Giving In*, 2nd ed., ed. Bruce Patton (New York: Penguin Books, 1983), 36.

10. Martin Luther, "Smalcald Articles: Article IV. The Gospel," *The Book of Concord*, trans. Theodore G. Tappert (Philadelphia: Fortress, 1959).

work out of these strengths, even after years of conflict avoidance, they rely less and less on piano wire and more and more on the Lord, along with their brothers and sisters in the faith.

"just enough" knowledge base	attitudes and beliefs
conflict techniques	God-centered hope
shifted conflict concept	preference for action
Biblical / traditional call	longing for discernment
skills	**behaviors**
adaptation and invention	hospitality
listening and speaking skills	slavehood for freedom

What underlying metaphor best describes congregations that engage in faith-based moral conversation, through which the future of their community will be generated? Based on our grid, the congregations who have healthy approaches to conversation and conflict see themselves as communities comprised of strangers who are more apt to hold differing views than similar ones. They don't presume agreement; rather, they assume otherness. They don't see their community as consisting of buildings erected of immovable granite but as changeable structures put up and taken down upon God's never-failing love. The community has to be on the move, changeable as its call to service changes, and as its neighbors' needs change. It is not randomly nomadic; rather, it goes where it is sent — to do the will of the Sender.

The metaphor of communities of strangers, of others, is rare among the hundreds of congregations we have encountered. Most of those congregations see themselves as families.[11] These families often cling for survival to their tradition and to the hope of children. They are good to one another and care deeply about the troubles each member faces. They do not spend much time thinking about their mission to others, though this is not out of selfishness per se, but out of a belief that all who are outside their family have had the chance to know Jesus and have already made up their minds one way or the other. Something about this image feels exactly right to them

---

11. Data from 186 congregations on Church Innovations' *Church FutureFinder*. When asked the questions "How do people participate in the life of this church?" and "How do you sense God's presence and activity in this congregation?" at least half the respondents used the word "family" or family-related language.

— perhaps ideal. But for a small but distinct number, the image does not fit, and they are uncomfortable with it, though they don't quite know why.

Conversation Leaders' Knowledge Base, Skills, Attitudes and Beliefs, and Behaviors

In the process of using a descriptive phenomenological analysis of leader interviews, three deep metaphors emerged that were operating in and under the text of the leaders' responses. These deep metaphors structured the way conversation leaders thought about what it means to be a leader of faith-based conversation in a congregational setting. These three metaphors were *pioneer, prophet,* and *servant-leader.* All six leaders we interviewed operated within all three metaphors to varying degrees. Some of their words appear in the following to provide the reader with some of the thick description out of which the metaphors grew. They also provide illustrations particular to each metaphor of various pieces of the Aristotelian grid for persons who lead faith-based conversation.[12]

Pioneer

Pioneers deliberately move beyond the status quo to create a new and/or alternative future for those who matter most to them. Pioneers on the North American frontier left a civilized region behind to claim and settle new land. Most did not do that alone, but in groups of families. They did not reject entirely what they had left behind; rather, they took some of the best parts with them, such as musical instruments, Bibles, family pictures, and heirlooms. All of these material objects expressed their traditions and customs and helped them establish a new civilization when they arrived at their new place.

Pioneers today change the place they occupy, even while they occupy it. They recognize the need for a change and discover a way to make it happen for the benefit of the community. Faith-based conversation pioneers recognize three ways of thinking that must change.

---

12. For more details and further listings in the grid, see Ellison, *Pioneer, Prophet, Servant-Leader,* 196.

1. In North America, people generally operate within a modern dog-matic system of thinking in which facts are separated from values.[13] People accept that there are a relatively small number of objective, provable facts and a huge number of subjective, personal values. Fur-thermore, people draw a line between those facts and values: they consider facts to be based on reason and scientific method (thus fit topics for public conversation) and values to be based on emotion and therefore irrational (fit topics for private conversation only).

2. It seems easiest for many people to think in dualities, preferring clear choices and simple answers, an either-or selection.[14] They want clear examples from their immediate life-world to help them make sense of life's complexity.[15] They want clear-cut choices partly because they are not practiced in making more difficult decisions themselves and partly because they do not have the wisdom of extended family and community to rely on.

3. Most people are comfortable with the hierarchical systems of leader-ship that thrive in our culture of experts. It is worth people's time and money to pay an expert to tell them what they should do rather than investing time and energy into figuring it out for themselves. This reliance on the expert affects public life across generational lines. The parents of the Baby Boomers allow leaders to lead out of respect for the leaders' position; the Baby Boomers and the members of Generation X allow leaders to lead because that is what they have paid them to do. If the leaders they have elected and paid do not lead, people fire them and hire others.

These three ways of thinking are a part of the status quo. Pioneers in faith-based conversation have some new direction in mind for community movement away from this status quo because they consider these three ways of thinking flawed. First, these pioneers believe that the separation of facts from values is arbitrary and unhelpful because it prevents any issue composed of both facts and values (virtually every moral issue) from be-ing the subject of public conversation. Further, if people cannot have pub-

13. Wayne C. Booth, *The Modern Dogma: The Rhetoric of Assent* (Chicago: University of Chicago Press, 1973).

14. Walter Wink, *Transforming Bible Study* (Nashville: Abingdon, 1989).

15. Robert N. Bellah et al., *Habits of the Heart: Individualism and Commitment in American Life* (Berkeley: University of California Press, 1985).

lic faith-based conversation, they cannot make the community decisions that are necessary as rapid social and economic change continues to occur.

These pioneers choose to reject the fact-value split in favor of an integrated picture in which every meaningful issue is attended by both facts and values, and each must be the subject of both public and private discourse. This amounts to a paradigm shift, one that is also underway in business and education. One of the conversation leaders placed it "under the heading of this continuous improvement, a process of getting people to work together to be more effective, to make better decisions, and collectively, actually talk about them, not have somebody just dictate."

Second, pioneers in public faith-based conversation believe that the simple dualities of either-or thinking are not sufficient for most group decision-making, particularly when conflict arises. If pioneers refuse to forever steer between the two ditches of simple dualities, then they must opt for a third way, a both-and framework. This alternative is neither pure inclusivity nor "anything goes." This alternative is accountable to honor all views as long as they are offered to further the community wisdom, to free one another for participation, and to help the group engage in spiritual discernment. This will help them make better choices, come to better decisions, and take wiser action. Of course, some participants still come to conversations in an either-or state of mind. One leader described some participants in a conversation he led this way: "Some came with a set agenda, and they were not at the next session because they hadn't succeeded in shutting it down. They weren't interested in looking at the whole issue. They just wanted to say their two cents' worth."

On the other hand, when the agenda is really open, anything might happen. Leaders need to have a commitment to that freedom of movement. One said: "You never know how it's going to turn out. By looking at the garden, you can't really tell what's there. There's stuff growing underneath that you have no idea about. I'm an adventurer. I like not knowing what it's going to be like. I'm never convinced it's going to be a disaster." A commitment to freedom of flow — a conversational "float" — opens up the group to seeing the Spirit's work more clearly.

Pioneer conversation leaders also understand that values can run deeper than particular positions on issues. One leader noted her growth as a conversation leader as she became aware, time after time, that where there seems to be deep separation, there is often deeper kinship. "When people have a strong feeling, there's an underlying value. We often share these wonderful, meaningful values although we don't come to the same conclusions. . . . [This awareness] has allowed me to hear a difference of opinion, and when people change the subject, to be able to sit back and take a look at what's happening."

Third, pioneers in faith-based conversation believe that hierarchical leadership by experts may work in situations that do not necessarily call for radical change. But in cases that do involve such change, decisions must be shared by the largest possible number of participants, and that calls for a group conversation process that will involve talking with God and with one another until a decision and an action emerge. One leader described this wideness of participation in this way: "I would suggest that there be a rich divergence of opinion, and maybe an openness to not having made up one's mind. Maybe we're over here when we come into the discussion, and we might be in a different place when we look at all this up on the board. We might see things pointing a different way than we'd originally thought." Another said: "Good moral conversations allow variety and differences, not solos. People who think they have the moral truth, they can pronounce it, and everybody else, you know, has to do it: that ceases to be music. I think moral conversation should be music in [the ensemble] way."

This group conversation and discernment process cannot be led effectively by a typical hierarchical leader who claims and supports a particular position. Such a claim by a leader will automatically suppress participation by many people, whether in deference to that leader or via a delegation of responsibility. Instead, the process must be led by someone who can provide enough structure to reduce anxiety but yet ensure a safe space for widespread participation without being directive or dominating. This leader needs to be one who is willing to get out of the way when the group begins to engage in meaningful conversation and spiritual discernment. One leader said that this model for faith-based conversation "gave me . . . the greatest comfort I ever had in trying to lead a group." Another said that using a ritual structure for the conversation "gave more of a sense of safety to people, particularly those who might not have spoken up or who would have been shut down. . . . Those people actually spoke up because they could do so in a less threatening atmosphere."

Another recalled objections to such nondirective leadership: "Many didn't want me to be neutral. They kept saying to me, 'Well, what do you want?' I kept saying, 'This is not my decision to make, this is why we're here together.' But several times they pressed, 'Oh, okay, but really, what do you want?'" This leader disciplined himself to encourage the responses of others. If on occasion he felt compelled to add some missing pieces to the conversation, he sat down among the participants to do so, spoke, and then rose to his feet again to continue taking notes on the conversation for the group.

What does our grid look like now, containing the reflections of these six pioneer conversation leaders? Here is a new version, containing three items for each of the Aristotelian elements. Pioneers opt out of what they see as unhelpful status quo, are willing to help others shift into what works better. They possess discipline and understanding about human nature (their own and their neighbors'), and they do what it takes to give the new way a fair test. They create safety and trust as they go along. They scout, choose locations, and erect new structures in which the community of strangers can live.

LEADER AS PIONEER

"just enough" knowledge base	attitudes and beliefs
• paradigm shift in business from top-down to grassroots planning • values run deeper than positions • the faith-based model itself	• not either-or but both-and • experimentation can be enjoyable • openness to change
skills	**behaviors**
• discipline to set aside own position • creating safe space for leader and participants • set new leader expectations	• refuse to lead directively • use the model for structure • assist people to attend and assert

Prophet

In biblical times people recognized prophets as persons who were out of the ordinary because "they had a special relationship with God."[16] Even more important is the prophet's role of bringing messages from God to humans,

16. John Barton, *Oracles of God: Perceptions of Ancient Prophecy in Israel after the Exile* (New York: Oxford University Press, 1986), 103.

messages intended to persuade a person or group to repent, or turn from something or someone toward God. Prophets spoke truly about the past, present, and future, inspired by and in conversation with God.[17] In the Judaeo-Christian tradition, the prophets were often killed for doing their work by people who did not want to hear or acknowledge the message.

Today, a *public prophet* may seem to be an anachronism, largely because religious belief, having been placed into the fact-value split on the side of irrational values, carries little weight in everyday public life. Spirituality is considered something either for individual and private musings or for church bodies separated from the public sphere.[18] At best, a modern public prophet seems to be a caricature to many people, a relic of an older time trying to represent some ethical truth. At worst, today's prophet is seen as an irrational zealot who has the passionate power to seriously harm himself or herself and others — as well as the social order. Of course, since the prophet's job is to get people to turn in a new (or old) direction, toward God, interruption of the social order is a goal of prophecy. Faith-based conversation prophets reject the fact-value split that places the prophetic role at either extreme in the first place; instead, they rely on an integration of faith within the whole fabric of their lives.

The relationship between the Christian prophetic messenger and the God who creates and sends the message is built on fear, love, and trust.[19] The prophet is in awe of God's power and sees God as presently active in the world. The Christian prophet understands God's nature as love and mercy as revealed in Jesus and trusts in God's faithfulness above all else. Prophets see the world in which we live as first belonging to and inhabited by God. What does this theocentric view of the world mean for today's prophets? How does it place them in conflict with the culture? These three assumptions of modern Western culture run counter to a Christian prophet's orientation:[20]

1. Much of American culture views the God of the Bible as largely mythical, perhaps meaningful at one time but no longer.

17. Gerhard von Rad, *Message of the Prophets* (London: SCM Press, 1968).

18. Bellah et al., *Habits of the Heart*, 6, 82.

19. "You shall have no other gods. What does this mean? We should fear, love, and trust in God above all things." Martin Luther, "Small Catechism — The Ten Commandments," *The Book of Concord.*

20. Bellah et al., *Habits of the Heart*, 16.

2. If God exists, that existence is distant and irrelevant to today's real world.

3. Human lives and talents have little or nothing to do with God, although if people choose to believe in God, that private choice may lead to healthier ethics and community support.

Today, prophets in a faith-based conversation process understand but do not accept this human-centered, occasionally God-related worldview. First of all, prophets say that God is: that is, God exists apart from human ability to perceive or explain God. And if God is unfathomable, then God is uncontrollable. Two leaders had this conversation: "You're always at the mercy of things completely outside of your realm of control or influence, like the Holy Spirit working in the place. This might not be the right time for this kind of discussion, here or there, and no amount of tinkering can get it to happen." "Yes, God only knows how many times you're going to have this shown to you before it takes. . . ." Another leader put it this way: "Your image of God should always be larger than your image of God . . . it's very subtle. Who am I following? Have I created God in my image, or am I really discovering who and what God is and, therefore, I'm being remolded in that image?"

Next, conversation leader-prophets say that God is not distant and separate from human life. God is present. God is on the loose.[21] These leaders feel God's presence in life. When asked what God was up to in congregational conversation, one leader said, "God is up to creating servants." Another said: "'To help us honor the gift of complexity' came to my mind; that's what God is up to, and maybe that's what I can hopefully be. So how do we honor the gift of complexity, the gift of ambiguity, living in the paradox?" If God's work is indeed ours, the human action will be more effective if we center our work, our thoughts, and our trust in the God who is in the midst of us. Conversation leader-prophets place a high reliance on prayer. "When it comes really right down to it," one conversation leader observed, "we need individual relationships with God." Another said: "To me, to have a better prayer life, to be in touch more often with God than I had ever been before maybe — now that's critical." We

---

21. Donald Juel and Patrick Keifert, "God in the Classroom: Teaching the Bible as a Theological Discipline," paper presented at the Consultation on the Bible and Theological Education, Apr. 1995, Luther Seminary, St. Paul, MN.

are partners with God, albeit unequal partners. Partners work better when they work together.

A focus on God as intrinsic to faith-based conversation is what makes this model complete. One leader said: "It is very different from Robert's Rules of Order, which lacks that spiritual dimension. This is what makes this model unique and so wonderful. . . . To ignore what contributes so much to our value system or spirituality, to completely ignore it when we're talking in secular settings, school board meetings, whatever, when moral deliberation and values are based so much on the spiritual element, it has to be taken into account."

Third, faith-based conversation prophets say that humans exist because God has always loved the world. God has given humans powers and talents in abundance, and when God calls on them, they can put those gifts to work in God's service as a response to God's generosity. One leader favors group decision-making on tough issues precisely because it's a better use of all of their gifts: "It's probably going to be a better decision, one that's owned by a number of different people. . . . People are empowered by this process, by the Spirit, by our prayers, by our being together, to be God's people and do what's appropriate as they face an issue and answer a question." Prophets urge people to listen to God's call to use our gifts in God's work and to respond by dedicating our gifts to serving our community. One conversation leader put it this way: "I was teaching in schools, and suddenly I felt pulled to turn my talents toward the work of the church, as if that work were the reason I'd been given my talents in the first place. . . . This leadership activity is God's foot in the door to my life."

Skills of confident teaching and public prayer were listed by faith-based conversation leaders as crucial. One expressed it this way: "I define myself differently having [training or teaching] as a talent. Wherever I've worked, that's just something I'd do. I just train. Well, God is just somewhat more perceptive than restaurant managers, but even restaurant managers, you know, saw me as a training person. I think God is using me to do just that." Confidence that she could train others, no matter what the task, built trust among the participants who learned from her. She added: "I also needed to know how to pray in the [conversation] sessions because prayer as the center of these moral conversations is critical to our way of doing them."

Deliberate focus of attention on God was mentioned often. "You ask people to be aware of the Spirit's leading, to try to erase from their minds some of their previous prejudices, thoughts, opinions, and to see what happens under the leadership of the Spirit." "[Christians] do that all the time: we say a prayer . . . and then run off and maybe we don't even listen or check for signals. . . . We have devotions at the beginning, but we don't refocus spiritually during a business-type meeting like a council or committee meeting." One conversation leader used the model in confirmation class: "They didn't even want to take a break. We were reading *Night* by Wiesel — his moral conversations around the holocaust. The kids worked on how that changes your image of who and what God is. . . . I feel I'm called to do that, to have those conversations."

What does our grid look like now that we have added the reflections of these six conversation leader-prophets? Here is a new version, containing two items for each of the Aristotelian elements. Prophets understand God to be beyond human power and to be present now. They see God as the one who calls us and gives us gifts so that we can accomplish specific work. They understand that they are to lift the focus of all faith-based conversation to rest on God, God's call, and God's work in that congregation. They remind people of the foundation and the future of their community.

LEADER AS PROPHET

"just enough" knowledge base	attitudes and beliefs
• God is beyond human power. • God is present in life and in conversation with humans.	• The church is a body called by God. • People's talents are God-given.
skills	**behaviors**
• teaching • public and private prayer	• focusing attention on God • encouraging talk about God

Servant-Leader

Robert Greenleaf describes the servant-leader as servant first and leader later. The best test of whether one is a servant-leader, he says, is whether those who are served grow as persons, have their deepest needs met, and become more likely themselves to become servants.[22] Of course, for Christians, Jesus is the primary model of servant-leader and demands that very behavior of his disciples.

In these days, even purely situational leaders are referred to metaphorically, either as *up* or *above* or *ahead*, as those who "rise to the surface" or who "rise to the challenge." They step forward, and followers can see the person they are following. People are used to this directive style, a hierarchical scheme that places leaders ahead of or above their followers by virtue of their education, experience, or zeal for a cause. In contrast, though servant-leaders may have extraordinary education, experience, or zeal, their style is not hierarchical. Instead, their understanding of leadership is exactly that: *under*-standing. That is, they stand beneath what is happening, doing whatever they can to make sure that everyone else has the opportunity to speak, lead, hear, and grow. They do have a vision of what they stand under: that is how they make their plans, imagine the task, and work with other participants. But instead of being the focus of the project, these leaders are its servants. In short, they are able to lead by getting out of the way.

Servant-leaders agree that communities need leadership — some directive and some servant style. They also realize that many people consider nondirective leadership as no leadership at all. First of all, servant-leaders understand that we live in a culture that is led by experts.[23] These experts become advisors as people try to make sense of chaotic life lived at a frenzied pace. People are comfortable allowing these leaders to be directive in such matters as investments and taxes, the law, and medicine, matters that seem to belong to the fact side of the fact-value split. Many people have options that an expert can simply lay before the uninitiated decision-maker. Public leadership on factual matters is allowed, even expected, to be mostly directive.

Second, servant-leaders also understand that people must decide and act on matters that do not feel simply "factual." For example, many decisions have moral or ethical aspects, and those decisions require attention to both facts and values. But public leadership now becomes tricky. In matters of values, which in North America are usually only privately dis-

---

22. Robert Greanleaf, *Servant Leadership: A Journey into the Nature of Legitimate Power and Greatness* (New York: Paulist Press, 1977), 244ff.

23. Alvin Toffler, *The Third Wave* (New York: Bantam Books, 1984).

cussed, directive public leadership will not work. Individuals have made personal-values decisions for so long that, when public groups need to take some action on a morally disputed issue, they can only do it individually and privately — not together as a community. An expert leader will only polarize the group. Should it seem better to have no leader, we must realize that, left leaderless, the group would probably never convene, a public discussion would never take place, and a group decision would never be made nor any action taken.

A different kind of leadership is required. Servant-leaders want to diminish the passive, spectator mentality fostered by the expert culture characteristic in modern society; instead, they want to foster active involvement and honesty about people's fears and hopes.[24] Congregations may certainly invite experts to help them with difficulties, even difficulties with moral conversation. But their typical mode of operating should be grounded in the belief that every congregation has within it the necessary gifts to carry out the work God has called it to, and that God is engaged with it in creating a trustworthy world.[25] This understanding means that, instead of just looking outside for the necessary resources to get the job done, congregation members need to look for leadership and talent within the congregation itself. A process of deep, faith-based conversation and spiritual discernment, led by persons whose main goal is to serve, will lead congregations, over the long haul, to a more active role in their spiritual growth and their living out their faith.

Those who are servant-leaders of faith-based conversations are grounded in an understanding of God as revealed in Christ Jesus, particularly in the Christ Hymn in Philippians that David Fredrickson has elucidated above. These leaders understand their purpose as church *[ekklēsia]* to be an active, called-out community that is determining its future by means of speaking with God and with one another. As leaders, they are dedicated to the equal participation of as many as possible in the conversation. As Jesus opened the way for us to converse with God, so we enlarge the circle for others. A solid working knowledge of the model helped leaders improve wide participation. One leader said: "This model helps you look at things from historical, community, and personal experience angles.

24. Toffler, *Third Wave*, 367.
25. Patrick R. Keifert, *Welcoming the Stranger: A Public Theology of Worship and Evangelism* (Minneapolis: Fortress, 1990).

You tried to include all of these elements in your discussion, so it was satisfying. No matter what someone wanted to share, there was a dimension for them to share from."

In our research, conversation servant-leaders shared beliefs about the biblical appropriateness of a servanthood that helps others to be active. "It's a way of involving people sort of from the grass roots, from the bottom up, to make decisions and carry them out, to be responsible for and own the decisions that are made. . . . That's what Jesus meant when he said, 'Who would be great must be the servant.' Disciples have to do that. It's a far better thing for disciples to do this together than for someone simply to send down lightning from [headquarters] or whatever."

In our research, conversation servant-leaders also shared real fears and hopes. "There's always the concern, 'Will I look dumb, will I misspeak, will I forget to say what I really want to share with the group?' But with this model I had to be concerned about the other participants more than myself." "At the end there's always the feeling of unfinished business, that you wish you could have heard more from this person or that person." "I wasn't sure if the conversation would float or if it would just be like pulling teeth to get people to talk. . . . Some people came up afterwards and said it was really good . . . some said they talked more than they thought they would." "There's warmth in the group and kind of mutuality about sensing this is good to do, and we feel closer to each other because we're working on this question together as disciples, as brothers and sisters in Christ."

Regarding the public moral conversation process itself, servant-leaders look for opportunities to avoid hierarchical or directive styles of behavior, opting for an approach that looks less like making a point and more like making the coffee. That is, they make all the arrangements so that the group itself can take over the work. They are not threatened by low-status work as long as that work contributes to the movement of the conversation into a floating state during which spiritual discernment can take place. Leaders made analogies about their role as humble leaders: "a poor struggler going up a down staircase," "a toilet cleaner, getting into things people would never want to dirty their hands with," "a patient gardener, encouraging things to grow," "a hermit on the hill," without anything except the view down the other side.

Listen to the descriptions of letting go of top-down leadership concepts that some of these leaders expressed: "I don't have to be perfect. I think I'm a lot less obnoxious now that I don't have to be perfect. I share a little, and then others add their parts." "This role often calls for teaching with neutrality." "I'm going to share what I care about and become a true listener for what other people care about and value." They coach, encourage, enforce rules, point to model diagrams and brainstormed lists, take notes, get snacks, and clean up afterward if that's what it takes.

Conversation servant-leaders described their actual behavior, some up to a year after the experience: "I kept on plodding and things." "I stood first, and then I sat and listened." "I was taking notes and realized I was out of space and they were talking about something else . . . and then I'd have to tear that sheet off and put it up and try to get started on the next sheet." "Asking the right questions and not getting involved in the debate, so to speak." "I was the stenographer, writing things down." "When we started getting sidetracked, I'd walk over to the chart of the process and would redirect where we were." "We put the coffee on." "We were by the door, greeting people." Servant-leaders do whatever it takes for the group to have a meaningful exchange of ideas and to enlarge their imaginations in a safe and engaging environment. They are not obsequious. They are active and perceptive. They are servants.

What does our grid look like now that it contains the reflections of these six conversation servant-leaders? Here is a new version, containing two items for each of the Aristotelian elements. Servant-leaders know that God invites us into conversation, and they know a method that helps them to do the same for others. They are active in their service, they need not be perfect, only helpful, and they do what has to be done so that others are welcomed into the conversation and the life of God. They are those who build homes and trust and freedom for the community of strangers with the work of their bodies and minds.

SERVANT-LEADER

"just enough" knowledge base	attitudes and beliefs
• solid theological framework for model • working knowledge of model	• self as servant • having real fears and real hopes
skills	**behaviors**
• release self from perfectionism • helping skills	• myriad serving acts • monitoring self when tempted

Drawing the Pieces Together

Did leaders of a God-centered model for congregational faith-based conversation find that work rewarding and energizing? In fact, each one did. Each was excited about being on the leading edge of a new activity, about pointing to God in the midst of it, and about doing whatever was necessary to help people participate. These metaphors are also coherent with the Box, the Triangle, and the Pyramid models (described in my earlier essay in this volume). For these six persons, leading was good.

While it will be tempting to use these "leader" metaphors in recruiting new leaders, we know that the descriptive phenomenology used to lift those metaphors out is exactly that — descriptive. Those metaphors apply to the six leaders I interviewed, but they may not be descriptive of all excellent leaders of moral conversation. I imagine that, with a theocentric, faith-based model, most leaders would be helped by the prophetic beliefs and behaviors that I have discussed here; and given the nature of conversation on controversial issues, a leader must always work in service of the participants on the many small and crucial details that permit such talk to flourish.

May our Lord, who charts courses for pioneers, embraces the prophet, and models for us true servant-leadership, continue to bless the workers who lead and the congregations they serve. And may we as scholars and researchers continue to be blessed by their generosity as we learn from what they do.

The Dialectic of Idolatry and Profanation:
On Discerning the Spirit in Congregational Studies

Lois Malcolm

The contributors to this book have sought, in concert with the Spirit of God, to build up and empower congregations.[1] What knowledge base, skills, attitudes and beliefs, and behaviors do members of congregations need in order to faithfully and effectively enact their identity as those who, in the power of the Spirit, have been baptized into Jesus' death and resurrection (Rom. 6)? A key question in our deliberations has been how spiritual discernment might occur within the activity of theological reflection on practices that constitute the life of a congregation.[2] We have engaged a

---

1. On the burgeoning field of congregational studies, see Carl S. Dudley's introduction to "Giving Voice to Local Churches: New Congregational Studies," *The Christian Century* (Aug. 12-19, 1992), 742-46. See also James P. Wind and James W. Lewis, eds., *American Congregations,* 2 vols. (Chicago: University of Chicago Press, 1994); Jackson W. Carroll, Carl S. Dudley, and William McKinney, *Handbook for Congregational Studies* (Nashville: Abingdon, 1986); Carl S. Dudley, Jackson W. Carroll, and James P. Wind, eds., *Carriers of Faith: Lessons from Congregational Studies* (Louisville: Westminster John Knox, 1991); James Hopewell, *Congregations: Stories and Structures* (Philadelphia: Fortress, 1987). See, most recently, Matthew Guest, Karin Tusting, and Linda Woodhead, eds., *Congregational Studies in the UK: Christianity in a Post-Christian Context* (Aldershot, UK: Ashgate Publishing Company, 2004).

2. Practices are defined as those socially established patterns of human activity and meaning that mediate between the personal and subjective, on the one hand, and the corporate and objective, on the other. Oriented toward ends that inhere in the practices themselves, they may not necessarily have a product in addition to those internal ends. See David Kelsey, *To Understand God Truly: What's Theological About a Theological School* (Louisville:

range of disciplines in this effort, including congregational studies, theological education, and practical theology, among others, in addition to the classical fields of biblical, historical, and systematic theology. Nonetheless, the focus of our attention has been on a single subject matter: the reality of God. As members of the Congregational Studies Research Team, we have approached our respective tasks in this project from the vantage point of our own academic disciplines and distinct vocations as theological educators. Yet we have all been focused on a singular task, that of spiritually discerning truth within the presence of the Spirit of God. Our theological reflection on congregations has found a shared locus in the activity of spiritual discernment.

Our reflections in these essays have been organized around Bernard Lonergan's eight functional specialties.[3] We have moved from descriptions of congregational practices to initial understandings and assertions about them, to judgments about these assertions, and finally to analyses of the deeper dialectics uncovered in our conversations. This chapter focuses on one of these core dialectics. It reflects on three approaches relevant to congregational studies from the fields of theological education[4] and practical

---

Westminster John Knox, 1992); see also Rebecca Chopp, *Saving Work: Feminist Practices of Theological Education* (Louisville: Westminster John Knox, 1995). This focus on "practice" can be contrasted with the attention given to "doctrine" in classical forms of Roman Catholic and Protestant orthodoxy and "experience" in modern liberal theologies. Compare Edward Farley's calls for a renewal of the classical concept of *habitus* in theological education, the ethos that cultivates the soul's dispositions and orientations in its knowledge of God, which he spells out in *The Fragility of Knowledge: Theological Education in the Church and the University* (Philadelphia: Fortress, 1988) and in his earlier *Theologia: The Fragmentation and Unity of Theological Education* (Philadelphia: Fortress, 1983). See also Francis Fiorenza's discussion of the turn to practical reason in "Theological and Religious Studies: The Contest of the Faculties," in Barbara G. Wheeler and Edward Farley, eds., *Shifting Boundaries: Contextual Approaches to the Structure of Theological Education* (Louisville: Westminster John Knox, 1991), 119-50. Craig Dykstra describes the centrality of practices to congregational studies in "Reconciling Practice," in Wheeler and Farley, *Shifting Boundaries,* 35-66. This turn to practice is reflected in a broader turn toward practical philosophy; see, e.g., Hans-Georg Gadamer, *Truth and Method* (New York: Crossroad, 1982); Richard J. Bernstein, *Praxis and Action* (Philadelphia: University of Pennsylvania Press, 1971); and Bernstein, *Beyond Objectivism and Relativism: Science, Hermeneutics, and Praxis* (Philadelphia: University of Pennsylvania Press, 1983).

3. See Bernard Lonergan, *Method in Theology* (New York: Crossroad, 1972).

4. On the relationship between congregational studies and theological education, see Joseph Hough, Jr., and Barbara G. Wheeler, eds., *Beyond Clericalism: The Congregation as a*

theology,[5] as represented by Don Browning, David Kelsey, and Rebecca Chopp, with respect to the theological practices of two major twentieth-century theologians: Karl Barth and Karl Rahner.[6] I use those two as exemplars to illustrate how theological reflection as a critical exercise might be rooted in basic Christian practices for understanding God truly. In particular, I focus on the Reformation act of preaching and the Ignatian practice of spiritual exercises. The fundamental dialectic I have uncovered in this analysis is that of the Reformed critique of idolatry (the treatment of what is profane as sacred) and the Roman Catholic critique of reductionism, or what could be called profanation (the treatment of what is sacred as profane).[7] What I examine in this chapter is the relevance of this dialectic for discerning the presence and activity of God's Spirit within paradigmatic practices of Christian faith that lie at the heart of a congregation's moral discourse and action.

The Problem and Context

Let us begin with an analysis of three theological approaches to the study of congregations, approaches that correspond to broader movements in theological education and practical theology. Don Browning's *A Funda-*

Focus for Theological Education (Atlanta: Scholars Press, 1988). For related discussions on theological education, see Don Browning, David Polk, and Ian Evison, eds., *The Education of the Practical Theologian: Responses to Joseph Hough and John Cobb's "Christian Identity and Theological Education"* (Atlanta: Scholars Press, 1989); Joseph Hough and John Cobb, *Christian Identity and Theological Education* (Chico, CA: Scholars Press, 1985); Max Stackhouse, *Apologia: Contextualization, Globalization, and Mission in Theological Education* (Grand Rapids: Eerdmans, 1988); and Wheeler and Farley, *Shifting Boundaries.*

5. On the relationship between congregational studies and practical theology, see Don S. Browning, "Congregational Studies as Practical Theology," in Wind and Lewis, eds., *American Congregations*, vol. 2, *New Perspectives in the Study of Congregations*, 192-224. See also Browning's influential *A Fundamental Practical Theology: Descriptive and Strategic Proposals* (Minneapolis: Fortress, 1991). An exemplar of theological reflection with the congregation as a focus is Patrick Keifert's *Welcoming the Stranger: A Public Theology of Worship and Evangelism* (Minneapolis: Fortress, 1992).

6. See Lonergan, *Method in Theology*, chap. 10, "Dialectic." In the analysis of these positions, I have sought to follow in a general — if not a detailed fashion — Lonergan's description of the "structure" of a dialectic (see *Method*, 249ff.).

7. On the distinction between "idolatry" and "profanation," see Paul Tillich, *Systematic Theology*, vol. 3 (Chicago: University of Chicago Press, 1963).

mental Practical Theology is our first exemplar.[8] His intent is explicitly to relate the theological dimensions of congregational practices to their sociological, historical, psychological, and ethical dimensions.[9] The distinctive thrust of his argument is to argue that theology as a whole should be conceived as a "fundamental or critical practical theology." Informed by the turn to practical reason in hermeneutical and critical social theories, he intends to reverse traditional models of theological education that begin with theories and then apply them to practice. Instead, he contends that not only practical theology, but indeed all theology, needs to be conceived of as a fundamental, or critical, practical theology. Such a theology has four movements: descriptive, historical, systematic, and strategic. And a fundamental practical theology such as this begins with the practical questions that emerge within congregational life as descriptive theology. It then handles these questions more generally and critically as historical and systematic theology, and finally allows these new insights to shed light on concrete situations within congregations themselves as strategic practical theology.

Browning notes the parallels between his position and David Tracy's proposal for a revisionist theology that critically correlates Christian witnesses with other interpretations of culture and experience.[10] Nonetheless, Browning contends that Tracy's attempt to determine the transcendental truth status of such a correlation obscures the *practical* character of all theology. Hence, Browning confines his correlation approach of validity claims to more modest pragmatic, or hermeneutical, criteria. In a similar vein, he criticizes confessional theologies such as Barth's for simply applying the theory of divine revelation to the practice of, say, giving sermons.

Our second exemplar is David Kelsey's *To Understand God Truly*. In this book Kelsey seeks to provide a framework for assessing and reshaping the ethos and polity of theological schools.[11] His goal is to identify not only what unifies these schools, their construal of the *Christian thing*, but to do justice to the pluralism of ways this Christian thing is construed. His contention is that the diverse subject matters of theological schools are best understood with respect to their place and role in the actual practices

---

8. Browning, *A Fundamental Practical Theology*.

9. Note the five dimensions he includes in practical theology: the visional, obligational, tendency-needs (or anthropological), environmental-social, and rule-role.

10. See David Tracy, *Blessed Rage for Order* (New York: Seabury, 1975).

11. David Kelsey, *To Understand God Truly*.

of existing congregations. In his attempt to identify the Christian thing, he rejects any essentialist construal that would limit it to an essence or structure that remains the same in all times and spaces. Therefore, Kelsey shies away from anything more substantive than a merely nominal depiction of Christian congregations. He defines them merely as that "group of persons that gathers together to enact publicly a much more broadly practiced worship of God in Jesus' name."[12] Such a nominal approach can best be described as "cultural-linguistic," because it defines its criterion for Christian identity primarily in terms of the linguistic practices of congregations.[13]

Our third exemplar is Rebecca Chopp's *Saving Work: Feminist Practices in Theological Education,* in which she reflects on feminist practices in theological education. In an analysis of the presence of women in theological education and the current state of feminist theological scholarship, she highlights the importance of feminist practices to theological education by describing three practices: (a) narrativity, how women compose or write new narratives for their lives; (b) ecclesiality, how women have attempted to reconstruct ecclesial practices; and (c) feminist theology, how women are reconstructing theology along feminist lines. She traces how such practices deconstruct patriarchal forms of theology and reconstruct Christian theology in a feminist vein. That reconstruction is informed by a range of feminist values, such as "particularity," "embodiment," "creativity," "mutuality," "friendship," "justice," and so on. Like Browning, Chopp is critical of traditional notions of divine transcendence. In her early work, she rejects Tracy's transcendental correlation approach in favor of what she calls a "praxis correlation."[14] In *Saving Work* she rejects a traditional notion of divine transcendence, identifying it with a patriarchal emphasis on separation and detachment. Instead, she emphasizes the importance of connectedness and embodiment, not only in relationships among human beings, but also for speaking about God's relationship with human beings. She does speak of the importance of openness, but her emphasis is on openness to diversity and difference among human beings.

These three approaches differ in how they identify the central truth

---

12. Kelsey, *To Understand God Truly,* 137.

13. Cf. George Lindbeck, *The Nature of Doctrine* (Philadelphia: Westminster, 1992).

14. Rebecca Chopp, "Practical Theology and Liberation," in Lewis Mudge and James Poling, eds., *Formation and Reflection* (Philadelphia: Fortress, 1987), 120-38.

and meaning of Christian theology. For Kelsey, it is the practices performed in the name of Jesus that constitute the Christian identity of congregations and theological schools. For Browning, it is the critical correlation of the range of validity claims — metaphysical, normative, natural, social, and ecological — that emerge in the study of congregations. For Chopp, it is the feminist praxis that transforms patriarchal Christianity.

However, we can note three points of similarity among these positions. First, all three accept such modern notions of historical consciousness and a nonteleological view of the natural world. They are not advocating a return to premodern Christian orthodoxies. Second, all three advocate the turn to practical reasoning characteristic of much postmodern thought: they all recognize a deep interconnection between rationality and such factors as commitment, desire, and shared systems of belief and practice. Finally, all three are critical of traditional theological concepts of divine transcendence or philosophical forms of transcendental argumentation. This is the case whether they are conceived of in essentialist terms (Kelsey), in confessionalist or transcendental and metaphysical terms (Browning), or in the patriarchal terms of detachment and separation (Chopp).

Instead, Kelsey opts for a *nominal* criterion for truth: the name of Jesus. Browning and Chopp opt for *pragmatic* criteria: what enables human life to flourish. Such criteria enable these theologians to criticize some distortions in classical theology: (a) the reduction of what is distinctively Christian to a universal essence within human experience (Kelsey); (b) the reduction of concrete practices to theoretical abstractions (Browning); and (c) the reduction of Christianity to a patriarchal religion (Chopp). These criteria, in turn, enable them to criticize possible distortions of each other's positions. Kelsey might detect an essentialism in Browning; Browning might detect a narrow confessionalism in Kelsey; Chopp might detect patriarchialism in both Browning and Kelsey, and they, in turn, might detect a tendency by Chopp to reduce Christian faith to the concerns of a particular cause or movement.

The criticisms these positions offer each other can be situated within the long tradition of rational criticisms of distorted religion. These extend from Heraclitus's and Plato's critique of ancient Greek beliefs to Kant's and Hume's critiques of classical theism, to the later critiques of Christianity by Marx, Freud, Feuerbach, and Nietzsche. Nonetheless, in addition to these rational criticisms there have also been, throughout the history of both Judaism and Christianity, distinctively *theological* forms of critique: these are the *prophetic* and the *mystical*.[15] Prophetic critique is identified with the Old Testament prophets, some of the movements of monasticism, the Reformation, and evangelical radicalism. This kind of critique attacks the sin of *idolatry*, what I have identified above as the sin of treating as sacred or divine that which is profane or mundane. By contrast, the mystical critique within Christianity negates any form of *profanation*, what I have identified as the sin of treating as profane or mundane that which is sacred. This is found among patristic and medieval theologians. These two sins can be thought of as constituting the polarity of methods for understanding God truly.

In my analysis of Barth and Rahner,[16] I will show how these two forms of critique mutually test each other's theological distortions — each other's possible sin.[17] And yet, each form of critique is rooted in the same

15. See David Tracy's use of the contrast between the "mystical" and "prophetic" in *Dialogue with the Other: The Inter-Religious Dialogue* (Louvain: Peeters Press; Grand Rapids: Eerdmans, 1990); see also his earlier contrast between "manifestation" and "proclamation" in *Analogical Imagination: Christian Theology and the Culture of Pluralism* (New York: Crossroad, 1987). See also Paul Tillich's contrast between the prophetic and mystical in *Systematic Theology*, vol. 1 (Chicago: University of Chicago Press, 1951), 81ff., 172ff.

16. For another study that examines how Barth and Rahner might contribute to a conception of "critical theology," see Gareth Jones, *Critical Theology: Questions of Truth and Method* (New York: Paragon House, 1995). His argument is compatible with the one I am making in this chapter. On the question of a "critical theology," note the following comment by Hugh T. Kerr in his essay "Time for a Critical Theology": "A critical theology, taking seriously the revelatory dimension of the gospel, could be our best safeguard against selling out completely to a 'religionless Christianity' which is no more distinguishable from secular humanism" (*Our Life in God's Light: Essays by Hugh T. Kerr*, ed. J. M. Mulder [Philadelphia: Fortress, 1979], 60, quoted in Gareth Jones, *Critical Theology*, 6, n. 7). But note also Kerr's comment on "critical theology": "It is perhaps not unduly summary to say that this means systematic theology (a rarely practiced inquiry in the ancient English universities) is critical of its own grounds and disturbing to the faithful (a rare phenomenon in confessional institutions). The task of the critical theologian in this sense is — or would be — to reflect, theoretically and critically, upon the first-order levels of more or less spontaneous religious (in this sense Christian) existence as they are found in symbolic, linguistic, and institutional forms" (in Kerr's review of Nicholas Lash's "Doing Theology on Dover Beach," *New Blackfriars* 60 [1979]: 237; quoted in Jones, *Critical Theology*, 6, n. 6).

17. This critique will be related to their respective notions of "hiddenness" (Barth) and "incomprehensibility" (Rahner). On the theological concept of "hiddenness," see B. A. Gerrish, "To the Unknown God: Luther and Calvin on the Hiddenness of God," *Journal of Religion* (1973): 263-93. For Rahner's definition of "incomprehensibility," see "Thomas Aquinas on the Incomprehensible God," in David Tracy, ed., *Celebrating the Medieval Heritage: A*

theological criterion, which is the God known by Christians as the God re-vealed in Jesus Christ by the power of the Holy Spirit.[18]

An Appropriation of Karl Barth's and Karl Rahner's Theologies

In the prolegomenon to his *Church Dogmatics,* Barth contends that the task of dogmatics is to test the proclamation of the church against the be-ing of the church, the revealing and reconciling address of God in Jesus Christ.[19] His theological method is rooted in the core act of Reformation piety, which is the preaching of the Word that sanctifies and justifies and that leads to obedience and self-denial. Barth's theology criticizes both a Protestant liberalism that locates the criterion for Christian theology in a more general ontology or anthropology and a Roman Catholicism that judges Christian theology in terms of the infallible teaching of the church. For Barth, theology's task is to test church proclamation against the crite-rion of the revelation of God. This revelation is given in a free divine act, rather than being the result of any human possibility or necessity. None-theless, this task is inherently difficult. In preaching, God's speech and ac-tion is only indirectly expressed in the two direct forms, proclamation and Scripture, forms that are in and of themselves human and not divine. Hence we encounter the challenge of dogmatics: how to discern God's speech and action when it is only found in a human form.

Colloquy on the Thought of Aquinas and Bonaventure, Journal of Religion Supplement (1978): S107-26. For an appropriation of Karl Barth's concept of hiddenness, see Eberhard Jüngel, *God as the Mystery of the World: On the Foundation of the Theology of the Crucified One in the Dispute between Theism and Atheism,* trans. Darrell L. Guder (Grand Rapids: Eerdmans, 1983).

18. Note Lonergan's perceptive comment: "It is to be observed that while for secular man of the twentieth century the most familiar differentiation of consciousness distin-guishes and relates *theory* and *common sense,* still in the history of mankind both in the East and the Christian West the predominant differentiation of consciousness has set in opposi-tion and in mutual enrichment the realms of *common sense* and of *transcendence*" (*Method in Theology,* 266; italics added). The thrust of my argument in this chapter is for the central-ity of the latter differentiation of consciousness (between common sense and transcen-dence) to theological reflection without negating the importance of the former differentia-tion (between theory and common sense).

19. See Karl Barth, *Church Dogmatics,* vols. 1-4, ed. G. W. Bromiley and T. F. Torrance (Edinburgh: T&T Clark, 1936-77).

Barth understands God's hiddenness in revelation. Thus, God's speech and action is always, on the one hand, a law that judges all human pretensions and projections onto divinity; on the other hand, God's speech and action is expressed in concrete human forms. These include the humanity of Jesus, the preaching that gives witness to that humanity, the church in which that preaching occurs, and so forth. These forms tangibly articulate the gospel, God's revelation and salvation. Preaching repeats the Word of God in the here and now; it recollects and expects Jesus' death and resurrection. The sacramental reality at the heart of time is God's election of Jesus Christ, an election that culminates in his life, death, and resurrection. It is this life, death, and resurrection that, by the power of Jesus' resurrected Spirit, is repeated in the church's recollection and expectation of its eschatological and cosmic implications. These are always simultaneously past, present, and future. The theologian's task is patterned after that of an exegete and preacher committed to the hearing and doing of the Word. In this regard, Barth explicitly links his hermeneutical method with a Law/Gospel dialectic that actually speaks of God's judgment and mercy. The theological task must be an act of prayer and of gratitude, an act of response to a divine address, both *there and then* and *here and now.*

Rahner's theology, by contrast, is deeply informed by the Ignatian exercises and the act of discerning divine will and presence in the concrete and ordinary circumstances of life.[20] At the heart of his work is a depiction of the divine-human encounter as a dialogue in which human beings are understood to have an ecstatic or transcendent movement beyond strictly empirical experience. This orientation or openness toward the divine is radicalized by grace in such a way that humans do not experience God merely as the infinitely distant Other, but they also experience God as immediate and attainable. God can be apprehended, as in the beatific vision, in loving ecstasy and rapture. The task of theology entails depicting this fundamental encounter philosophically. It entails presenting the fundamental teachings or mysteries of the faith theologically so that they render an encounter with the divine and not merely a teaching of church tradition. Finally, it entails describing existentially the process whereby human

---

20. Karl Rahner, *Foundations of Christian Faith: An Introduction to the Idea of Christianity* (New York: Crossroad, 1987); *Theological Investigations,* vols. 1-6 (Baltimore: Helicon Press, 1961-69); vols. 7-10 (New York: Herder and Herder, 1971-74); vols. 11-16 (New York: Seabury Press, 1974-79); vols. 17-23 (New York: Crossroad, 1981-92).

beings may surrender themselves unconditionally to the abiding presence of mystery in the concrete circumstances and decisions of their lives. But these tasks are fraught with a problematic similar to that of Barth's dogmatics. How can divine and infinite reality be said to be present within human forms that are always conditioned by finitude, realities such as space, time, history, and language?

Rahner understands God's incomprehensibility in self-communication to speak of the way God is experienced in one's abstraction from concrete particulars. Such abstraction, in turn, leads to the categorical experience of God in concrete experiences and thoughts, the finding of God in all things, and the mediated immediacy of God's presence in all reality. Explicit and more frequently implicit acts of prayer, for Rahner, enact the dynamism whereby God's offer of grace is accepted. We find this, for example, when decisions are made between good and evil, right and wrong in light of a conception of absolute truth or absolute good. For Rahner, the center of human and cosmic history is also Christological: that is, it is defined in terms of Jesus' incarnation, where the divine became human. All human actions and thoughts — and within them, all history — find their *telos,* their true meaning and purpose, from the incarnation. Rahner's mode of theological reflection is patterned after that of the person who leads others in contemplation and action, through an attitude of *indifference* toward all things so that one can then find God in all things. His very concept of the interpretation of doctrine is that it is such a person that leads one to an actual encounter with abiding mystery. The goal of interpretation is to lead one to see how the innumerable beliefs within Christianity actually have to do with the mystery of God's self-communication.

These two theologies offer criticisms of the potential distortions in each other's positions. Rahner's fear is that a position like Barth's fails to grasp what lies at the heart of God's incomprehensibility, which is the very inexhaustibility and limitlessness of God's own life. This is a mystery that cannot be reduced to the finite expressions of revelation or grace, even though these serve as the very grammar of divine self-expression. Rahner wants to emphasize the fact that it is always God, and therefore uncreated grace, who is present in the experience of Jesus and the Holy Spirit. He stresses this even though this experience is always mediated by the finite person experiencing it. This leads him to criticize all forms of positivism, which can include a metaphysical *ontologism,* a biblical and dogmatic *extrinsicism,* or a scientific *positivism* that denies the sacred presence of

God in all finite reality. The key to Rahner's criticism lies in his critique of distortions concerning God's revelation or the experience of grace. He is concerned that God not be viewed as simply another agent, even if the largest agent, among human agents.

Barth's fear would be that Rahner fails to grasp the particular character of God's mystery as address: this is the election of Jesus Christ and his life, death, and resurrection, and the church's distinctive witness to it. For Barth, God's hiddenness even in this revelation entails that God cannot be circumscribed in ways that comprehend God's free act, as though this event could be circumscribed within human existence. He criticizes all forms of the analogy of being — whether of a liberal or Roman Catholic variety — that would reduce the free act of God's revelation to a category of being or subjectivity. The force of Barth's criticism lies in the critique of distortions that would treat the free act of God as yet another realization of a possibility within human existence.

What is at stake in the contrast between Barth and Rahner? Is it that Barth is a revelational positivist? Does he disallow human autonomy, the full knowledge and experience of God, or any possibility of a sacramental presence of God in the world or the church, and so on?[21] Is it, in turn, that Rahner is an experiential expressivist? Does he not do justice to either the mystery of God or the concrete media that mediate the church's witness to the distinctive life, death, and resurrection of Jesus Christ?[22]

Where Barth and Rahner differ is over what each considers to be the central distortion of faith. For Barth, the central distortion is any false identification of some aspect of human experience — nature, reason, or history — with the knowledge and experience of God. This distortion presents the danger of being an idolatry that would sacralize some finite reality and absolutize it. By contrast, Rahner's idea of the central distortion

21. Barth has often been depicted as a "revelational positivist" who fails to deal adequately with human experience, both inside and outside the church, by subsuming all reality within the single act of God's election of Jesus Christ. For the first use of this phrase, see Dietrich Bonhoeffer, *Letters from Prison*, ed. Eberhard Bethge (New York: Macmillan Co., 1971), 28.

22. Rahner has been depicted as an "experiential expressivist" who fails to deal adequately with not only linguistic and cultural experience and natural constraints, but most importantly with what is distinctive to the Christian ecclesial experience and its witness to the life, death, and resurrection of Jesus Christ. For the first use of this phrase, see George Lindbeck, *The Nature of Doctrine*.

is not a false identification with the divine, but the negation of divine presence.[23] What he criticizes is not false spirituality but a false secularism. This is the case whether it takes an ecclesial or a humanist-scientific form, any form that fails to perceive God's sacred presence in all reality. For Rahner, the central theological distortion is the profanation that negates or refuses to recognize the presence of the sacred in all things, including one's own and others' agency and power.

A Critical Conversation with Congregational Studies

What relevance does this excursus on Barth and Rahner have for congregational studies? These two figures are relevant because they appropriate classical notions of hiddenness and incomprehensibility in ways that enact the presence and mystery of God in the actual practices of congregations. Such practices include listening to and appropriating sermons and Bible reading, and discerning God's will in specific choices on issues. Practical theology, along with its subdisciplines of theological education and congregational studies, has made important strides in rethinking how theological reflection might be done, given both modern and postmodern shifts in thinking. Nonetheless, the concern with what is distinctively theological in these fields of study could be intensified. Seeking to address this concern in this section, I set Barth and Rahner in critical conversation with Browning, Kelsey, and Chopp, the three exemplars of current thinking in theological education and practical theology.

Browning's central contribution to the study of congregations is his comprehensiveness. His fundamental practical theology has within its purview the whole range of goods, needs, and desires that constitute human and creaturely existence before God. He offers in this an antidote to a linguistic positivism that would reduce the totality of human existence to

---

23. Note the similarities between Karl Rahner's notion of sin and that of Lonergan: "Sinfulness similarly is distinct from moral evil; it is the privation of total loving; it is the radical dimension of lovelessness. That dimension can be hidden by sustained superficiality, by evading ultimate questions, by absorption in all that the world offers to challenge our resourcefulness, to relax our bodies, to distract our minds. But escape may not be permanent and then the absence of fulfillment reveals itself in unrest, the absence of joy in the pursuit of fun, the absence of peace in disgust — a depressive disgust with oneself or a manic, hostile, even violent disgust with mankind" (*Method in Theology*, 242-43).

specific cultural expressions, to particular forms of Christian identity. Nonetheless, Barth's notion of hiddenness brings to the fore a possible danger in this position. It might subordinate Christian theology to criteria derived from other disciplines and thereby commit the idolatry of establishing an external vantage point from which to view God's self-revelation. An antidote to such a distortion may be found in Rahner's understanding of the radical depth and irreducibility of divine incomprehensibility. The depth and irreducibility is, in fact, the condition for the possibility of all creaturely existence and all human knowing.

Kelsey's central contribution to congregational studies is his focus on the constitutive role the name of Jesus has for defining what is Christian in the practices of congregations. He offers an antidote to an experiential expressivism that would de-emphasize linguistic practices that constitute Christian congregations as Christian in favor of transcendental experiences of God. But Rahner's concept of incomprehensibility brings to the fore a possible distortion in Kelsey's position, the reducing of the Christian thing to a nominal — in Rahner's term, "extrinsicist" — conception of divine presence. As an antidote, we can recall Barth's emphasis that it is finally the resurrected Spirit of Jesus who is disclosed in the preaching and teaching of the church, the Spirit who is present precisely as the ascended Lord in that proclamation.

Chopp's argument for the importance of feminist practices in theological reflection is a definite critique of all forms of patriarchalism in Christian theology. But she also offers the corrective of emphasizing the centrality of concrete human experiences and movements that are taking place in our time. And yet, from a Barthian standpoint, the danger in her position is that it tends to blur the distinction between God's Word as an address from the Other and one's own particular experience of salvation or liberation. Once again, Rahner's concept of incomprehensibility provides a way of thinking about God as the abiding presence that is tangibly present within all human activity. This is true especially in human experiences of liberation, even though this presence cannot be reduced to any particular thought or action or experience of liberation.[24]

24. Having outlined these insights from Barth and Rahner, I should also comment on how the emphases of our three contemporary thinkers offer correctives to their work. We have noted Kelsey's focus on cultural-linguistic practices, Browning's integration of a range of specific dimensions of human experience, and Chopp's focus on women's experi-

On the basis of this critical conversation, I offer three insights for an interdisciplinary approach to understanding God truly in congregations.[25] These insights revolve around the threefold task of how Christians might: (1) test the spirits in moral conversation and action; (2) reflect on that lived practice; and (3) understand how God is active in both activities.[26]

The first task involves testing the spirits in conversation and action. Following our reading of Browning, this entails placing within the compass of theological reflection the totality of creaturely existence, including the metaphysical and religious, the social and linguistic, and the biological. It is especially important that theological reflection encompasses the whole of human existence in our highly complex, differentiated modern

---

ence. These three emphases indicate a strong trend in recent theology toward the concrete and particular in human experience. Barth and Rahner have been criticized for their lack of attention to concrete human history and experience: Barth for collapsing all creaturely existence (historical and natural) into the figure of Christ, and Rahner for collapsing all reality, including biblical history and public human history, into the creature's dynamism toward transcendence. See, e.g., Kendall Soulen's critique of Barth and Rahner in *The God of Israel and Christian Theology* (Minneapolis: Fortress, 1996). Among Protestants influenced by Barth, Wolfhart Pannenberg has placed a greater focus on human rationality, human history in general, and the proleptic expectation of the future. See, e.g., his *Systematic Theology*, vol. 1, trans. Geoffrey W. Bromiley (Grand Rapids: Eerdmans, 1988). Eberhard Jüngel places greater focus on the death and resurrection of Jesus as the locus for naming God's identity; see Jüngel, *God as Mystery of the World*. Finally, Jürgen Moltmann has emphasized both the cross and human creaturely freedom within history; see, e.g., *The Crucified God: The Cross of Christ as the Foundation and Criticism of Christian Theology*, trans. R. H. Wilson and John Bowden (San Francisco: Harper & Row, 1974). Within Roman Catholicism, Johann Baptist Metz has emphasized similar themes, giving greater attention to the future and to the suffering of Jesus and human beings in general within history; see *Faith in History and Society: Toward a Practical Fundamental Theology* (New York: Seabury, 1980). Hans Urs von Balthasar, in turn, places greater emphasis on the death and resurrection of Jesus and the centrality of that event within the life of God; see *The Glory of the Lord: A Theological Aesthetics*, 3 vols. (San Francisco: Ignatius Press, 1983-88), and *Theodramatik* (Einsiedeln: Johannes-Verlag, 1973-83).

25. I also develop some of these themes in another paper, entitled "Cultivating Wisdom in a Complex World," in L. Gregory Jones and Stephanie Paulsell, eds., *The Vocation of the Theological Teacher* (Grand Rapids: Eerdmans, 2001).

26. My analysis follows the threefold pattern William Schweiker outlines in his essay "Beyond the Captivity of Theology: Toward a New Theology of Culture," presented at the American Academy of Religion, Nov. 2000: (1) socio-cultural *analysis;* (2) conceptual-linguistic *articulation;* and (3) religio-moral *attestation.* See also his *Power, Value and Conviction: Theological Ethics in the Postmodern Age* (Cleveland: Pilgrim Press, 1998).

societies. In these societies we have multiple subsystems that are reflexive, that is, they act on and are affected by each other. In such societies, each social system, such as the law or the economy, must adapt itself as it interacts with information coming from other domains.[27] But how can one speak about this differentiation and still speak about God and thus the *whole* of one's existence? Following Luther and Calvin, the Reformation practice of preaching, with its reading, exegeting, and appropriating Scripture, cannot be divorced from the activity of enacting one's vocation. What is the meaning of "vocation" in classical Reformation theologies? It is the institutionally embodied expression of how individuals and groups might enact God's purposes in all of life, including the family, the government, and the church. In a similar vein, the Catholic practice of discerning the spirits presupposes a differentiated and hierarchical conception of human goods or ends. What does this conception of human goods or ends entail? It entails that human beings have a natural right to self-preservation even as they participate in a common social good.

Both sets of theological resources — that of a Reformation understanding of vocation or a Roman Catholic understanding of differentiated goods — presuppose God's presence and activity. In the former, the norms and purposes of life are rooted in patterns of interaction founded ultimately on God's fidelity to creation. In the latter, the natural ends of humans flourishing as individuals and in communities serve supernatural ends. These two legacies offer complex symbolic and conceptual resources for thinking about how we might order our lives as individuals, families, and congregations. More important, they offer resources for thinking about how Christian communities are indeed "ecumenical, worldly forces that can and may and must counterbalance [even] transnational, global agents."[28]

The second task involves reflecting on particular lived practices. Following our reading of Kelsey, this entails naming within the concrete practices and face-to-face encounters of Christian communities precisely what

---

27. See John Tomlinson, *Globalization and Culture* (Chicago: University of Chicago Press, 1999), and Roland Robertson, *Globalization: Social Theory and Global Culture* (London: SAGE Publications, 1992). See also William Schweiker, "Beyond the Captivity of Theology."

28. See William Schweiker's discussion of these two legacies in "Responsibility in the World of Mammon," in Max L. Stackhouse and Peter J. Paris, eds., *God and Globalization*, vol. 1 of *Religion and the Powers of the Common Life* (Harrisburg, PA: Trinity Press International, 2000), 105-39.

the God who raised Israel's Jesus from the dead would have us be and do (Rom. 12:1-2).[29] Precisely how is this God working all things together for good, not only in our lives but in the world as a whole, even when there may appear to be strong evidence to the contrary (Rom. 8:28)?

This is precisely why Christians exegete and appropriate Christian Scripture. They want to seek to discern God's will for their lives as they read and meditate on these texts. One can contrast the Reformation practice of preaching and exegeting the Word with the Roman Catholic practice of discerning the spirits. Nevertheless, these practices have a similar purpose. They both provide believers with a means for seeing and hearing how their lives are indeed affected by the historic and cosmic implications of Jesus' death and resurrection. Therefore, in these practices the task of interpreting the Bible is not simply that of repristinating the meanings of these ancient texts; nor is the task simply to find some singular essence that these texts were *really* intending.[30]

Rather, the purpose of these practices is to read the biblical texts inductively in their full complexity, as actual genres and actual traditions in their original settings in life.[31] Such an approach means reading these texts not only in their original settings in life but also in the range of ways they have been interpreted over time. Such a task will involve rethinking many of our highly abstract, commonsense notions of how God is active in the world in light of the rich and complex relationships among the pluralistic witnesses of Scripture.[32] And such rethinking will mean taking seriously the distinct ways God's presence and activity is actually depicted in biblical descriptions of creation, Jesus' life, death, and resurrection, and the ongoing presence of the Spirit.[33] The result of such rethinking is an even richer

29. See Robert Jenson's focus on the Trinity in *Christian Dogmatics*, vol. 1, ed. Carl Braaten and Robert Jenson (Minneapolis: Fortress, 1984).

30. See Paul Ricoeur, *Figuring the Sacred: Religion, Narrative and Imagination* (Minneapolis: Fortress, 1995). See also Ronald Duty's essay entitled "Discerning the Will of God," in this volume.

31. Thus the historical and literary criticism of biblical texts has been an important part of the use of Scripture in this study of congregations. See, e.g., David Fredrickson's essay in this volume.

32. See Michael Welker, "Christian Theology: What Direction at the End of the Second Millennium?" in Miroslav Volf, Carmen Krieg, and Thomas Kucharz, eds., *The Future of Theology: Essays in Honor of Jürgen Moltmann* (Grand Rapid: Eerdmans, 1996), 73-88.

33. See Welker's reference to John Polkinghorne (*The Faith of a Physicist: Reflections of a Bottom-up Thinker* [Princeton, NJ: Princeton University Press, 1994], 4) in his essay

understanding of God's power and wisdom — and the creative freedom of creatures. It also entails correcting distorted ways of thinking and speaking about God and God's relationship to the world. This enables humans to appreciate and experience more fully the "real joy in God's vitality, genuine fear of God, and the vitality of human experiences of God."[34]

The third task involves discerning how God is active and present in life. Following our reading of Chopp, this entails discerning and responding to what God is doing in concrete, particular circumstances. As I have noted above, the very complexity of highly differentiated modern societies entails reflexivity: different domains act on each other and affect each other reflexively. This means, for example, that the mass media, the economy, and what is identified as the spiritual are in a very real way profoundly linked. As human agents, we cannot divorce ourselves from this reflexivity.[35] Indeed, to function in such a complex society, we need to have a high level of self-reflexivity. This is required even though we may find ourselves thinking, feeling, and acting amid circumstances in which we do not feel like individuals who have much control over such matters.[36] But for Christians the purpose of such reflexivity cannot simply be about self-mastery or achieving one's purposes in the midst of a rapidly changing and sometimes chaotic world. The purpose is to discern how best to participate in God's justice and mercy in this world.

We have been baptized in Christ's death, and thus have "died to sin." This means that we, too, like Christ, might be "raised from the dead by the glory of the Father, so that we might walk in newness of life" (Rom. 6:4). Partly at issue here is dying to being self-centered in an individualistic sense, of seeing only our own ends and not the broader sweep of things. But also at issue is how we participate in systems, such as the economic,

---

"Christian Theology," 78. Following Polkinghorne's observation in the Gifford Lectures of 1993-94 that "many theologians are instinctively top-down thinkers," Welker suggests an inductive "bottom-up" reading of Scripture.

34. Welker, "Christian Theology," 75.

35. Note the ongoing relevance of Lonergan's perceptive analysis of reflexivity; see esp. his discussion of Bruno Snell's *The Discovery of the Mind* (e.g., in *Method in Theology*, 260ff.). For an insightful discussion of "spiritual reflexivity" from a sociological perspective, see Wade Clark Roof, *Spiritual Marketplace: Baby Boomers and the Remaking of American Religion* (Princeton, NJ: Princeton University Press, 1999).

36. See, e.g., Peter Senger, *The Fifth Discipline: The Art and Practice of the Learning Organization* (New York: Doubleday, 1990).

political, and cultural systems in which we find ourselves. We use these systems to pursue particular interests, many of which are incompatible with God's reign of truth and justice, as is evident in Romans 8:38-39: here is a list of things we might fear would separate us from God's love.[37] But in the final analysis, it is not critique and death that we are about — but life. The purpose of testing our biases and distortions is for us to perceive the rich density of God's goodness in the very webs of interconnectedness we find ourselves in, whether on an interpersonal or institutional level.[38]

In the words of François Roustang, a modern Jesuit spiritual writer: "To discern God's will, our first care must be to let things and beings assume their own value and their own weight, to thrust aside previous impressions and to welcome as a living reality this world in which God is at work."[39] This requires spiritual discernment, what St. Paul calls the "wisdom of God": it is allowing the Spirit, who searches all things, to reveal to us the "deep things of God," the "mind of Christ."[40] Such intelligence is not measured by scholastic aptitude tests; rather, it lives out of the truth of the future. This future is entailed in the promise that all things will indeed work together for good and that nothing can separate us from God's love in Christ Jesus (Rom. 8). But such discernment also respects the past: it recognizes how the present is constituted by previous situations, events, relationships, acts, and thoughts. Of course, this past derives its value from the future that God is preparing for us. Nonetheless, the future can also be a dangerous myth if it does not accept the past, and if it does not fully recognize where and what things really are in the present.

Thus the spiritual cannot be divorced from the cognitive in congregational studies. Spiritual or theological wisdom *(sapientia)* must embrace the other disciplines in the study of congregations *(scientia)*, such as history, the social sciences, education, and so on.[41] We must not aban-

---

37. Welker makes this point in "Christian Theology," 84-86.

38. Lonergan's very helpful discussion of biases and distortions in theological reflection should not be overlooked. See *Method in Theology,* esp. chap. 10 on "Dialectic" and chap. 11 on "Foundations." Iris Murdoch is also helpful on this; see, e.g., *Metaphysics as a Guide to Morals* (London: Penguin, 1992).

39. François Roustang, S.J., *Growth in the Spirit,* trans. Kathleen Pond (New York: Sheed & Ward, 1966), 141.

40. On the "mind of Christ" in Phil. 2, see David Frederickson's essay in this volume.

41. Again, Lonergan is helpful on the relationship between the "sapiential" and the "cognitive," or, to use his categories, intellectual, moral, and religious conversion. "I would

don empirical description and rational analysis, for they have a role in our fully understanding the entanglements of our lives: to whom we commit ourselves, what we buy, how we vote, how we spend our time — the basic attitudes, beliefs, and values we allow to influence our perception of the world. These are precisely the places where we experience the beauty and goodness of God's creation, the reality of sin and tragedy, and the healing and forgiving power of Jesus' resurrection and the new creation it entails.

The specific form such discernment takes will vary. The complexity of the biblical texts themselves, and their rich diversity of genres, is testimony to that variety. Note the range of these texts, from the wisdom that accounts for the best in nature and human intelligence (Prov. 8) to the folly of the cross that confounds the wise and the debaters of the age (1 Cor. 1:20-25). In this chapter I have focused on the dialectic that these two classical forms of wisdom represent. We have seen these in Rahner's depiction of grace and Barth's depiction of the gospel. We have also noted the two distortions, or forms of sin, that they wish to reject. But this analysis has not simply focused on critique. The point of the dialectic we have analyzed is to assist congregations in discerning how God is at work *in*, *with*, and *under* the reality of our lives. The point is to enable us to discern when and how God's goodness is being replaced by some idolatrous effort to be God, and when and how to enact God's justice and mercy in the often messy complexity of life.[42]

---

use [the notion of 'sublation'] in Karl Rahner's sense rather than Hegel's to mean that what sublates goes beyond what is sublated, introduces something new and distinct, puts everything on a new basis, yet so far from interfering with the sublated or destroying it, on the contrary needs it, includes it, preserves all its proper features and properties, and carries them forward to a fuller realization within a richer context" (*Method in Theology*, 241).

42. Cf. Michael Welker's comment about "realistic theology" in *God the Spirit* (Minneapolis: Fortress, 1994), xi: "Many theologies grounded in human experiences and forms of experience need to take as their points of departure both actual demonstrations of God's power within creation and people's search for God in the realm of that which is creaturely. This is true whether the orientation of such theologies be empirical, pietistic, moral, epistemological-philosophical, or otherwise. A realistic theology mediates this need of theologies grounded in human experience with the concern of classical, Reformation, and dialectical theologies 'from above' to take God's divinity seriously and not to obstruct enjoyment of the fullness and glory of God."

Conclusion

In summary, throughout these discussions of congregations we have been arguing that God can only be understood indirectly. God is always both hidden and revealed in the church's proclamation (cf. Barth); God's mystery and incomprehensibility remain even as we come to know and love God more deeply (cf. Rahner). Nonetheless, as Christians we affirm that God has revealed who God is in the life, death, and resurrection of Jesus. By the power of the Spirit, we have been called and sent to tangibly attend, assert, decide, and act on this within the totality of our lives. But that means that we must risk thinking and speaking about God, and thus we risk the sins of either idolatry or profanation.

Within Protestantism, the main fear has been of the danger of idolatry. If anything, modern culture has sought to base its public life on what is universal, objective, and abstract, and not on what is sectarian. Indeed, one could argue that the Enlightenment critique of particular religions could be seen as a secularized version of this Protestant critique.[43] The Congregational Study Research Team has presupposed that the finite is capable of bearing the infinite: this means that the worldly and mundane can indeed embody God's presence. What I have argued for here is an appropriate balance of this polarity. Of course, in addition to the danger of idolatry, there is also the danger of profanation. Therefore, what I have offered by way of a comparison of Barth and Rahner is an analysis of precisely this dialectic and how it might function in the discerning of God's presence in actual congregational practices.

43. Immanuel Kant, *The Critique of Religion within the Limits of Reason Alone* (Cambridge, UK: Cambridge University Press, 1999), would be the paradigmatic exemplar of this.

The Use of Scripture in Congregational Research

Donald H. Juel

Among the features that make up the working agenda of the Congregational Studies Research Team (CSRT) is the explicit use of the Bible: we have self-consciously used the Bible at every level of the program. The purpose of this brief essay is to make some observations about the various ways Scripture has been used, to offer a preliminary assessment of the effect on the research, and to suggest some ways to think about biblical interpretation as a feature of this program.

To speak of the "use" of Scripture sounds almost irreverent. It would seem more appropriate to read the Bible for its own sake. However, things are not always what they appear. Talk about Scripture and its authority often proves empty. The respect accorded the Bible may well be inversely proportional to the influence it exercises. As a cultural icon, Scripture occupies a prominent place in our public rituals, such as in trials, installations to public office, and even in political campaigns.

Yet it is increasingly apparent that the Bible is not read by the vast majority of those who grant it such respect. It is not a small matter that the Bible has been handed on through the centuries by people who were convinced that it is good for something. The Congregational Studies Research Team has proceeded with the conviction that the Bible is important to the extent that it is used. In this essay I will seek to examine the various ways the Bible has been used in the whole research process and to draw some major hermeneutical implications.

The Bible and Christian Imagination

The Bible is principally important as a way of shaping Christian imagination. That suggests that its major function is in the formation of an ethos within which individual believers and congregations may understand themselves. Of course, this has already happened as the Bible has been read and appropriated, as the biblical words and sentences have been set to music and sung in hymns and liturgies, and as they have shaped the prayers that generations of believers have prayed. But to the degree that people inhabit a world increasingly shaped by a secular culture, the Bible can have an increasingly important role in changing people's minds. This role is not, first of all, by providing specific answers to questions about particular moral issues; rather, it is by creating a different world in which people live and move and have their being.

This is a distinctive approach to Bible reading. Among those in the church who tend to have a high regard for Scripture, the majority have been trained to view the Bible as an answer book, particularly on moral *issues.* In congregations where the authority of Scripture is an explicit topic for discussion, in virtually every instance the real issue is a debate about moral issues. These debates are notably about such controversial matters as abortion or human sexuality, and interpretation consists principally in locating answers to those major questions. This is true not only for those who seek biblical answers that will settle conversations ("Bible bullets"), but also for those who enlist scholarly methods to disarm Scripture and disqualify it from consideration. Both of them view the Bible essentially as a book about what we are to do. The number of biblical texts they actually discuss is remarkably small, and the portions of Scripture that are apparently irrelevant to such conversations are remarkably extensive.

The approach to reading the Bible owes a great deal to views of language. For many people, words are containers of meaning that point to something more real. Students speak of what stories "mean" or "stand for" or "represent." The assumption seems to be that the biblical works are *about* something else. They are either statements of historical fact, or, in the case of moral issues, propositions that can be stated in the form of declarative sentences. And thus the task of interpreters is to formulate those sentences.

There are several problems with such a view of biblical language. One is that the approach bears little fruit. Seeking to derive an answer to a controversial question from the Bible seldom settles anything. Such interpretations merely provide insulation from opposing views or weapons to use against others. They change few minds. Another problem is that few biblical works were written to be reduced to a sentence or two. It's true that Jesus told parables whose meaning can perhaps be formulated concisely in a sentence or two, such as, "God is generous in forgiving sinners." However, the formulation does not *do* to readers what the parable does. In the story that Jesus tells about a vineyard owner who pays laborers who have spent only one hour in the vineyard the same as those who have worked all day, one can experience the generosity of God in a way that can still evoke powerful reactions from readers today. Propositions do not shape an imagination; parables do. They work by giving readers an experience of truth in the form of extended analogies that rearrange our mental furniture.

The use of the Bible by the Congregational Studies Research Team has sought less to find answers in biblical passages than to invite groups into a world created by the biblical words. Such a world is one in which God is an active agent and in which there are possibilities for fruitful interaction. The use of Scripture seeks to create that world by allowing different experiences of Scripture to provide different habits of reading and interpretation.

Locating Ourselves

The Bible fruitfully requires some hunches. Readers need some hints about what they are to look for. People already come to the Bible with *prejudices,* some of which we have already noted. Those prejudices may need to be called into question. The tradition of the church provides hunches about the biblical story that have stood the test of time. These might be called "fruitful prejudices."[1] Perhaps the most important prejudice is one we might call "evangelical." We read the Bible, first, not to learn what we are to do, but rather to learn what God has done. The Gospels spend far more time speaking about what Jesus did, and what was done to him, than about what we are to do. The good news is that God is unwilling to leave our world to its own destructive devices. Particularly in the ministry of Jesus

---

1. The notion of "fruitful prejudices" draws on the important contribution in the field of hermeneutics by Hans-Georg Gadamer, *Truth and Method,* 2nd rev. ed., trans. Joel Weinsheimer and Donald G. Marshall (New York: Continuum, 2003; originally published in German in 1960).

and in the subsequent church's preaching of the crucified and risen Christ, God works to make of the world a place for life. Our conviction as Christians is that it is the intrusive act of God on behalf of a world still in bondage to sin that sets faith in motion. God was and will be the primary agent in our lives as Christians. Trinitarian formulations are an attempt to make that statement in a way that takes most fully into account the experience of the God who created the heavens and the earth. This is the same God who in Jesus continues to redeem a world in bondage to sin. And this is the same God who through the Holy Spirit continues to freely give life until the day of the promised consummation.

Such prejudices require testing, reshaping, and modifying. However, without such hunches about the point of the biblical story, our reading of Scripture will lack direction and focus. This is a point at which the tradition of the church is a friend to those who seek to read and make sense of the biblical witness.

Interpreting Scripture

Scripture does not do its work automatically. Scripture must be read. Someone must give voice to the words if they are to exercise their power. It makes a great difference who gives voice to the Bible and how people understand their role. We regard the experience of actually reading and hearing the Bible as critical to the church's enterprise. Reading is a task that must be shared; it includes taking responsibility for making the words interesting and offering some sense of their meaning and import. Hearing is likewise a task to be shared, and it includes the responsibility to respond to the words. One person cannot dictate what the Bible means, particularly if the meaning of the words is bound up with the reaction it evokes in particular hearers. Some will find Bible words hurtful and offensive. In such cases, the task of Bible study leaders is not to correct their reaction but to explore what God is doing as the passages are read and discussed within a group. We may discover in the negative reactions of hearers systems of oppression for which the Bible has been enlisted. It has likewise often been the case that in shielding hearers from the genuine offense of the gospel, pastors and well-meaning teachers have prevented a deep encounter with God's grace.

Interpreting is a corporate effort. We do not come to the Bible without some help from the saints who have come before. Therefore, it is also true that we should not read it without the insights of others who are not the same as we are, whose experience of the world has been different. They may hear things we cannot. While private reading and meditation on the Bible is always appropriate, the major location for Scripture reading and interpreting should be within a group in which personal insights are challenged and supplemented. It is in such settings, we believe, that the Spirit of God works to bring Scripture to life. Because many Christians have had little experience reading and interpreting in such settings, the Congregational Studies Research Team took seriously its responsibility to model such forms of engagement with Scripture in which everyone is welcomed into the conversation.

In any encounter with Scripture there must be a critical moment. It may sound to some that the kind of biblical study we are encouraging is little different from the caricature of Bible study groups who gather to share ignorance and their individual feelings. That may explain why many in the academic community have little interest in what ordinary readers experience when they read the Bible. They have been trained to be suspicious of *experience.* Academic constructs often so distance the Bible historically and hem it in doctrinally that there is little risk anyone will experience a threat or a promise.

In fact, the problem is not engagement with ordinary readers. Rather, the problem is that, until the Bible engages the imagination of present-day hearers, it can exercise no power. However, it is crucial that audiences learn to see and hear things that are new and disruptive. What occurs in the most personal study of Scripture depends on the structuring of the conversation, the hunches that drive the process, and the goals that are articulated. Perhaps one of the most important features of any conversation is the acknowledgment that disagreement is not an enemy. Unless there are differences of opinion, no views will ever be challenged and no minds changed. While the use of scholarly resources is one way of expanding the horizons of ordinary Bible readers, it is at least as important to encourage all to participate while holding people responsible for their views.

Particular Experiences of Scripture Usage within the Research Program

How does this approach relate to the world of biblical scholarship and professional theology? Since its inception, the research team has experimented with Bible reading, and certain practices began to evolve. In one meeting the research team chose a passage from the Bible to study. The team began with a simple worship service, the reading of the biblical passage, and a brief discussion that might best be described as a reaction to the text. No one offered a sustained interpretation of the passage to begin the conversation. Members of the group were asked to react. Some comments responded to what someone heard, while others pointed to features of the passage in printed form that seemed interesting. Some questions were of a learned nature, and on occasion members wondered about the translation. However, most of the discussion focused on the experience of the passage within the group.

The passage came from Matthew, and we chose it for its appropriateness to the theme of our research. It deals with Jesus' instructions to his disciples as he sends them off to preach. Reading about the urgency of Jesus' mission and that of his disciples, an urgency that had to do with God's plans for the future and that involved leaving home to speak among strangers, gave a particular tone to our study of congregations. What came out in the conversation was obviously related to the purpose of our gathering, but none of us could have predicted the course of the conversation. Furthermore, there were numerous surprises as people contributed something that others had not seen or heard. The few disagreements provided some of the most interesting moments in the brief conversation.

After about a half-hour of conversation, we turned to the work of the committee. We did not try to make a smooth transition or obvious connections between the Bible study and our reports. Over the course of the two days we returned to the passage three more times, and a different person read each time. Something interesting arose from within each of those conversations. While the effects cannot be detailed, the repeated reading of a story about Jesus' sending the disciples to preach in strange villages had an impact on how we viewed the whole matter of congregational life.

Our task is to enlist the resources of the tradition to make the Bible come alive within congregations. There are things that need to be known, styles of interpretation that need to be cultivated, hermeneutical theories that need to be embodied, and imaginative hunches that need to be worked and tested. These are the knowledge base, skills, behaviors, and attitudes that make for such lively engagement with Scripture.